DARING COLOR

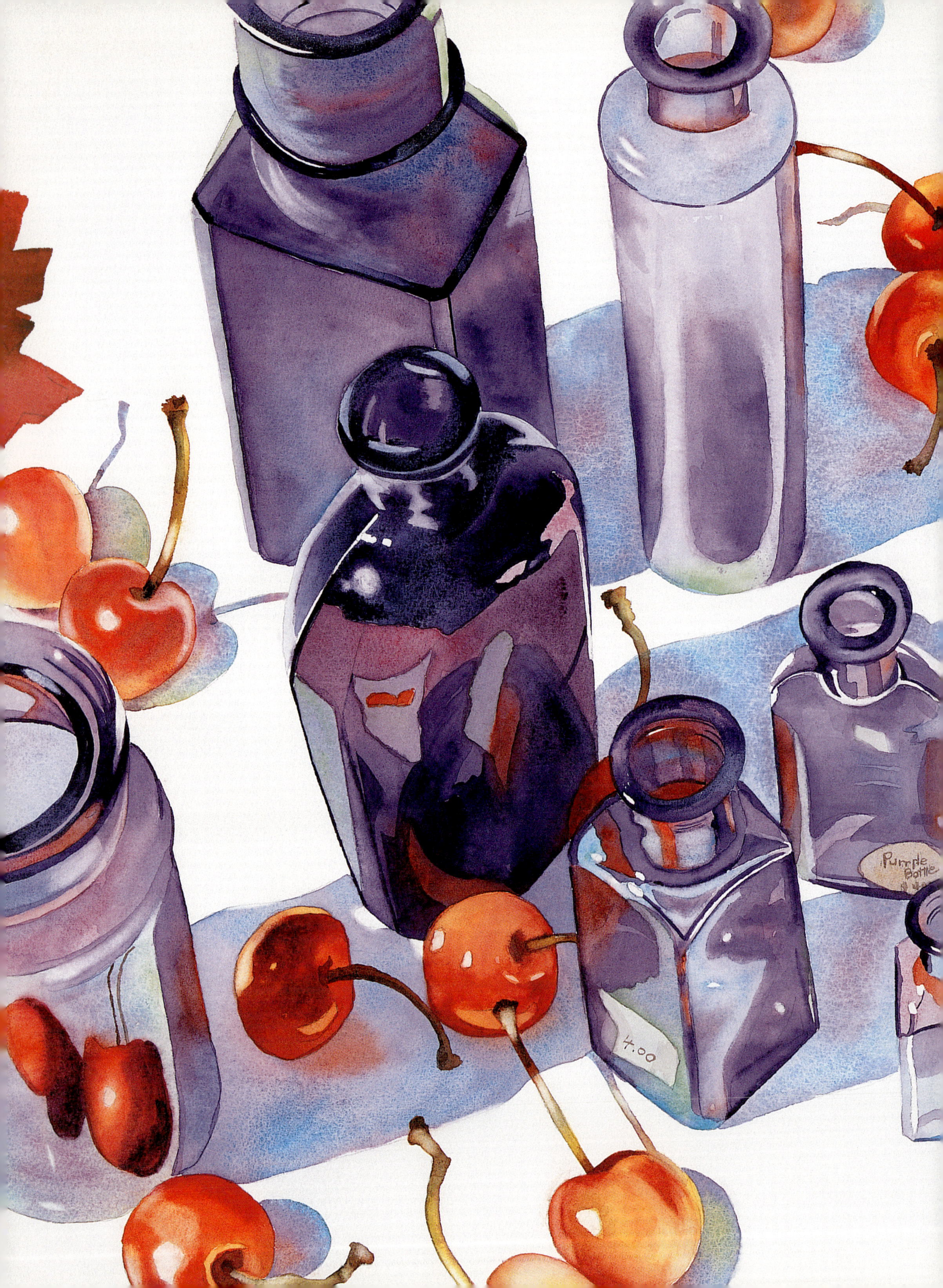
Purple Bottle
4.00

DARING COLOR

mix and mingle watercolor on your paper

Anne Abgott

NORTH LIGHT BOOKS
CINCINNATI, OHIO
www.artistsnetwork.com

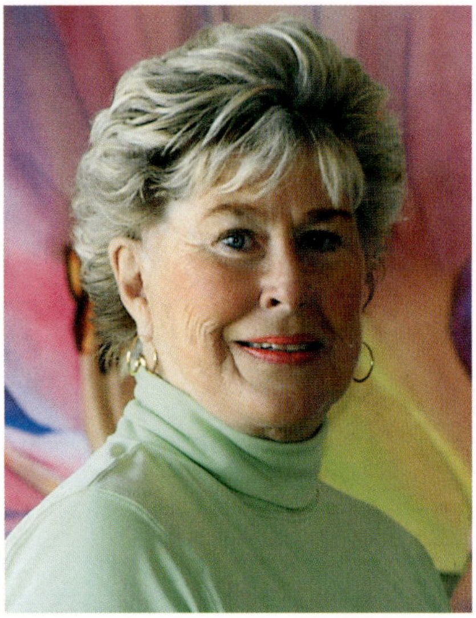

Photo by Sharon Davie Diskin

 Published by North Light Books, an imprint of F+W Publications, Inc., 4700 East Galbraith Road, Cincinnati, Ohio, 45236. (800) 289-0963. First Edition.

Other fine North Light Books are available from your local bookstore, art supply store or direct from the publisher.

11 10 09 08 07 5 4 3 2 1

DISTRIBUTED IN CANADA BY FRASER DIRECT
100 Armstrong Avenue
Georgetown, ON, Canada L7G 5S4
Tel: (905) 877-4411

DISTRIBUTED IN THE U.K. AND EUROPE BY DAVID & CHARLES
Brunel House, Newton Abbot, Devon, TQ12 4PU, England
Tel: (+44) 1626 323200, Fax: (+44) 1626 323319
Email: postmaster@davidandcharles.co.uk

DISTRIBUTED IN AUSTRALIA BY CAPRICORN LINK
P.O. Box 704, S. Windsor NSW, 2756 Australia
Tel: (02) 4577-3555

Library of Congress Cataloging-in-Publication Data

Abgott, Anne.
Daring color : mix and mingle watercolor on your paper / Anne Abgott. -- 1st ed.
p. cm.
Includes index.
ISBN-13: 978-1-58180-850-6 (alk. paper)
ISBN-10: 1-58180-850-X (alk. paper)
1. Watercolor painting--Technique. I. Title.
ND2420.A23 2007
751.42'2--dc22 2006100643

Edited by Kelly C. Messerly
Designed by Wendy Dunning
Interior production by Lisa Holstein
Production coordinated by Matt Wagner

ABOUT THE AUTHOR

Anne Abgott is a versatile artist whose range of subject matter includes animals, florals, architecture, still lifes and people. She uses a technique developed from endless hours of painting, and her passion for color and design are very personal and expressive. She maintains studios in Cortez, Florida and Linville, North Carolina. She was encouraged early on by a high school art teacher, and mentored by Alexandra Luke of the Canadian Painters 11 where she was tutored in oil painting. In 1992 she began painting in watercolor and was immediately captivated. She has studied with master watercolorists in the United States and Canada. She was on the faculty of Ringling School of Art and Design and she teaches widely, giving workshops in the United States and Canada.

Anne is a signature member of Florida Watercolor Society, Niagra Frontier Watercolor Society and Florida Artist Group, Inc.. She is also a member of the National League of American Pen Women and the Contemporary Women's Art Group. She serves on the board of Art Center Manatee in Bradenton, Florida, and is chair of the education department. She is past president of the Florida Watercolor Society.

Anne has received many awards, including twelve Best of Shows and First Prizes. She won the Florida Watercolor Society's Lattner Gold Award and the National Watercolor Society's Millard Sheets Award in California. Most recently she was accepted into the American Watercolor Society Show in New York City.

Anne's work has been featured in many books and magazines, including *Watercolor Magazine*, *The Artist's Magazine*, *Watercolor Magic*, and *International Artist*.

You can find her work in Art Uptown in Sarasota, Florida; Island Gallery West, Anna Maria Island, Florida; and Art Center Manatee in Bradenton, Florida. In North Carolina her work is in The Art Cellar in Banner Elk, North Carolina.

She can be contacted by e-mail at anneabgott@aol.com or on her web site www.anneabgott.com, where giclées of most of the prints in this book are available.

Art on cover: **Mexican Splash**, 22" × 22" (56cm × 56cm), transparent watercolor on cold-pressed paper, collection of Mr. and Mrs. Scott Murphy.

Art on page 2: **Moose Crossings**, 28" × 22" (71cm × 56cm), transparent watercolor on cold-pressed paper, collection of the artist.

METRIC CONVERSION CHART

To convert	to	multiply by
Inches	Centimeters	2.54
Centimeters	Inches	0.4
Feet	Centimeters	30.5
Centimeters	Feet	0.03
Yards	Meters	0.9
Meters	Yards	1.1

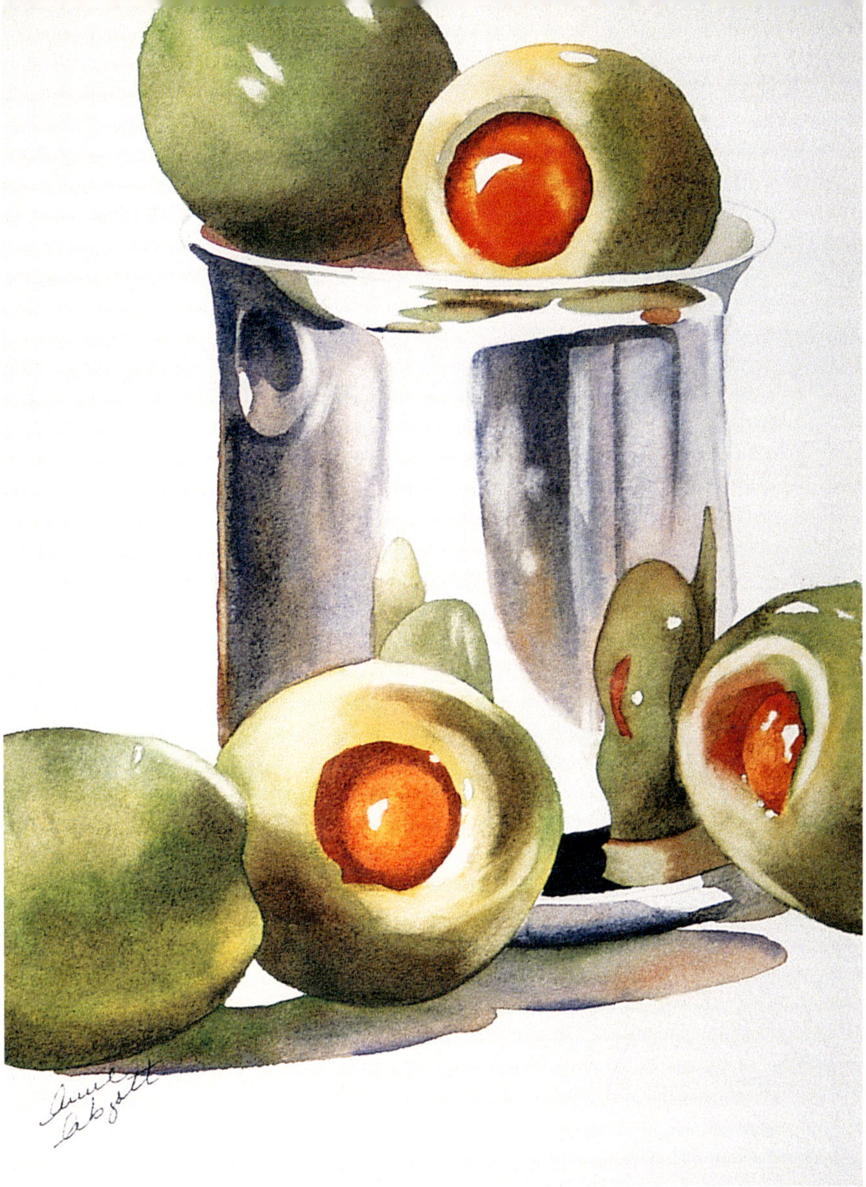

A DATE WITH JACK
16" × 20" (41cm × 51cm)
Transparent watercolor on cold-pressed paper
Collection of Mr. and Mrs. Harold Andersen

ACKNOWLEDGMENTS

To Bobbie Freeman, my partner in life and without whom I could not have done this book. His patience and calming influence helped me through many crises. Thank goodness he likes to cook and shop. His endless hours with the lights and cameras and the computer glitches made this experience a joy.

To my many friends who have taken care of me this past year, dropping off paintings at shows and picking up the pieces of a too-busy life. You know who you are.

To the students in the past years who have driven me to be the best teacher possible and above all inspired me by their own creativity. I came home many nights exhausted but unable to sleep because I couldn't wait to get my brush in hand the next day.

The generosity of the art community has always amazed me and rarely have I met someone who was unwilling to share their knowledge. I have to thank Roberta Carter Clarke, Margaret Martin, Mark Mehaffey, Suzanna Spann, Karen Vernon and the Rogers, Steve and Janet.

DEDICATION

In memory of Anthony Giglio: father, husband and son-in-law. A man I was honored to know and love for too short a time. And to my three children, Kelly, Craig and Mary—they make me proud of them every day.

Table of Contents

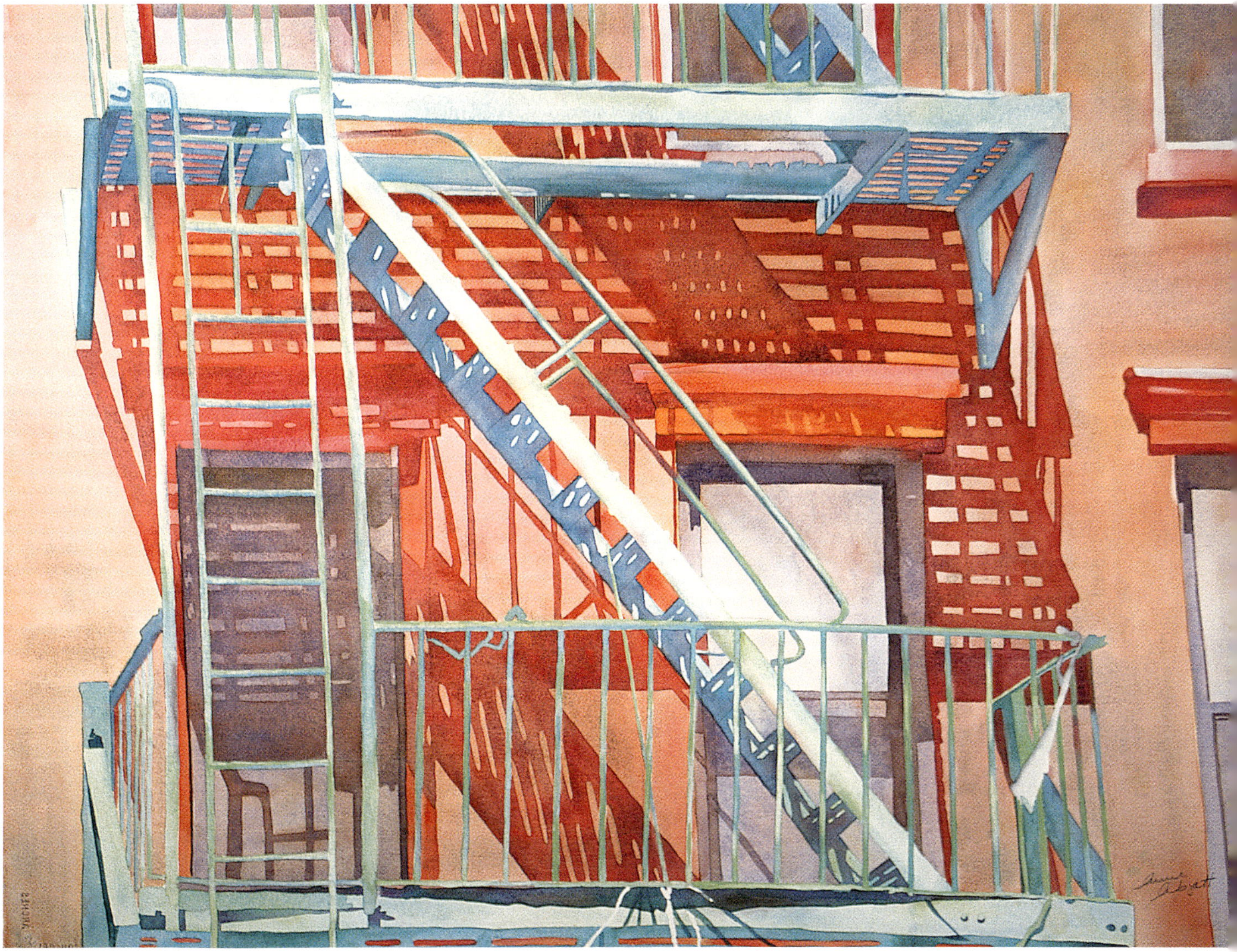

THE GREAT ESCAPE
22" × 30" (56cm × 76cm)
Transparent watercolor on cold-pressed paper
Collection of the artist

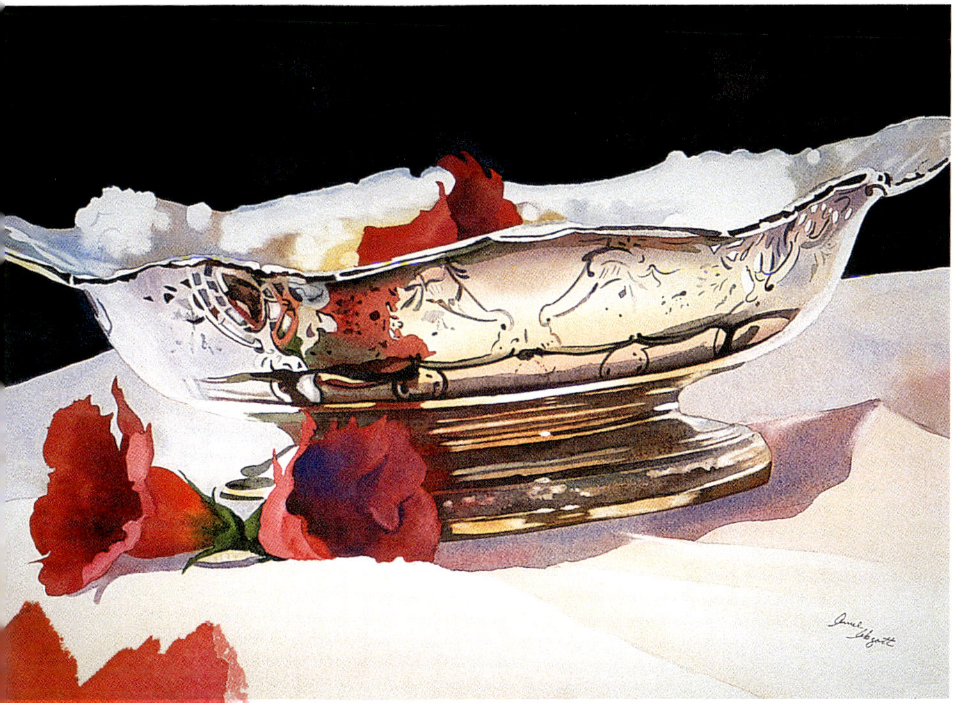

ANTIQUE REFLECTIONS
15" × 22" (38cm × 56cm)
Transparent watercolor on cold-pressed paper
Collection of Mr. and Mrs. Gary Allen

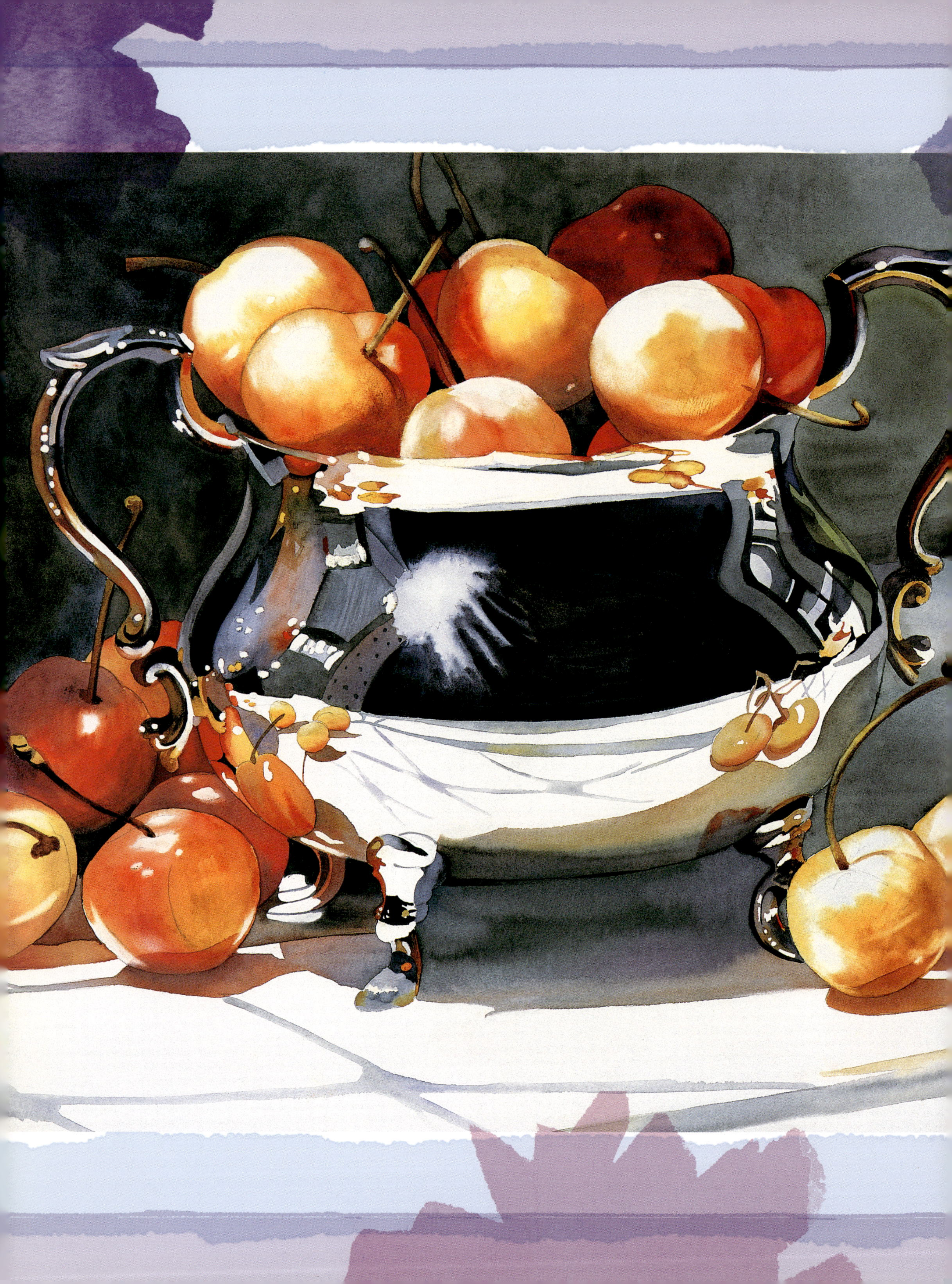

Introduction

Colors are the emotion of a painting. They are as important as the composition. There is a saying: "Value tells the story, but color gets the credit." How true!

Personally, I'm brave when it comes to color. My preferred technique of mingling transparent paints directly on the paper was a result of my desire to paint more quickly without having to glaze. This book is filled with tips and techniques to help guide you toward painting with daring color.

As a beginning watercolorist, I was told, "Watercolor is an unforgiving medium… Once it's on the paper, it can't be fixed." Wrong! If you use the right paper, pigment and brushes, watercolor can be easy and rewarding.

Sure, I had failures along the way as I learned. Every time you face blank paper, there is the potential for either greatness or disaster. Accept failure as part of the learning process, and don't expect every painting to be worthy of framing.

In this book, I reveal my personal tricks and techniques. To be successful, though, you must provide the most important ingredient: practice. The harder you work, the better you will become. Set goals for yourself and carve out time each week to paint. Challenge yourself by painting different subjects; if a subject scares you a bit, you'll work harder, and the effort will be more gratifying. Set yearly goals for yourself: complete twenty paintings; get accepted into a major college; enter at least six competitive shows. If you're willing to work, you will succeed.

I don't spend a lot of time thinking about interpretation, hidden meaning or philosophy. My work is representational, direct and uncomplicated. I paint what I see and what I love, and I try to present it with quality craftsmanship and technique. I paint pretty traditionally—using transparent paints, leaving the white of the paper and paying close attention to value. As for subject matter, I like to paint what I'm enthusiastic about. I capture these subjects with my camera lens; then the inspiration begins.

My creative process is never-ending. One idea leads to another. I find myself dreaming about potential subjects—images are there when I go to sleep, and when I wake up, I can't wait to get the brush in my hand. Watercolor painting is like a love affair in which I become totally immersed.

I hope you discover similar passion and feeling for whatever you want to paint. Above all, have fun!

Anne Abgott

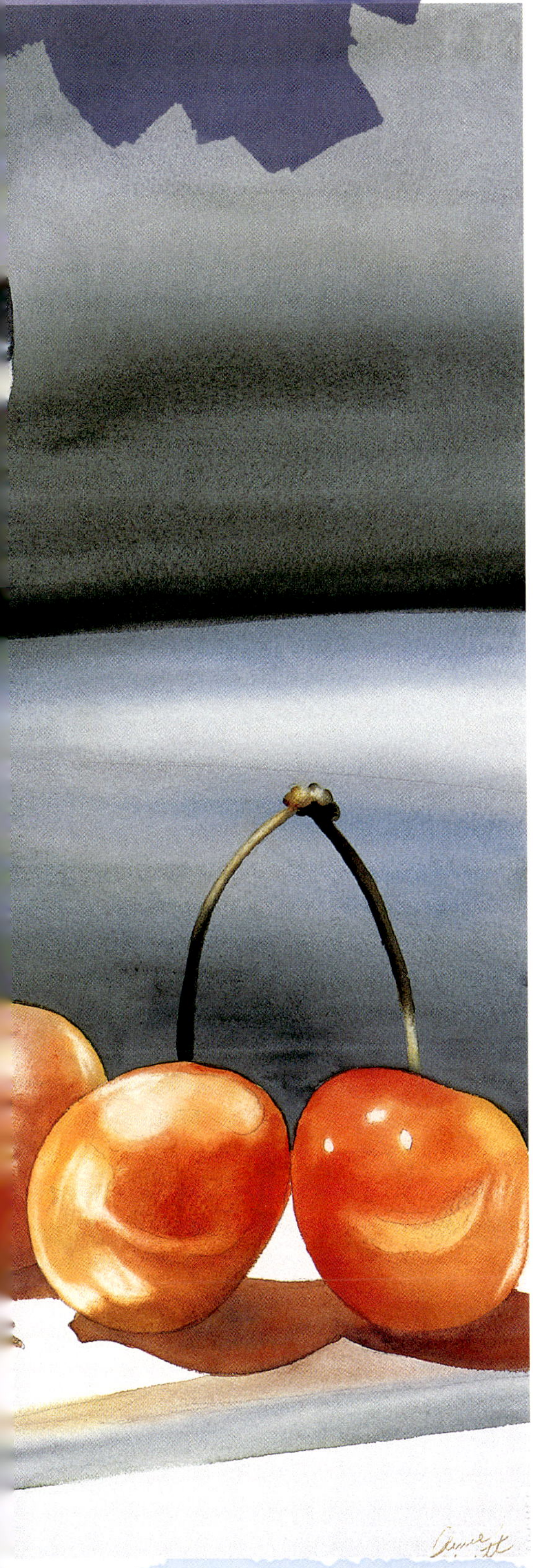

RAINIER REFLECTIONS
22" × 30" (56cm × 76cm)
Transparent watercolor on cold-pressed paper
Collection of the artist

Pigments

The key to clean, vibrant and daring color is to start with quality materials.

Choose your pigments carefully and be aware of the manufacturer, as the colors from different manufacturers vary in color and in transparency. I have developed my own favorite palette, but you should experiment with different paint brands to see which ones you prefer. See chapter one for more information on the different properties of pigments.

Some pigments are more finely ground and thus more expensive, but this is made up for by the brilliance and the color. Do yourself a favor and buy professional-grade paints. You can save money by buying the larger tubes, which give you three times the amount of paint of a smaller tube at half the price.

MIST PAINT FOR MORE CONTROL

I do not work with freshly squeezed paint. I fill the wells, let the paint dry, then mist the dry paint. The paint is fresh and the consistency ideal for my painting style because I can better control the amount of pigment on my brush.

ANNE'S FAVORITE COLORS

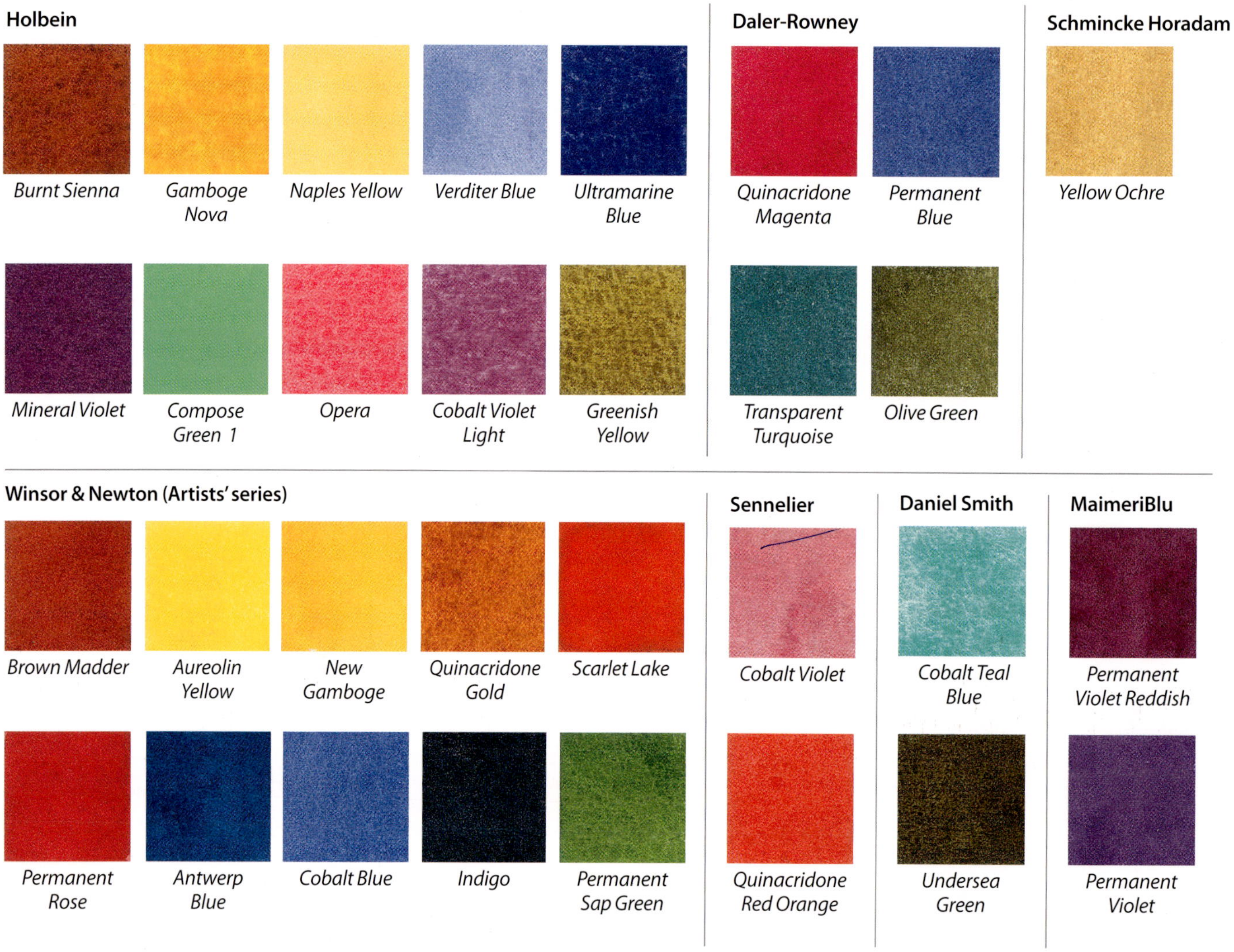

Paper and Palettes

PAPER

Choosing the right paper makes the difference between a painting you want to frame and a painting for the trash bin. I paint exclusively on 300-lb. (640gsm) Arches cold pressed natural color paper. Here's why I like it:

- The rag of this paper is extra absorbent, so the paper stays wet longer, letting you move and mingle colors for a much longer time.
- The transparent paint penetrates deeply into the paper's fibers and gives your subjects a rich brilliance.
- This paper is very tough and able to take a lot of scrubbing and abuse.
- It lies flat and does not buckle, so no stapling or taping is necessary. If you shop around, the cost can be quite reasonable. Cheap paper is frustrating to use and will add color only to your vocabulary, not your paintings.

I am often asked which side of the paper to use. I have used both sides of the Arches 300-lb. (640gsm) cold-pressed paper, and I find no difference between them.

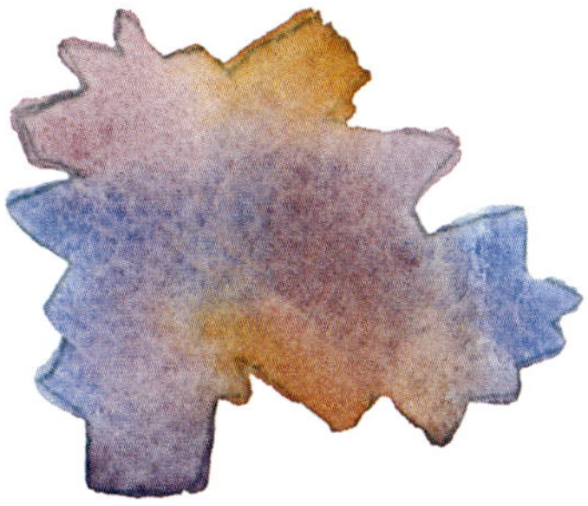

300-lb. (640gsm) cold-pressed paper

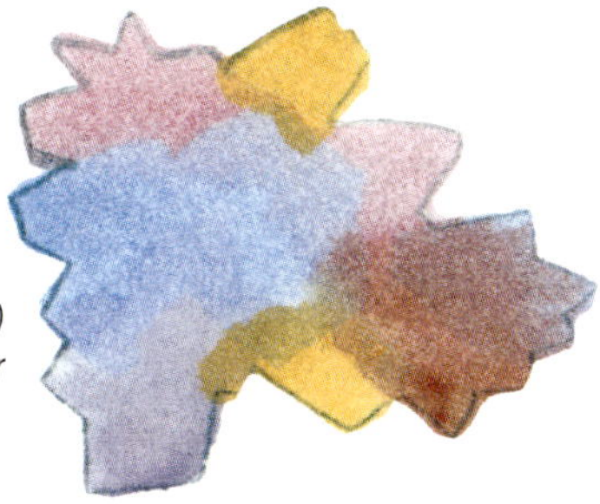

140-lb. (300gsm) cold-pressed paper

Comparing Paper Weights

See how the colors mingle better on the 300-lb. (640gsm) than on the 140-lb. (300gsm) paper. The colors seem to soak right in to the lighter-weight paper.

PALETTES

I use a large plastic palette with a large well in the middle for making big juicy puddles before mingling my colors on watercolor paper. My palette comes with a lid that I also use for mixing and mingling my colors. I use small portable palettes for extra pigments. These palettes easily fit into my larger palette for easy transportation when I take my paints to and from class. When the small palettes are removed, I still have my large palette space for making puddles. The palettes also fit easily into luggage.

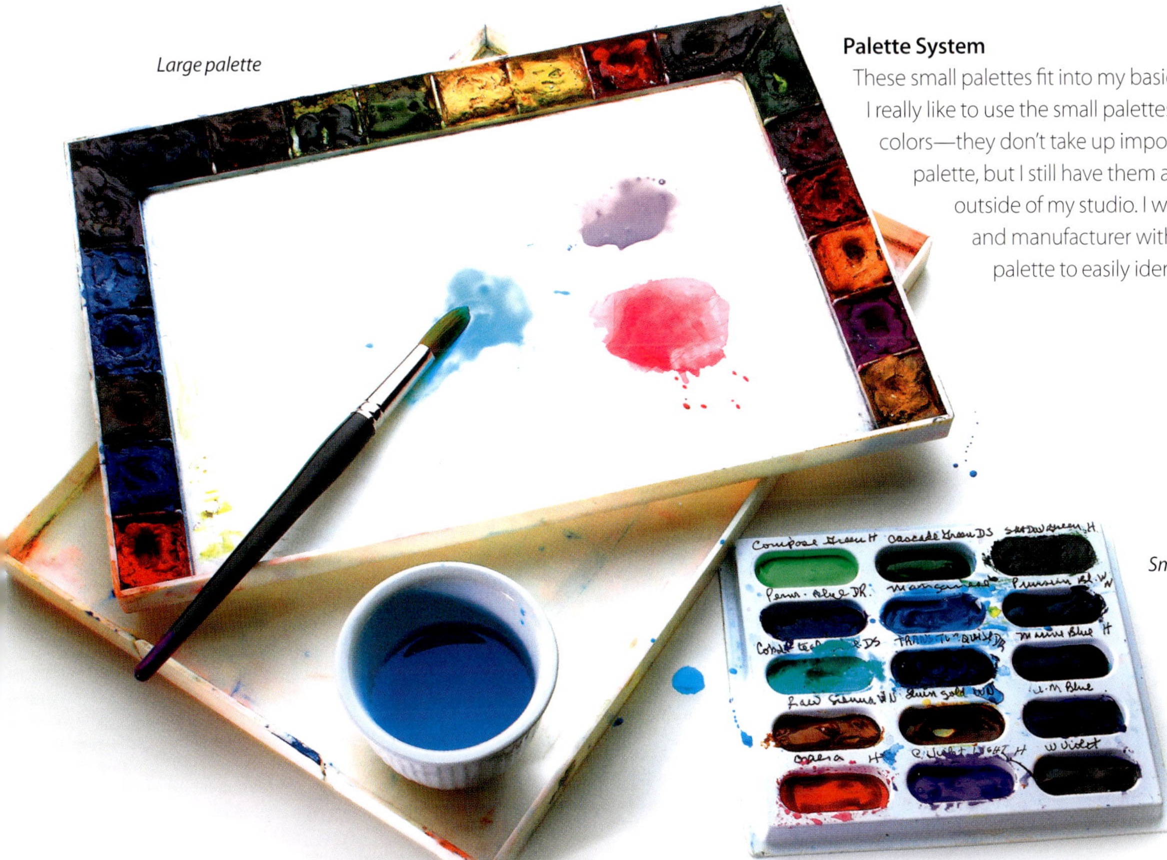

Large palette

Small palette

Palette System

These small palettes fit into my basic palette for easy transport. I really like to use the small palettes when I'm trying new colors—they don't take up important space in my main palette, but I still have them available when I paint outside of my studio. I write the pigment names and manufacturer with a permanent pen on the palette to easily identify the colors.

Brushes

Many good synthetic brushes have come on the market recently. I prefer Loew-Cornell synthetic brushes because they are hard-wearing, long-lasting, flexible and economical. However, you should experiment with various brands to find your favorites.

Brushes come in many sizes and shapes, but I mainly use rounds and flats. I use the rounds to lay water and pigment on the paper, and I use the flats to add even more pigment to the wet areas to darken the values.

The most frequent mistake my students make is trying to cover a large area of the paper with a small brush. Use big brushes for large areas and small brushes for small areas.

The brushes and the times to use them are very important to my painting techniques. You will find many places in the step-by-step demonstrations where switching brushes helps you maintain control of the water and your values.

BRUSH CARE AND MAINTENANCE

I don't wash my brushes with soap and water every time I use them. I generally wash them with soap once or twice a year. The soap also helps maintain their shape. Never leave a brush in water or lying flat on a table. Keep them upright in a jar or commercial brush carrier.

When a brush becomes ragged and some of the bristles are protruding in an awkward way, don't despair! Try dipping the damaged brush in and out of a pot of boiling water. Don't swirl the brush around the pot. Let the brush dry and it will be as good as new.

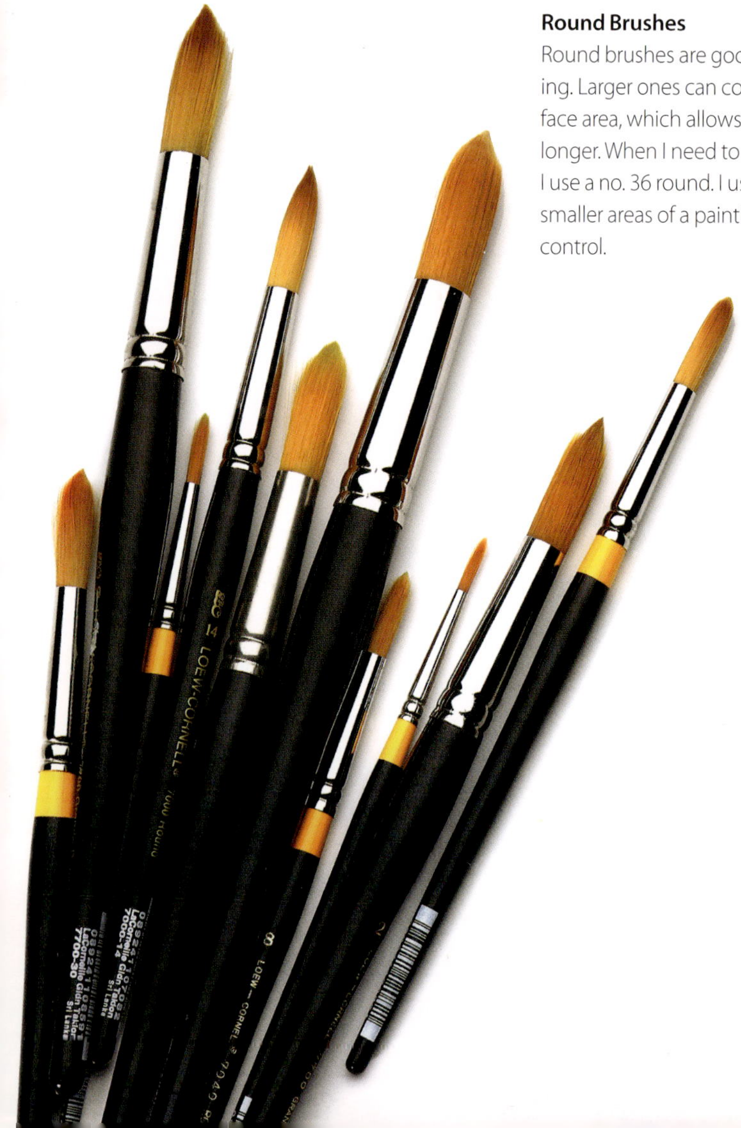

Round Brushes
Round brushes are good for washes and blending. Larger ones can cover a lot of the paper's surface area, which allows you to work wet-into-wet longer. When I need to cover a large area quickly, I use a no. 36 round. I use nos. 2 and 4 rounds for smaller areas of a painting where I need more control.

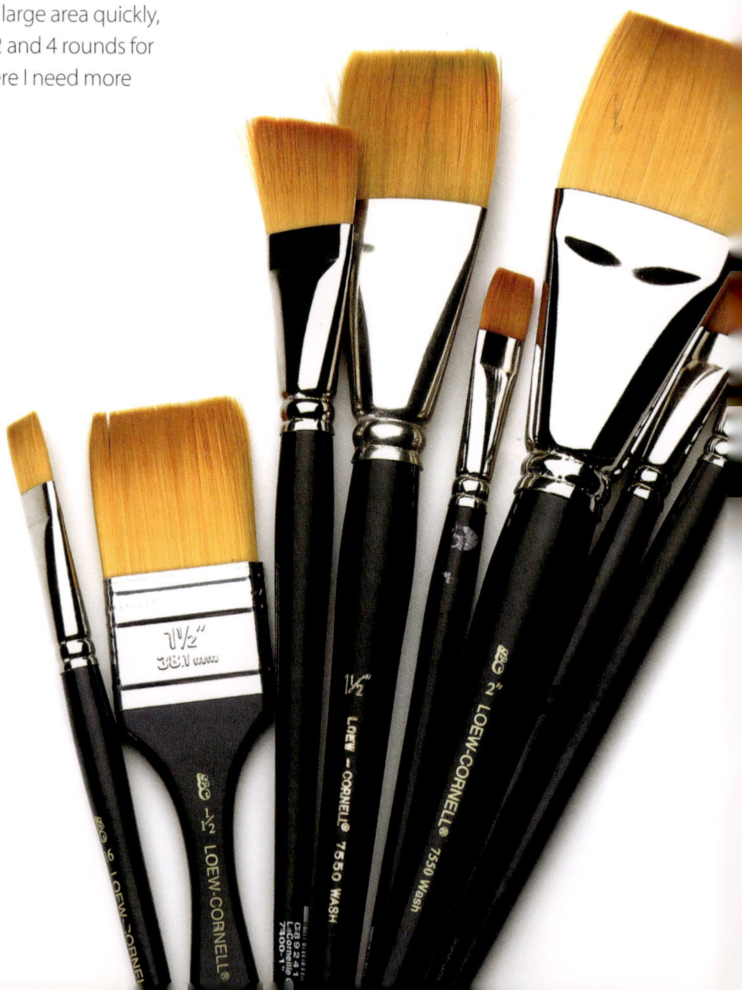

Soften Edges and Preserve Lights With Scrubbers

I lightened hard edges in this painting by first wetting them with a round brush. With a scrubber soaked with water, I began blending the dampened white paper into the dampened pigment, softening the edges. After you have lifted some of the pigment, use a paper towel to blot up the color. I repeated the process of wetting, lifting and blotting until I reached the desired effect. I also used the scrubber to soften and lift highlights in the birds' beaks and in some areas of the water. You don't have to worry about losing a light when you have a scrubber!

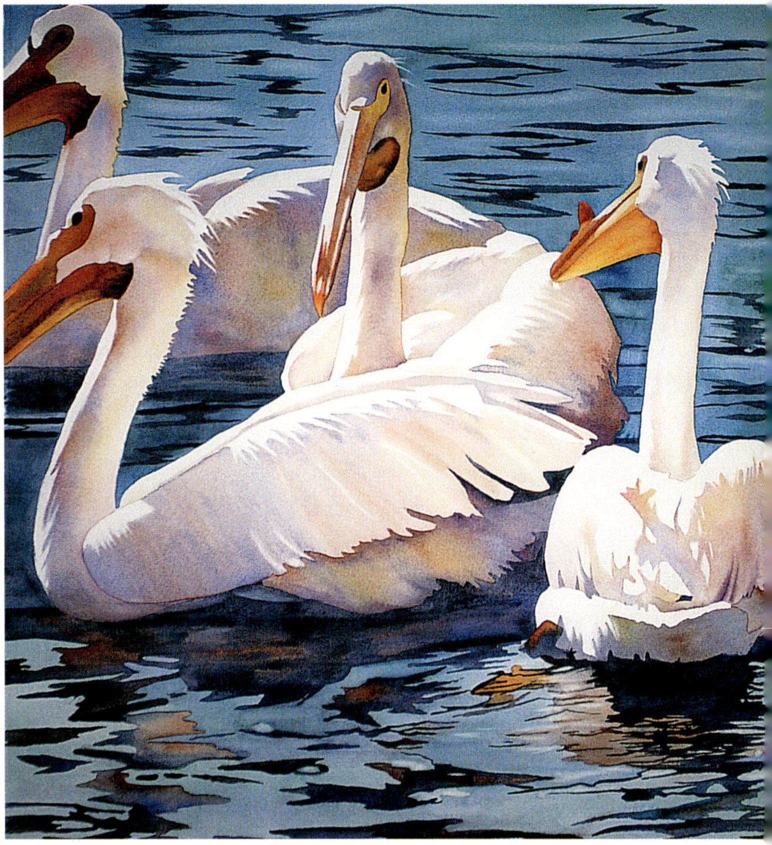

FEEDING TIME
22" × 22" (56cm × 56cm)
Transparent watercolor on cold-pressed paper
Collection of the artist

Different Brushes, Different Marks

Here you can see the difference in the flow and control that you get by using different brushes. Since rounds hold more water, the pigment will feather out if you drop it into a damp area. Flats hold less water, which creates a cleaner, more controlled area of dropped pigment.

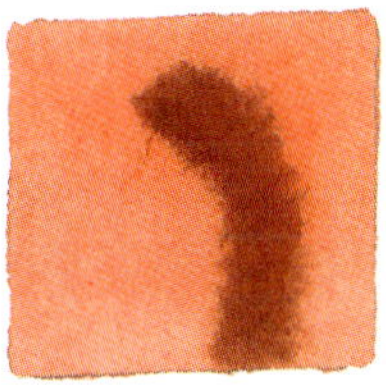

Round on wet surface

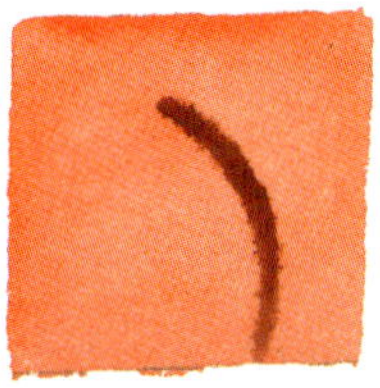

Flat on wet surface

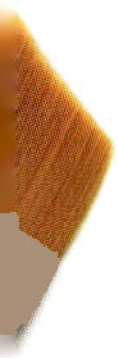

◄ Flat Brushes

Use flats for lifting and blending. Flats hold less water than rounds, so you can better control the flow of the paint. This makes flats ideal to use when you need only to drop pigment onto the wet surface. I use a 2-inch (51mm) flat and the 1-inch (25mm) angled flat for charging heavy pigment into my dark backgrounds. The tip of an angled flat is really good for getting into tiny corners.

Scrubbers ►

I prefer to use nos. 6 and 8 Fabric Dye Flats. They are stiff brushes made for painting on fabric, but I use them as scrubbers because they do not damage watercolor paper. Use them wet to lift out whites, soften edges, clean up spatters or even erase whole areas of a painting without damaging the paper. You can find them at your local craft or art supply store.

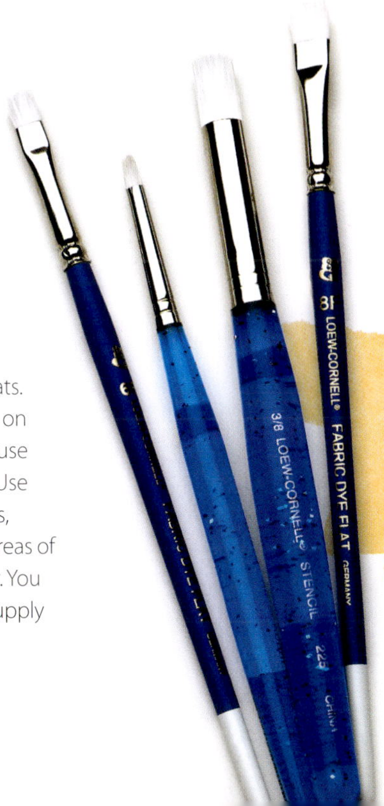

IDENTIFY YOUR BRUSHES

To keep track of your brushes, dip the end of the handle into nail polish, carve something into the handle or use tape. Whatever method you choose, mark your brushes as soon as you buy them to avoid mix-ups with other artists.

Masking Fluid

Masking fluid is a liquid latex solution. Applied to dry paper, it protects the masked area from paint and keeps it white or whatever color is underneath it. Masking fluid is often tinted to make it easier to see where you've applied it. Tinted mask also helps ensure that you won't miss a bit when removing the mask, which is important because mask will become impossible to remove if left on too long.

APPLYING MASKING FLUID

You can apply masking fluid with a brush, a toothpick or any sharpened stick. If you use a brush, make sure it is an inexpensive one, as mask will eventually ruin it. To minimize the damage to the bristles, dip the brush into four or five drops of dish soap diluted with water before dipping it into the mask. Reapply soap to the brush after every three or four strokes with the masking fluid.

TIPS FOR USING MASKING FLUID

- *Use a stick or brush handle to stir masking fluid. Never shake the bottle; shaking causes bubbles that can result in pinholes in the dried mask.*
- *Before you apply masking fluid to a painting, do a test run on a scrap piece of the paper.*
- *Masking fluid will thicken and dry out in larger bottles as the fluid level goes down. To prevent this, transfer the fluid to two or three plastic film canisters. This will keep the fluid fresh and make it easier to carry as well.*
- *Heat will adhere masking fluid to the paper, so don't dry masking fluid with a hair dryer—and don't leave your painting in the sun or under a lamp.*
- *Don't leave masking fluid on paper for more than ten days. It will turn brown and become impossible to remove.*

Make sure the paper is completely dry before you apply masking fluid. If the paper is the least bit damp, the mask will be impossible to remove. Also, be sure that the mask dries completely before you paint over it. Otherwise, the mask will get in your brush and will not completely cover the desired area. The mask is dry when it is sticky to the touch but doesn't come off onto your finger.

You should apply masking fluid as carefully as you apply your paint. A sloppy, quick application will only cause you grief. My students and I have ruined many paintings by slopping on masking fluid with a ragged brush. Be as precise as possible so you won't have sloppy, ragged edges and shapes that do not relate to the object you are painting. Take your time and do it carefully; you won't be sorry!

REMOVING MASKING FLUID

You can remove mask by rubbing it with your finger. For larger areas, use a commercial rubber cement pickup. This is a 2-inch (51mm) square of crepe rubber. Use it as you would an eraser. The sharp corners are good for picking up small areas of mask. When the corners get "gooed up," use a razor blade to cut off the corners of the rubber pickup and the buildup of mask.

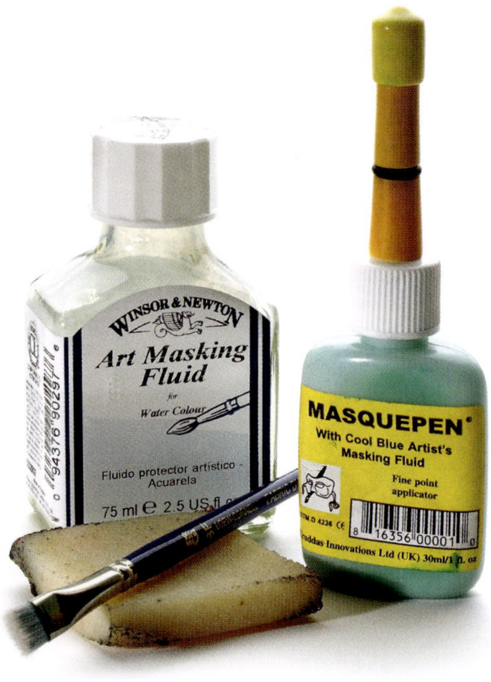

Masking Fluid and Supplies

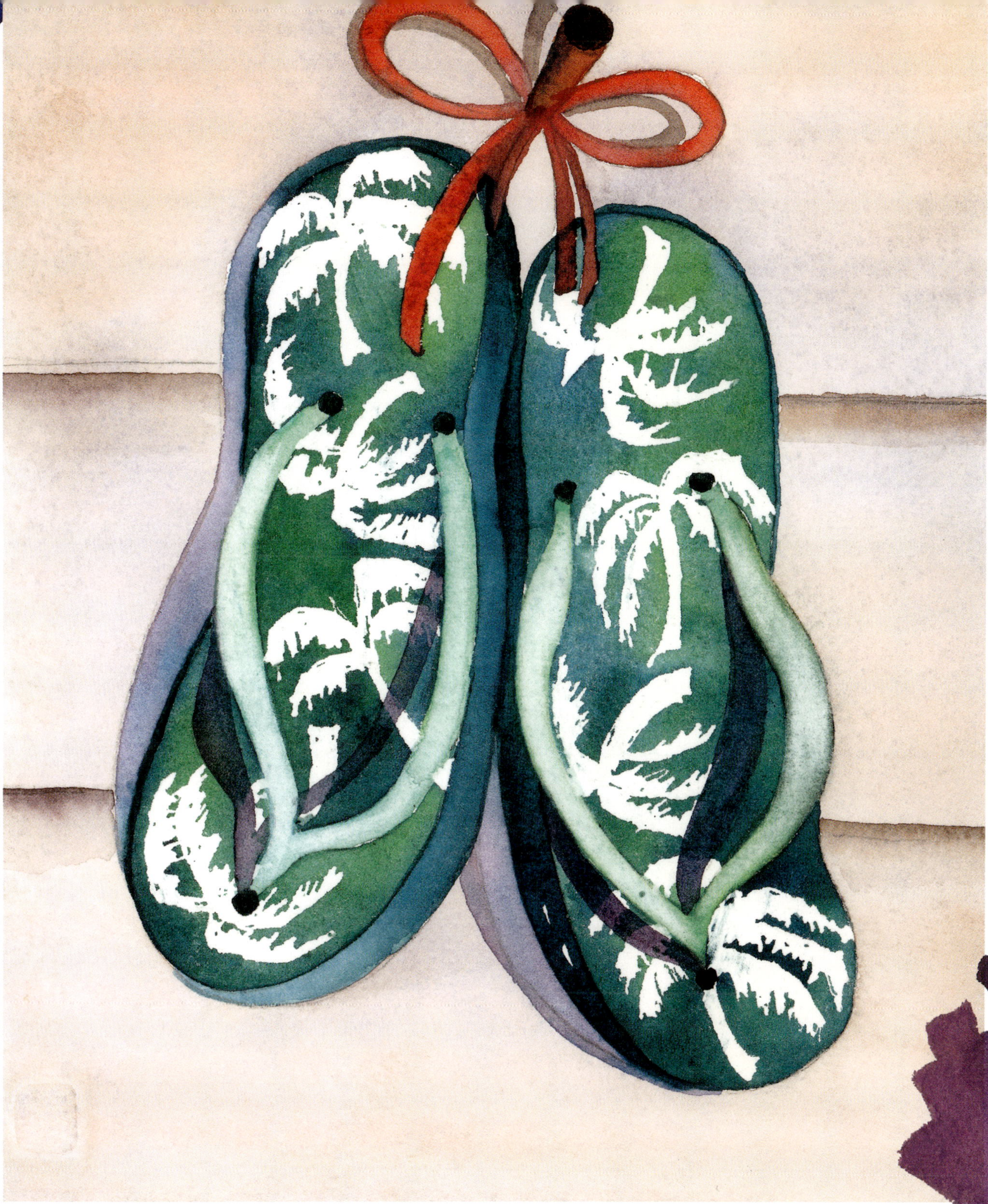

Masking Fluid in Action

Here I used a masking pen to loosely draw the shapes of the palm trees on the soles of these flip-flops. Once the masking fluid was dry, I used a no. 12 round to paint over the dry masking fluid with Transparent Turquoise and Aureolin Yellow. After the paint dried, I painted the tops of the flip flops and the sides of the soles . When the paint dried, I removed the masking fluid and painted the flip-flops' shadows. I then painted a nail head, a bow and some shadows to suggest that the shoes were hanging on a wall.

Try this using a masking pen with any design, and your creative juices will flow.

THE CAROL HOOD
14" × 11" (36cm × 28cm)
Transparent watercolor on cold-pressed paper
Collection of the artist

Other Supplies

Everyone has unusual tools in their "bags of tricks"—odd shapes of sponges, stamps, even dry iced tea—ideas picked up from other artists or teachers. Here are some of the essentials that I use to make my painting easier.

GESSO

Gesso is a water-based acrylic primarily used to prime surfaces before painting. I, however, do not use it to prime any surfaces. I use gesso as a fix-it tool. It has so many uses, I call it "the watercolorist's duct tape"!

I mix gesso with watercolor paints or use it straight out of the bottle on paintings. I use it to reclaim whites I have lost

MAKE AN ABSORBING PAD

It's important to get rid of the excess water on your brush before you paint or go into an already wet area. If you don't, you will drop water into that wet area. The water pushes away pigment, resulting in a bloom or blossom.

A small but crucial supply for my working method is an absorbing pad that I make and use to control the amount of water on my brush. This pad dries very quickly, can be put into the dryer and does not smell.

To use the pad: After rinsing out your brush and picking up more pigment, tap the tip of brush on the absorbing pad. Follow this process as you mingle your colors (see page 28).

Materials

- Nonwoven reusable wipes (plain, untreated with no cleaning products added)
- Good quality paper towels
- Stapler

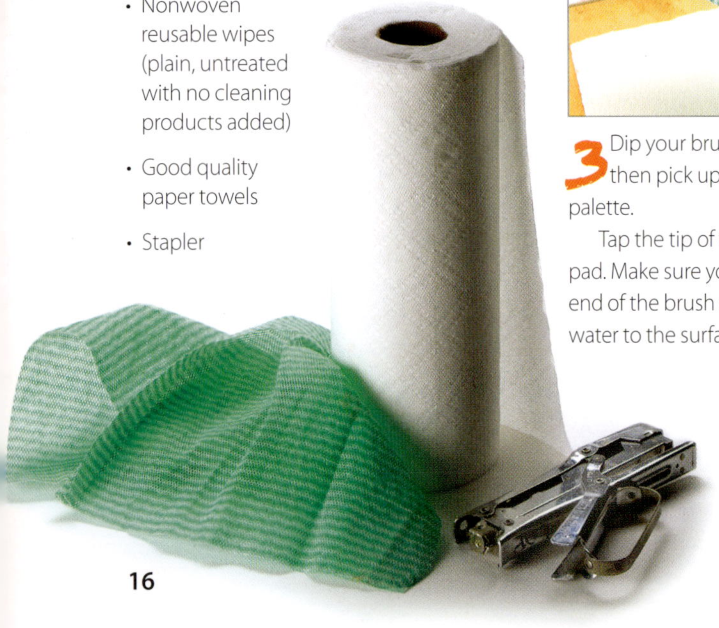

HOW TO MAKE IT

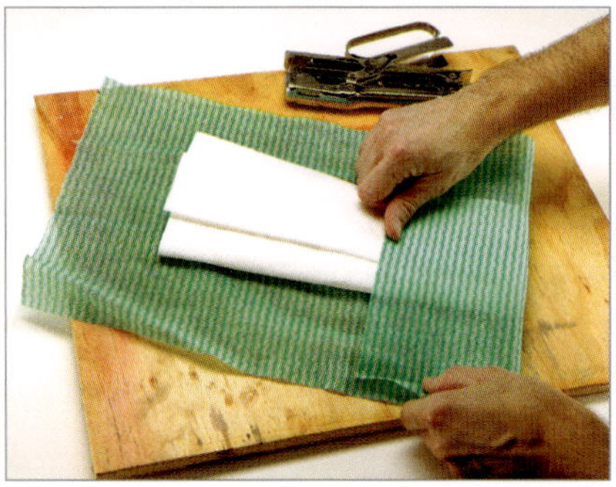

1 Simply fold ten sheets of paper towels into a long, skinny shape. Fold the nonwoven reusable wipes around the paper towels as you would wrap a package.

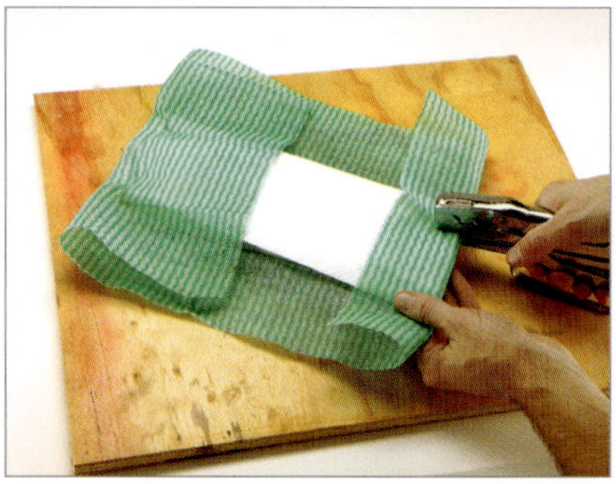

2 Staple along the edges to secure the reusable wipes around the paper towels. Make several absorbing pads at a time. Each one will last for months.

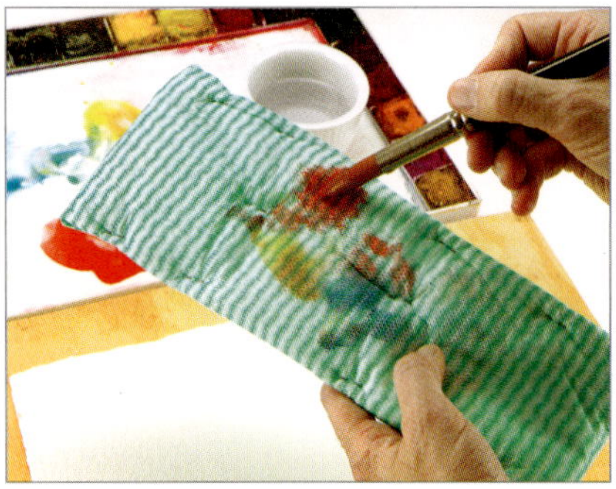

3 Dip your brush in water and rinse it out, then pick up some pigment from the palette.

Tap the tip of the brush on the absorbing pad. Make sure you get the "bubble" off the end of the brush so that you add no more water to the surface, only pigment.

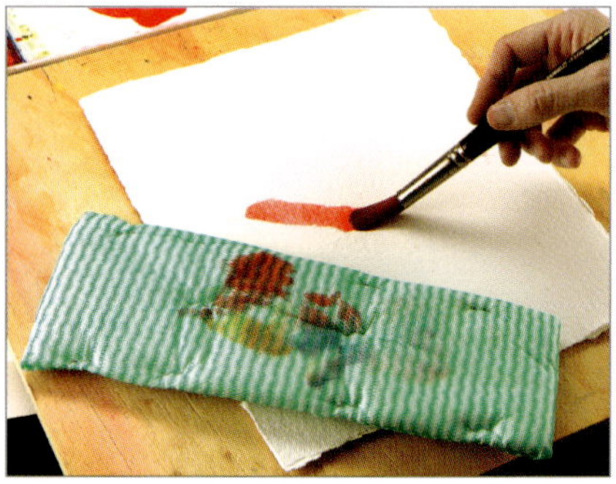

4 Drop pigment onto the surface of the wet paper. Do this with any brush you are using so you won't add extra water to the surface and will always have control.

There will be times when you will go from the paper to the pad and then back to the paper as the brush picks up extra water and pigment from the wet surface.

and to cover areas damaged by masking fluid. I have also used it to cover a bruise on the paper.

I dilute gesso with water and, using a large brush, paint over large areas of a painting to push subjects back. Diluted gesso is also a great way to depict fog rising off water.

I use it to spatter in dark backgrounds or mix it with pigments to create lighter shapes that suggest bushes or trees.

Gesso comes in large amounts, so transfer it to smaller containers so it won't dry out. You only need a little bit at a time.

Gesso
Use it to correct a mistake or reclaim white areas.

Spray Bottles
Purchase small spray bottles at a beauty supply store. Use them to moisten your paints before painting.

Plastic Cosmetic Case
Use plastic cosmetic cases to carry pencils, erasers, razor blades, film containers, dry cleaning pads, bottles to moisten paints and scissors. These cases are easy to see through and carry.

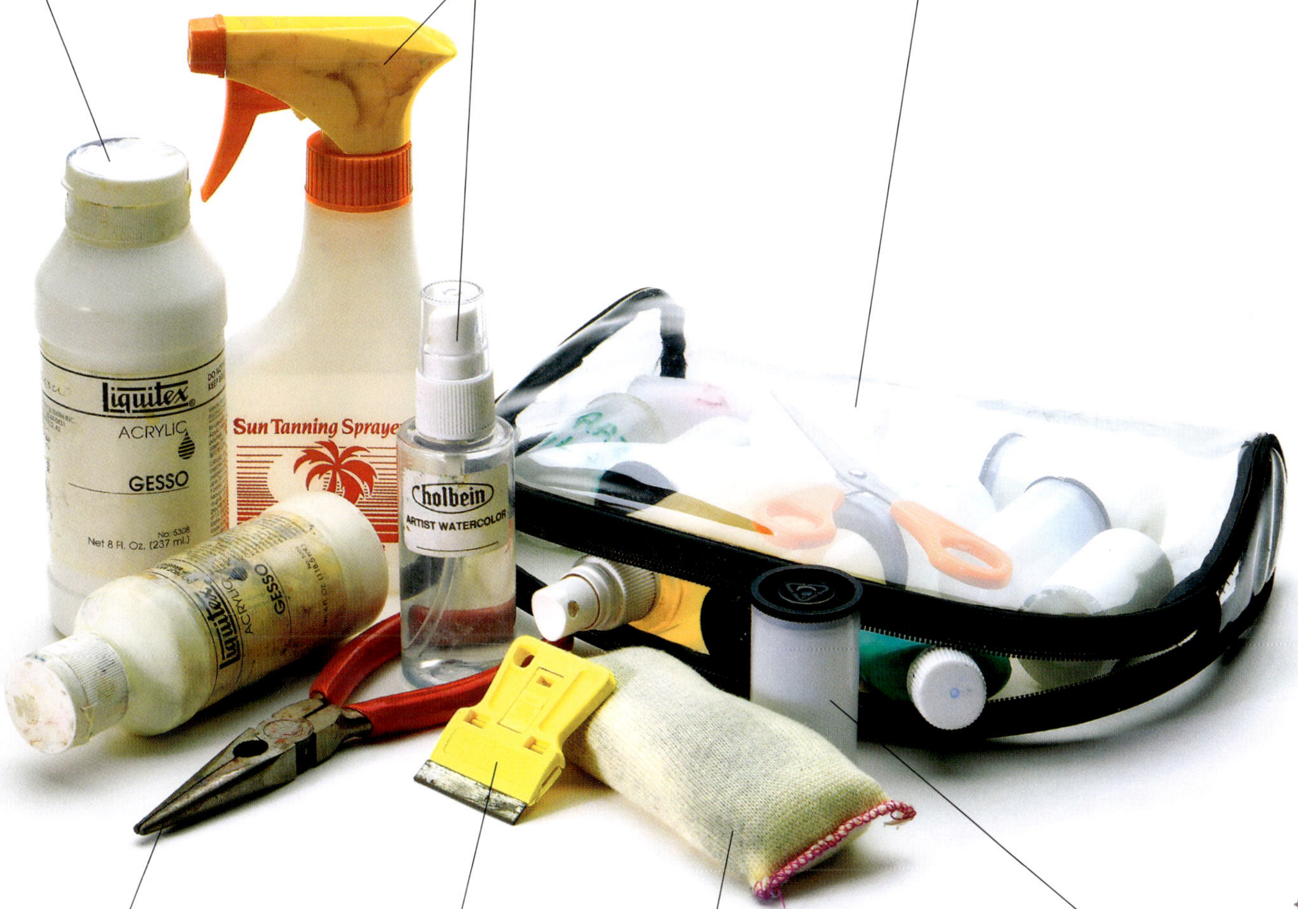

Pliers
Use pliers to squeeze every last bit of pigment out of the tube.

Razor Blade Holders
You can find these holders for razor blades at hardware stores. They keep the edges sharp, prevent rust and make it safer to transport the blades.

Dry Cleaning Pad
This architect's tool is used to remove excess pencil or graphite from your paper before painting. Good business supplies stores and some art stores carry this tool. It also works extremely well for clearing marks off mats. Store the pad in a plastic bag to keep it clean.

Film Containers
Use plastic film containers to carry liquid mask, soapy water, salt, gesso and extra razor blades. Label them to easily identify the contents.

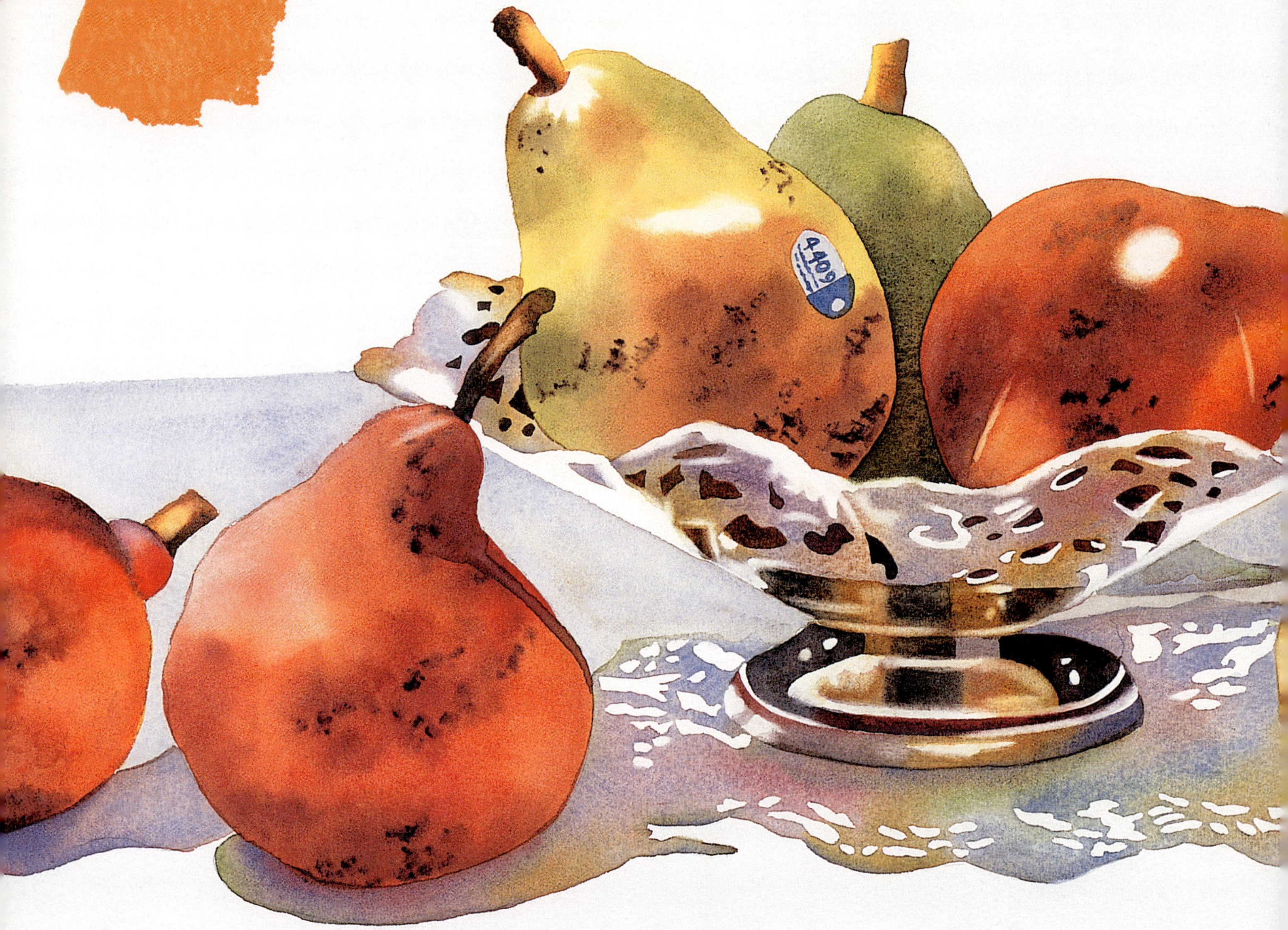
4409

1

Color

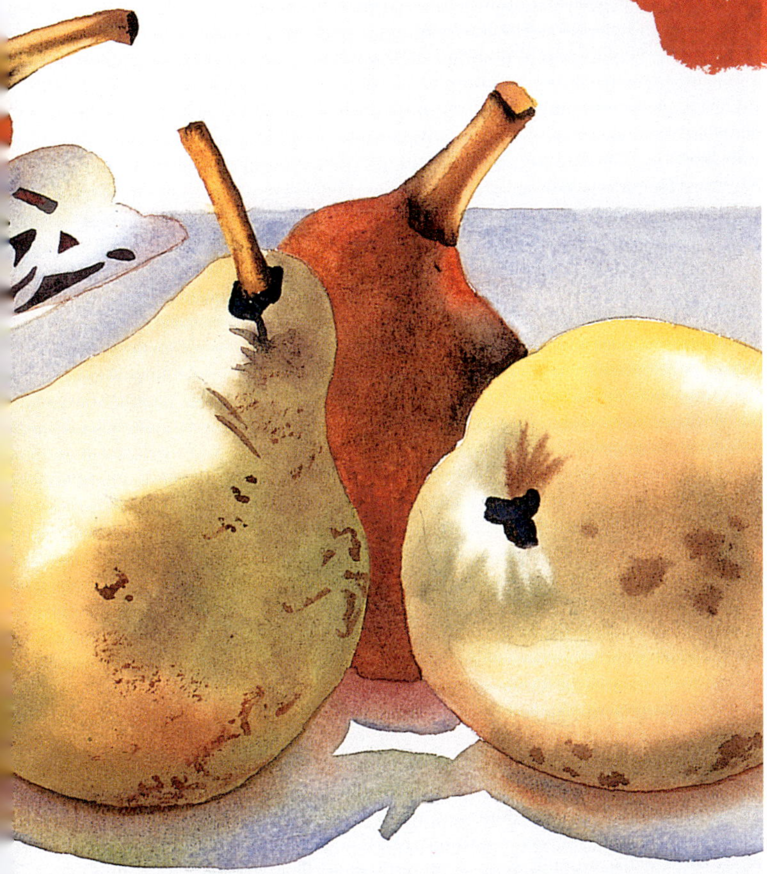

Using beautiful, daring colors is an important part of the way I paint. I find that each of my colors has a distinct "personality." Understanding the different aspects of the colors I use helps me achieve the results I want.

As you become familiar with the colors on your palette you'll find that a range of possibilities opens up to you. Understanding the difference between pigments that are transparent or opaque, staining or nonstaining and granular or nongranular will give you the power to make the best color choices for your artwork.

PICK A PEAR
22" × 28" (56cm × 71cm)
Transparent watercolor on cold-pressed paper
Collection of Mr. and Mrs. Ben Johnson

The Color Wheel

It's important to know your color basics so that you can combine your watercolors to their best advantage. Try creating your own color wheel with the colors on your palette.

TERMS TO KNOW

Primary colors: *Red, yellow and blue—the three colors from which all others can be mixed.*

Secondary colors: *The colors made by mixing any two primary colors. They are orange, green and violet.*

Tertiary (or intermediate) colors: *Colors made by mixing a primary color with an adjacent secondary color. They are red-orange, yellow-orange, yellow-green, blue-green, blue-violet and red-violet.*

Complementary colors: *Any two colors directly opposite each other on the color wheel. Complementary colors placed side by side tend to "vibrate" and attract the eye. Green is the complement of red; violet is the complement of yellow and orange is the complement of blue. When mixed together, complementary colors produce gray.*

Analogous colors: *Colors adjacent to each other on the color wheel. An example would be blue, blue-green and green. Analogous colors are naturally harmonious.*

Color temperature: *How "warm" or "cool" a color is. Red, yellow and orange feel warm; green, blue and violet feel cool. Color temperature is relative: a lemon yellow is cooler than a golden yellow. In fact, many artists like to have at least one cool version and one warm version of each of the primary colors on their palettes.*

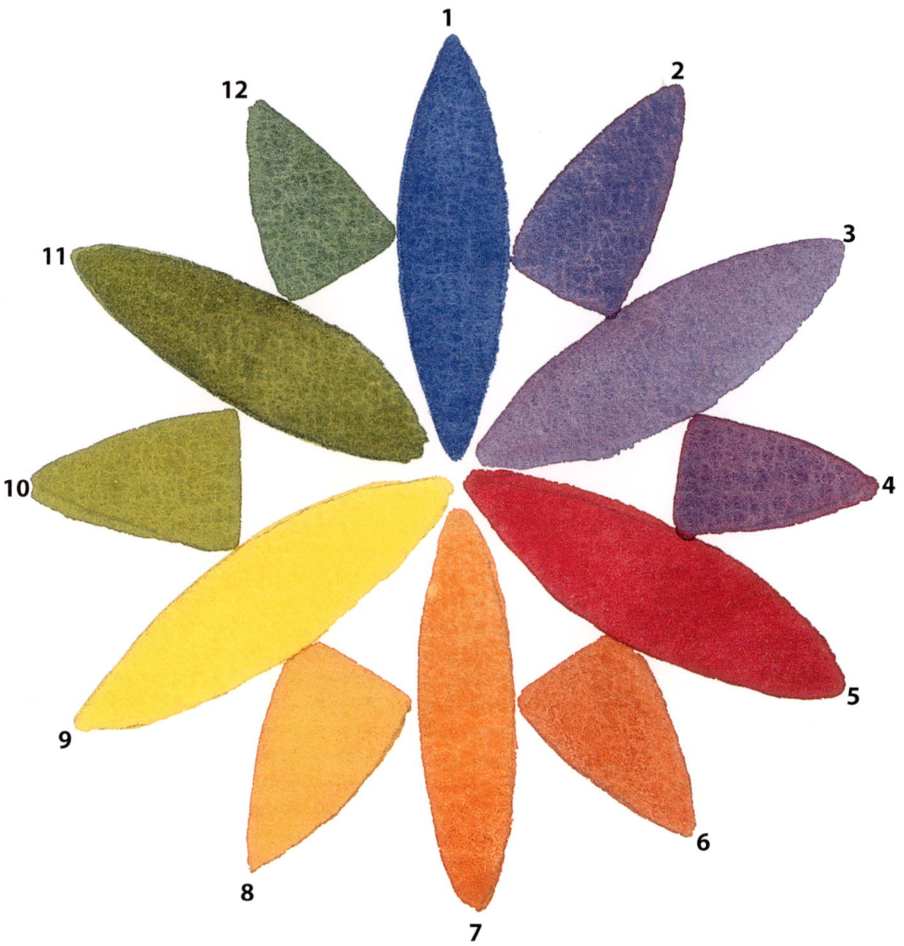

The Color Wheel

1. Blue
2. Blue-Violet
3. Violet
4. Red-Violet
5. Red
6. Red-Orange
7. Orange
8. Yellow-Orange
9. Yellow
10. Yellow-Green
11. Green
12. Blue-Green

Pigment Properties

Pigment properties can be used to predict clean color, avoid mud and achieve colorful darks. The basic properties of watercolor pigments are:

Transparency. A *transparent* pigment allows light to pass through. A pigment that allows little or no light to pass through is called *opaque*. Opaques flow much less easily across the paper than transparents do.

Granulation. Heavy pigments, such as the earth colors, tend to settle into the crevices of the paper as they dry, creating a mottled effect that can add wonderful texture if that is your goal. Such colors are called *granulating* or *sedimentary*. Like opaque colors, granulating colors do not flow as easily as transparents.

Staining. Some pigments lie on top of the paper and are easily lifted off if the paint film is re-wet. Those are called *nonstaining* colors. Other pigments tend to soak into the paper, making it impossible to fully lift out the color even if the surface is re-wet. Such colors are called *staining* colors.

Permanence. This refers to how well a pigment resists fading. A pigment with a high *permanence* or *lightfastness* rating will stand the test of time. Colors that are prone to fading are called *fugitive* colors. If you want your work to last, look for colors with a high rating for permanence.

CHECK THE PAINT LABEL

Most watercolor paint manufacturers rate their products for transparency, granulation, staining and permanence. If you don't see this information printed on the tube, ask your retailer for the manufacturer's color chart.

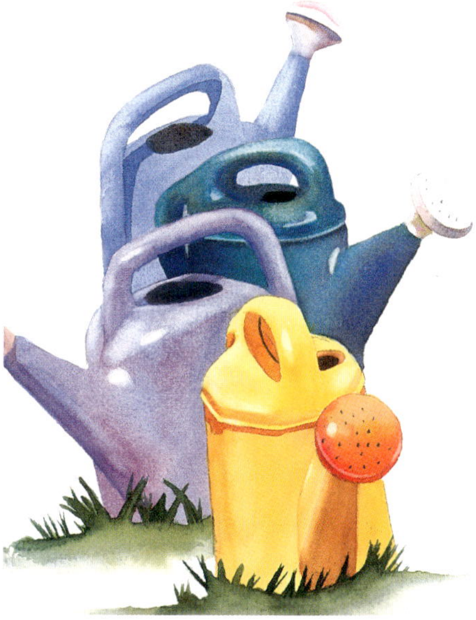

1. Granulating
2. Nongranulating

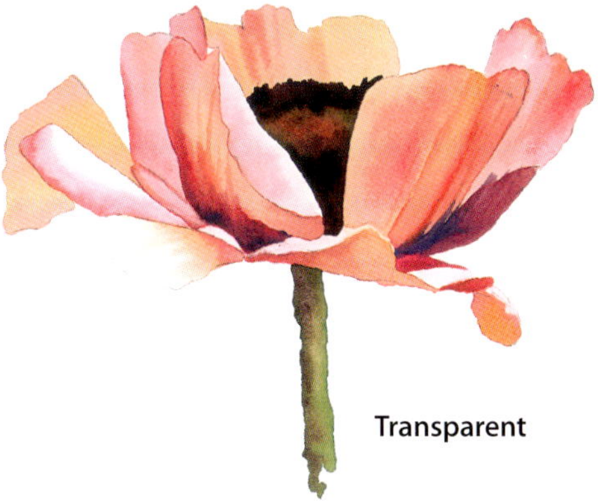

Transparent

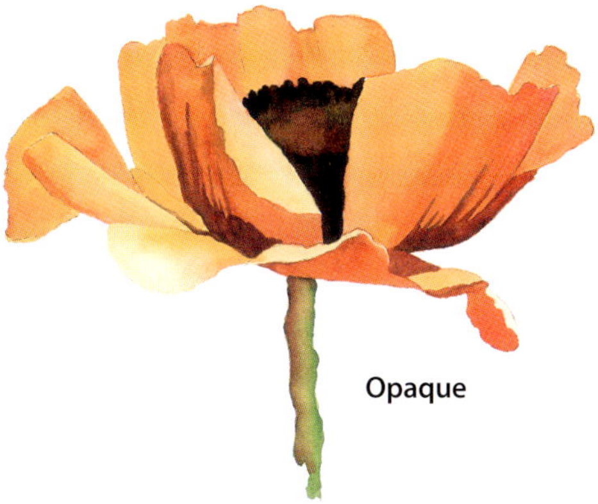

Opaque

Alizarin Crimson *Phthalo Blue* *Phthalo Green*

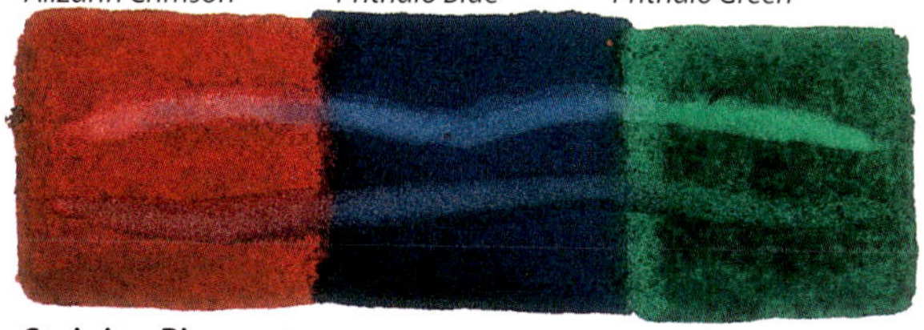

Staining Pigments

Permanent Rose *Antwerp Blue* *Undersea Green*

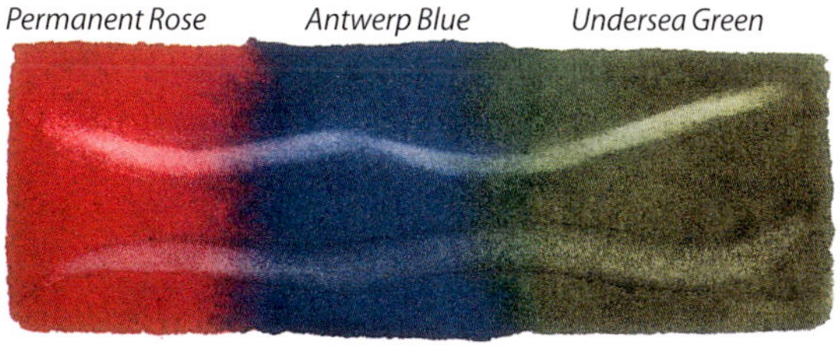

Nonstaining Pigments

Staining vs. Nonstaining Pigments As you can see, nonstaining pigments are much easier to lift out.

Color Charts

My colors suit me but may not suit you, so don't be afraid to experiment. Do your testing on scraps of different types of paper. The effect when the colors dry varies from paper to paper.

I stay away from cadmiums and most opaques; muddy colors are my enemy. When I do use the two opaques on my palette, I dilute them with a lot of water.

DON'T BE STINGY WITH YOUR PAINT

For my painting style—mingling and charging directly onto the paper—I like a palette with deep wells and large areas for mixing. The wells on my palette are large enough that I can get a 2-inch (51mm) flat into the well to pick up color by the heap. I fill the wells by squeezing out at least half of a 15mm tube.

Fill the wells, and give yourself more freedom. You won't be sorry.

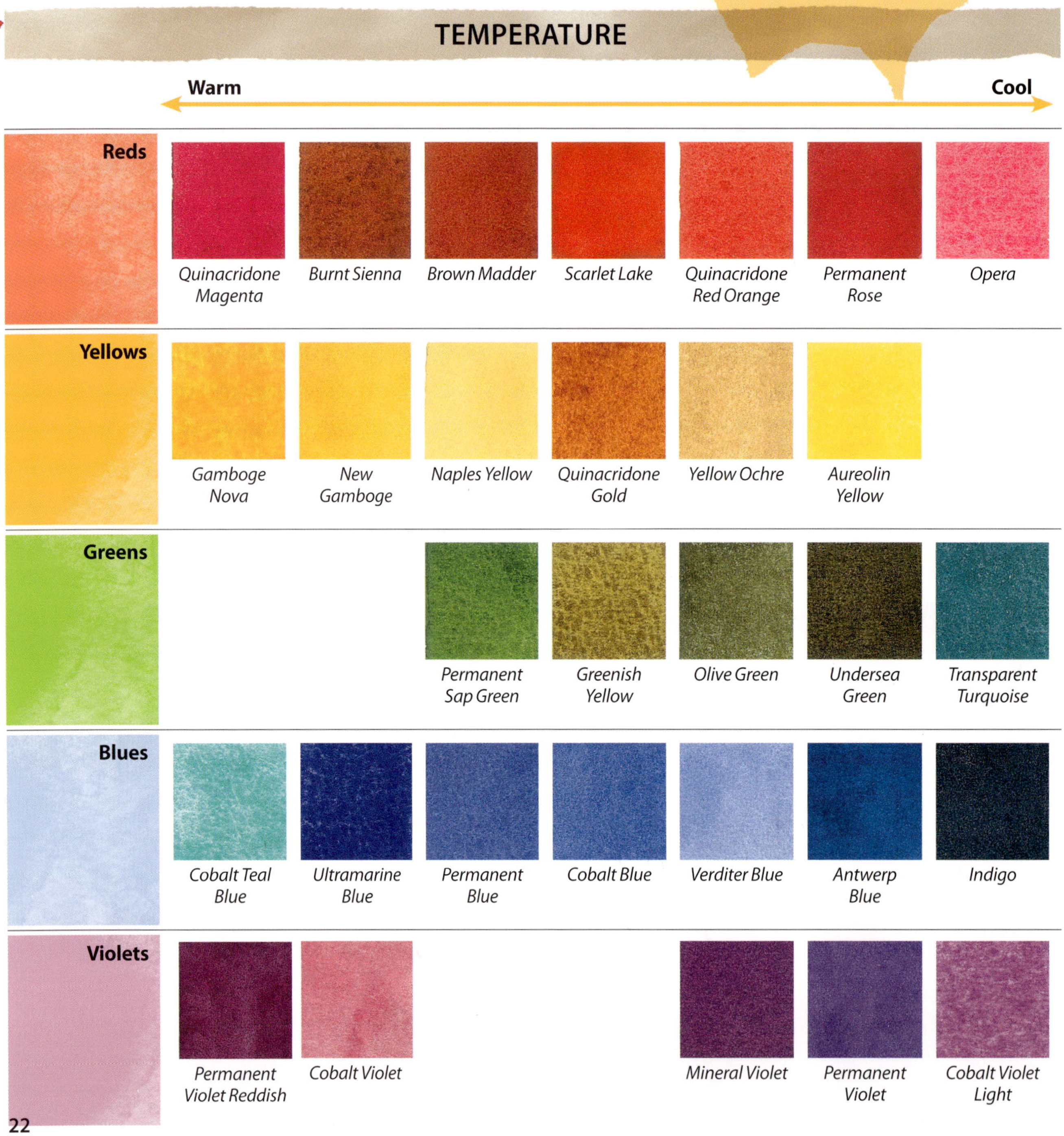

OPACITY

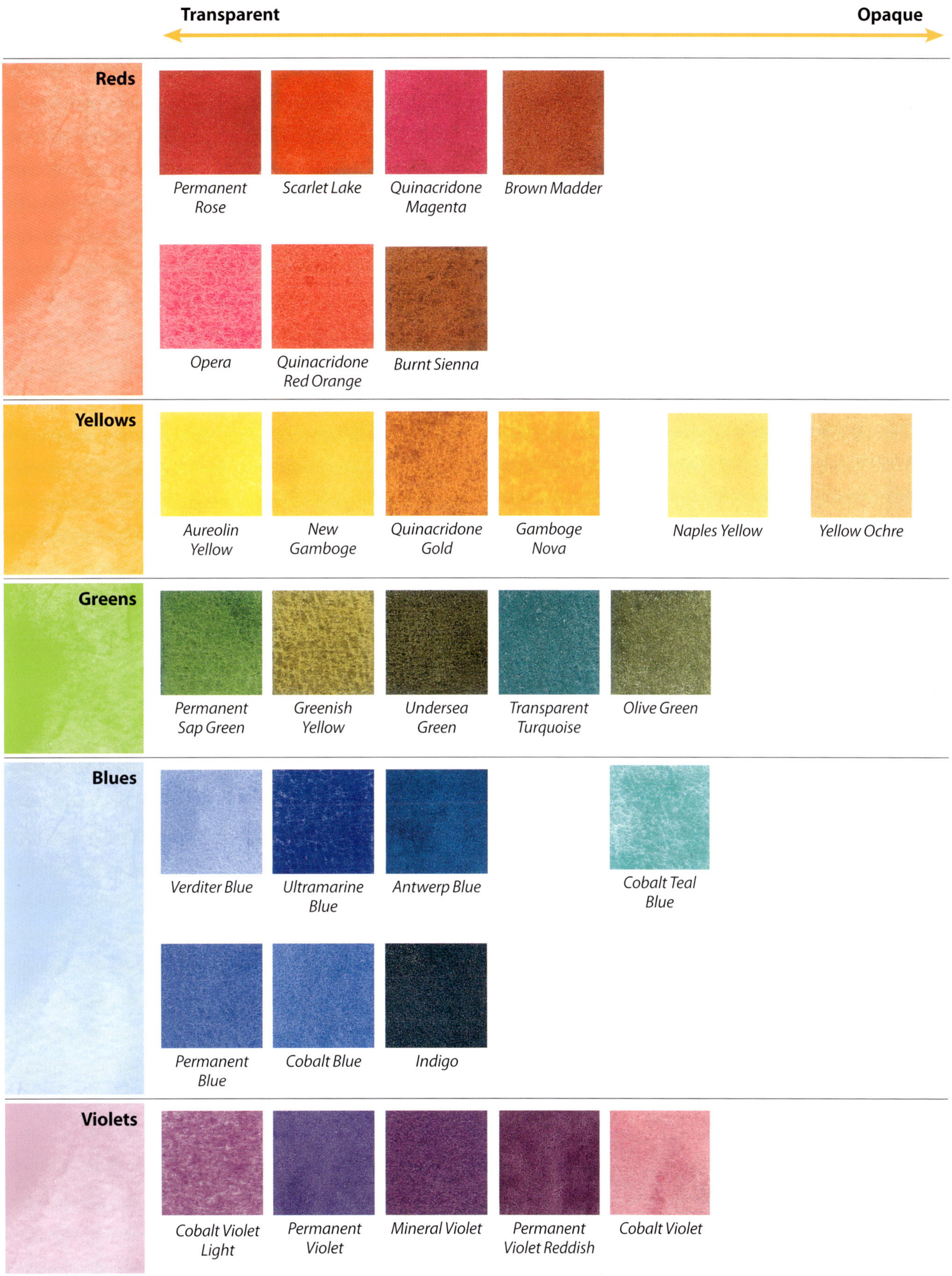
Transparent
Opaque
Reds
Permanent Rose
Scarlet Lake
Quinacridone Magenta
Brown Madder
Opera
Quinacridone Red Orange
Burnt Sienna
Yellows
Aureolin Yellow
New Gamboge
Quinacridone Gold
Gamboge Nova
Naples Yellow
Yellow Ochre
Greens
Permanent Sap Green
Greenish Yellow
Undersea Green
Transparent Turquoise
Olive Green
Blues
Verditer Blue
Ultramarine Blue
Antwerp Blue
Cobalt Teal Blue
Permanent Blue
Cobalt Blue
Indigo
Violets
Cobalt Violet Light
Permanent Violet
Mineral Violet
Permanent Violet Reddish
Cobalt Violet

GRANULATION

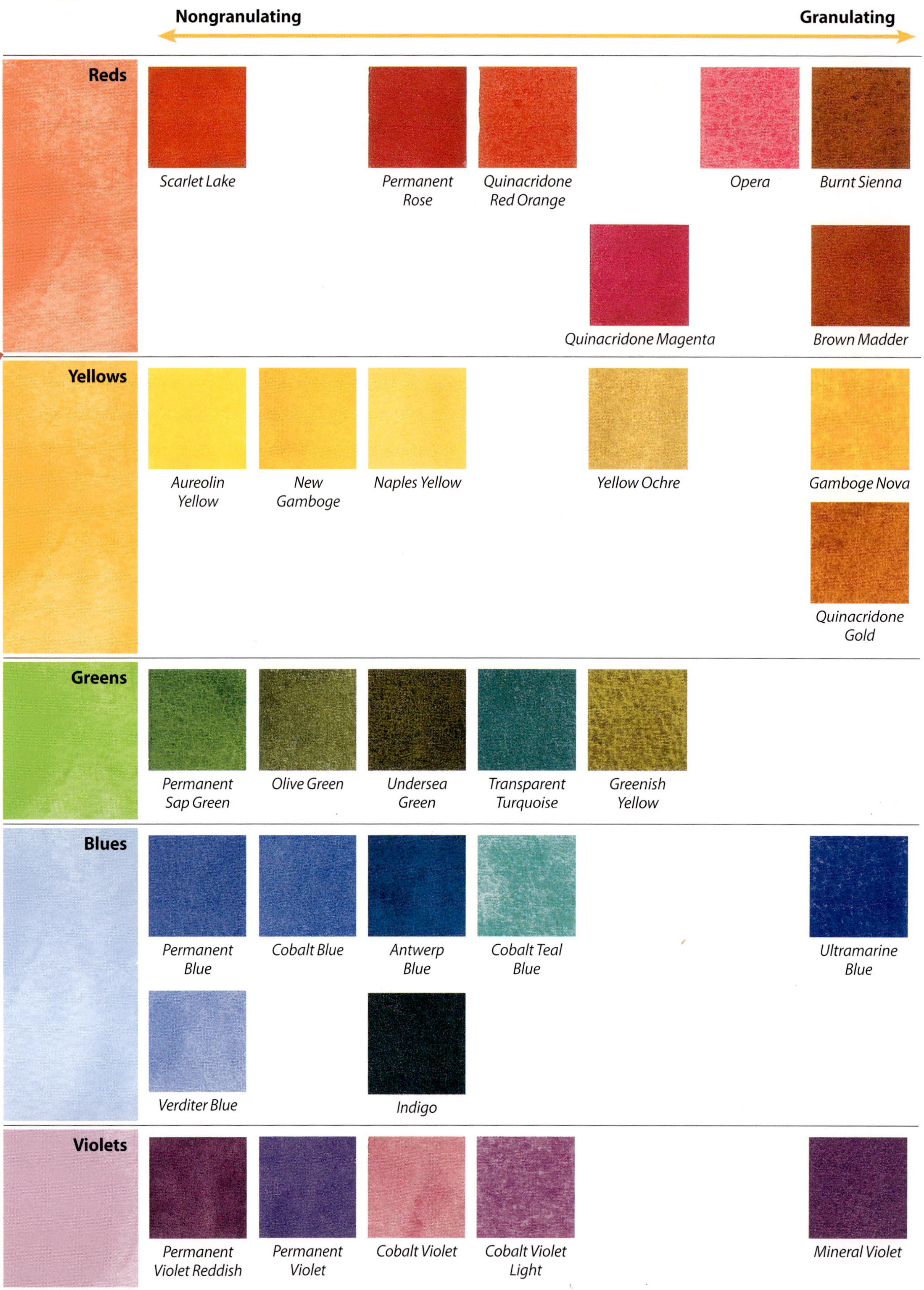

STAINING

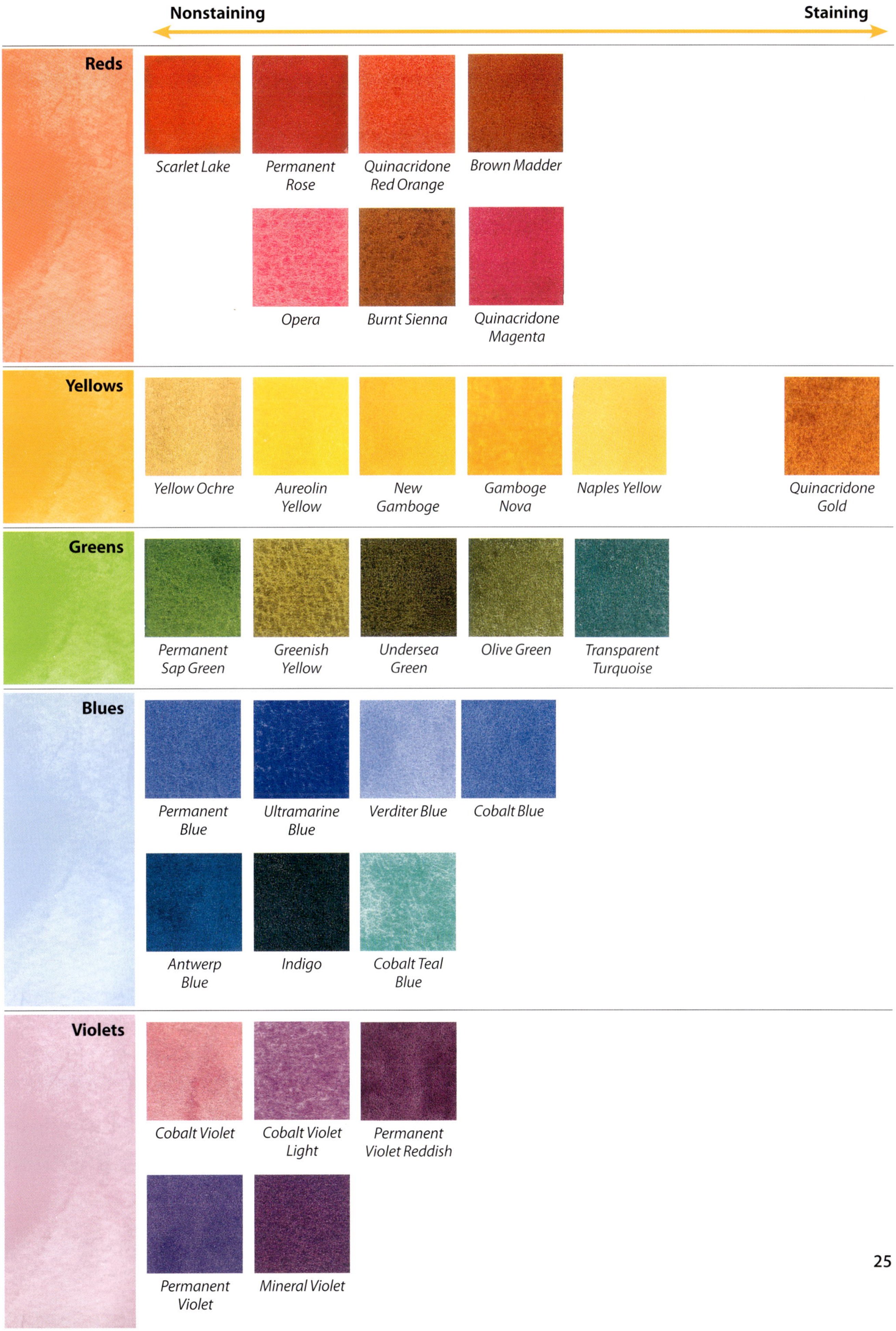
Nonstaining
Staining
Reds
Scarlet Lake
Permanent Rose
Quinacridone Red Orange
Brown Madder
Opera
Burnt Sienna
Quinacridone Magenta
Yellows
Yellow Ochre
Aureolin Yellow
New Gamboge
Gamboge Nova
Naples Yellow
Quinacridone Gold
Greens
Permanent Sap Green
Greenish Yellow
Undersea Green
Olive Green
Transparent Turquoise
Blues
Permanent Blue
Ultramarine Blue
Verditer Blue
Cobalt Blue
Antwerp Blue
Indigo
Cobalt Teal Blue
Violets
Cobalt Violet
Cobalt Violet Light
Permanent Violet Reddish
Permanent Violet
Mineral Violet

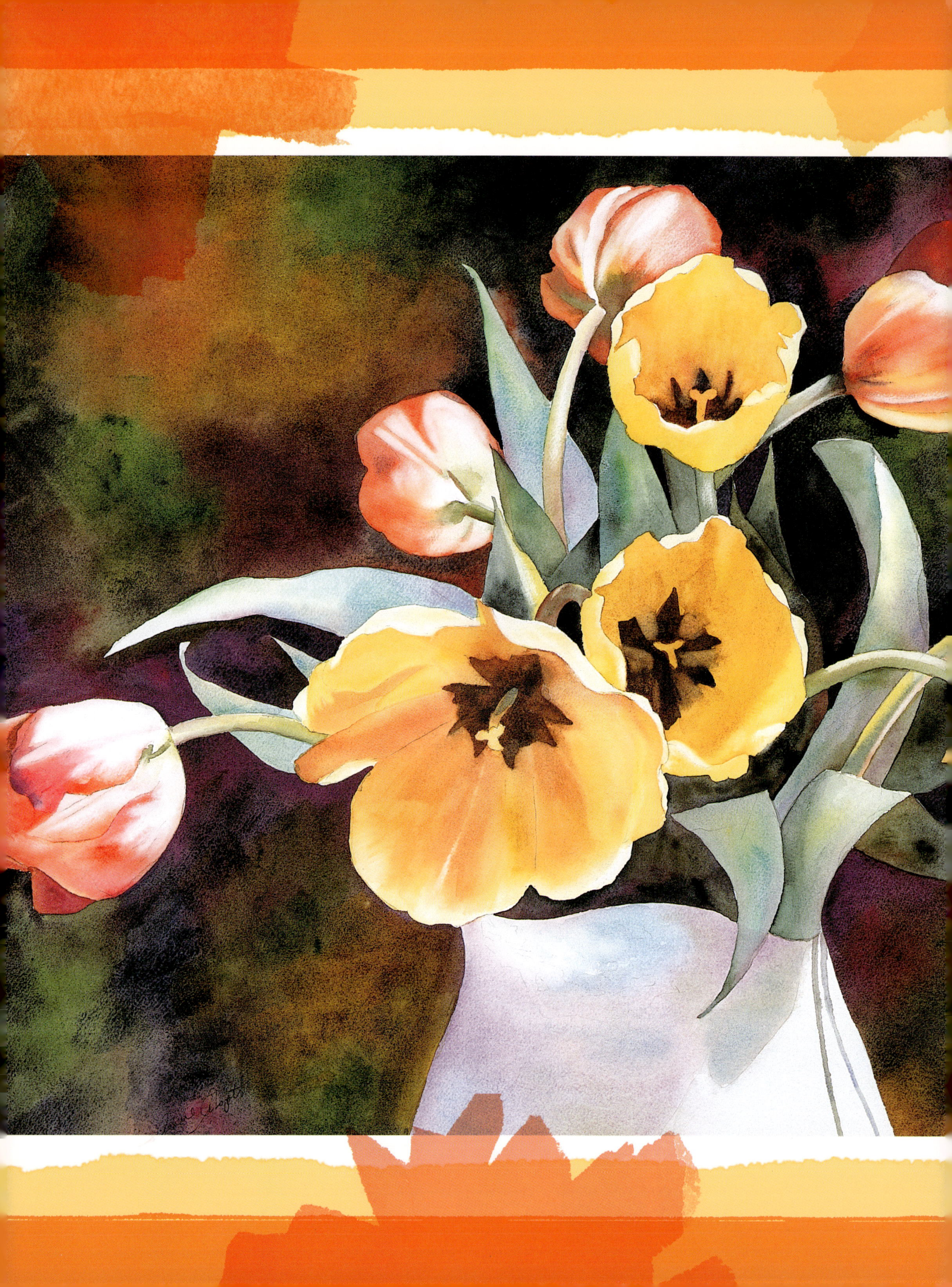

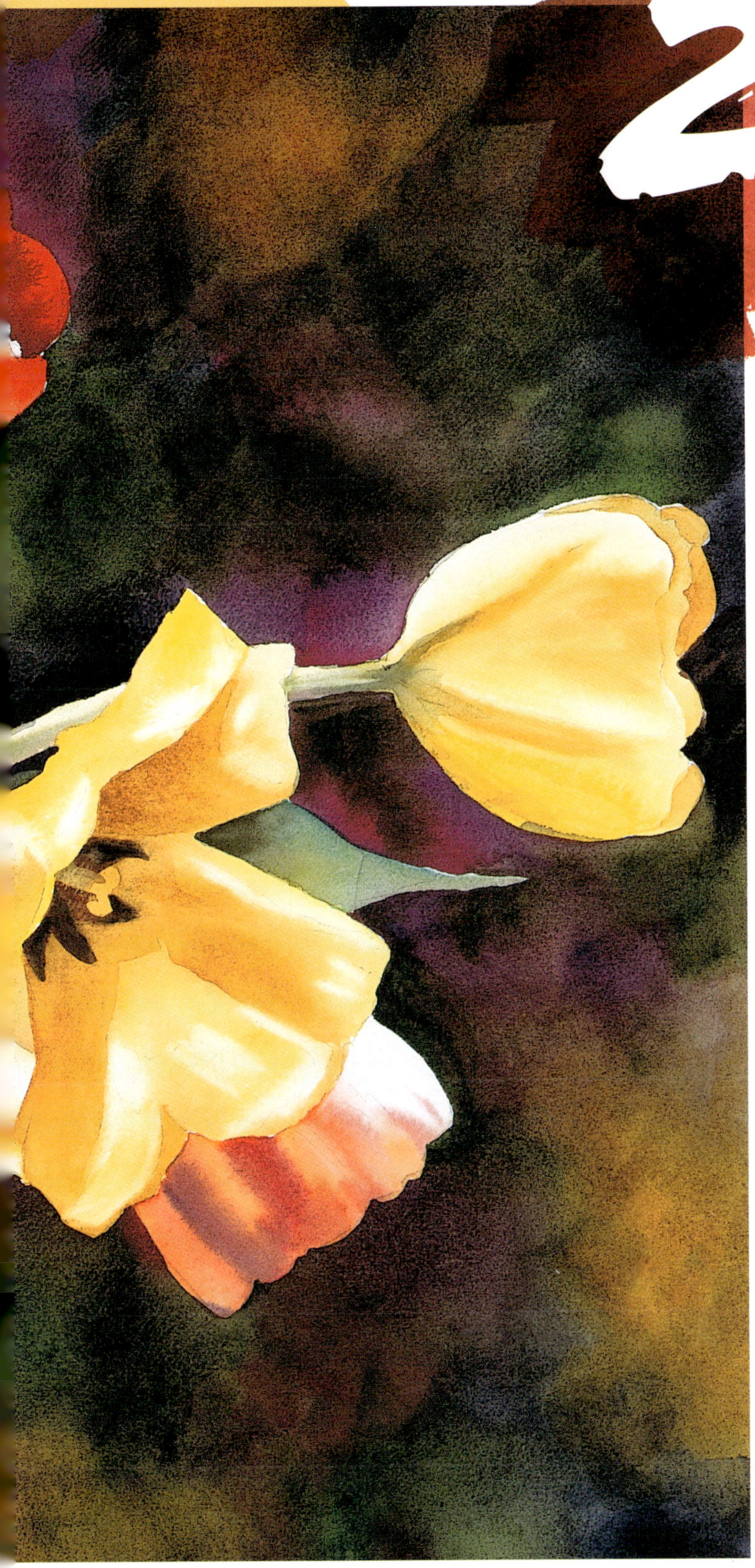

2 Color Mingling

Why do I mingle my colors and not mix them? I have discovered that mingling colors creates lively and vibrant color passages that cannot be achieved any other way. If the pigments and water are allowed to mingle and move on their own into the paper, you can apply paint directly to the paper thick or thin, side by side, warm against cool. This creates exciting and interesting areas and prevents flat passages that have nothing going on. Mingling also speeds up the painting process because I can get by with little or no glazing. As I went through the stages of developing my own style, I started to get comments on the glow, the color and the life my paintings had. When I had to write an article for a magazine describing my process, I suddenly realized I didn't mix colors—I mingled them. It was an epiphany!

SOME LIKE IT HOT
22" × 30" (56cm × 76cm)
Transparent watercolor on cold-pressed paper
Collection of Dede and Karl Kluckhohn

How to Mingle

MATERIALS

BRUSHES
No. 16 round

COLORS
Permanent Rose • Verditer Blue

SURFACE
300-lb. (640gsm) Arches cold-pressed paper

OTHER
Absorbing pad • flat work surface • water container

KEYS TO SUCCESSFUL MINGLING

For successful mingling, follow these tips:

- *When mingling, always choose transparent colors rather than opaque ones.*
- *Use 300-lb. (640 gsm) cold-pressed paper. It stays wet longer and allows the paints to mingle on the surface and into the paper.*
- *Work on a flat surface, not a tilted board, so the paints can move and mingle on their own.*
- *Get to know your colors before you start a painting by mingling swatches from your palette. This will eliminate any unwelcome surprises.*

Mixes are cleaner and richer when they're mixed on the paper. It's time to try it!

I primarily use Technique 1 for most of my painting. I rarely use Technique 2 except for grays.

TECHNIQUE 1: ONE COLOR AT A TIME

This is the method you use when you are laying in your base colors.

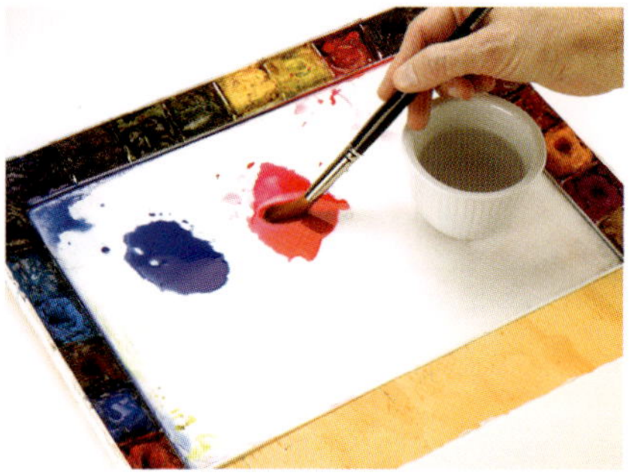

1 PREPARE THE PUDDLES
Mix two separate, juicy puddles of Verditer Blue and Permanent Rose with water. The consistency should be fairly liquid.

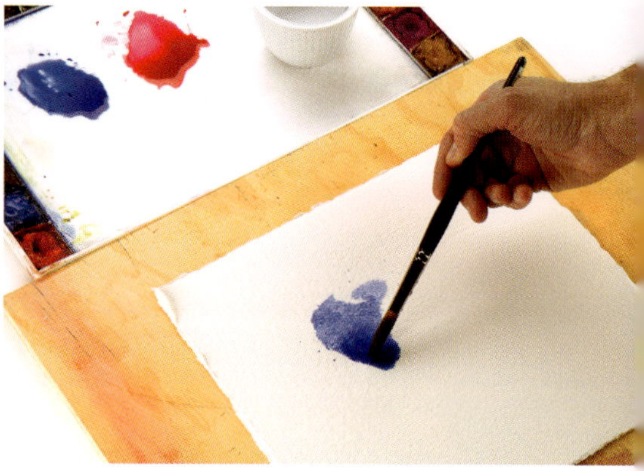

2 APPLY THE FIRST COLOR
Your paper should be dry and your work surface should be flat and level. Load the no. 16 round with Verditer Blue and apply it directly to the paper.

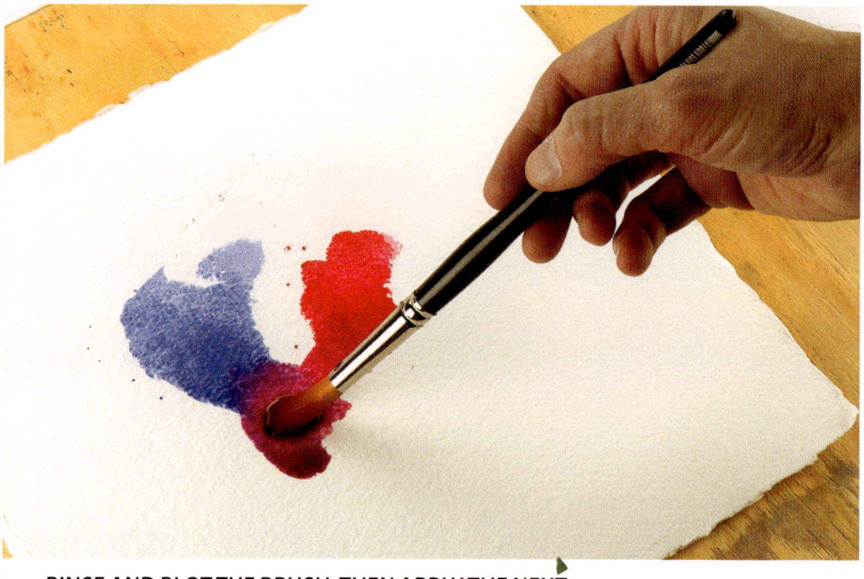

3 RINSE AND BLOT THE BRUSH, THEN APPLY THE NEXT COLOR
Swish the brush in water to clean it, then remove excess water from the brush with your absorbing pad. Load the brush with Permanent Rose from the puddle on the palette and paint this next to and touching the edge of the first color.

You can add more colors—for example, you may want to charge more than one red into an area of red, or change the temperature from warm to cool. Just be sure to rinse and blot the brush before each one.

TECHNIQUE 2: DOUBLE-LOADED BRUSH

This is the method you use when painting grays—especially when you're painting silver. The double-loaded brush allows the pigments to fall onto the paper with no control, creating grays with lots of life and color.

MATERIALS

BRUSHES
no. 16 or 26 round

COLORS
Aureolin Yellow • Cobalt Blue • Scarlet Lake

SURFACE
300-lb. (640gsm) Arches cold-pressed paper

OTHER
Absorbing pad • flat work surface • water container

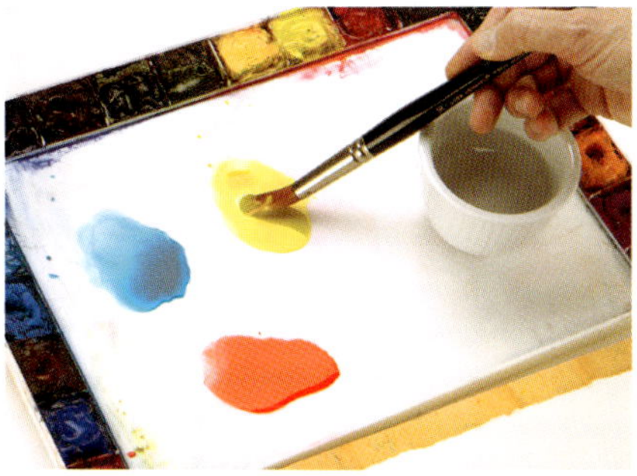

1 MIX THREE PUDDLES
Mix three separate, large juicy puddles: one each of Aureolin Yellow, Cobalt Blue and Scarlet Lake.

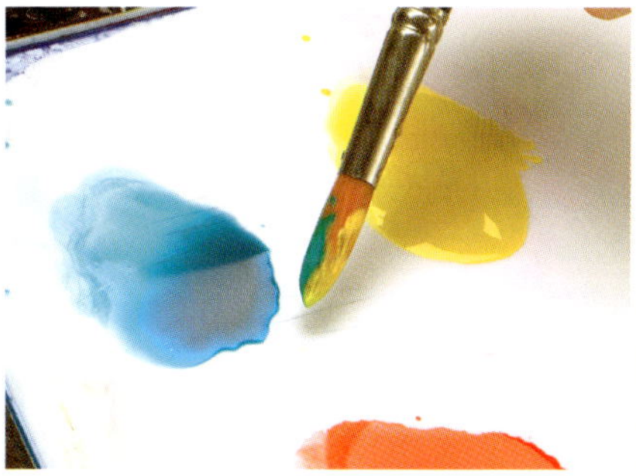

2 DOUBLE LOAD THE BRUSH, THEN APPLY
On dry paper, double load your no. 16 or 26 round brush with Cobalt Blue and Aureolin Yellow. To do this, swing one side of the brush into Cobalt Blue and the other side of the brush into the Aureolin Yellow. Don't blot the brush with a paper towel or pad. You need lots of fluid for flow so you can create a larger area.

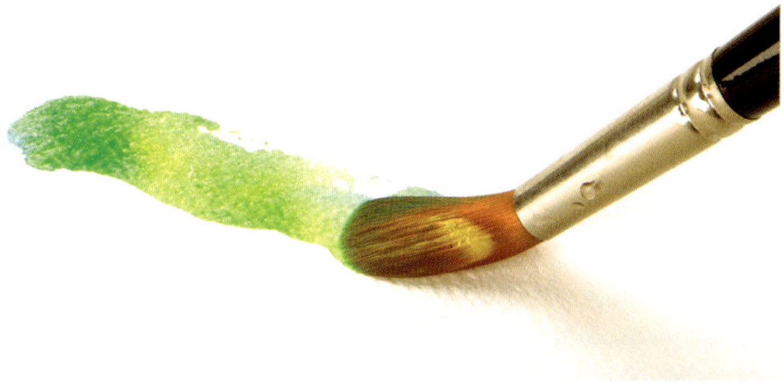

3 APPLY WITH A TWISTING MOTION
Twist the brush and mingle the colors on the dry paper.

HOW TO CHANGE A MINGLED AREA

When the whole area is wet, you may go back in to add or change colors. The key is to control the amount of water on your brush. Dropping more water into an already wet area causes blossoms; the weight of the excess water pushes away the surrounding paint. Carefully remove the bubble on the end of the brush before adding more to the mix by touching your brush to the absorbing pad. The brush is picking up moisture from the wet surface, so hit that absorbing pad before every application of paint.

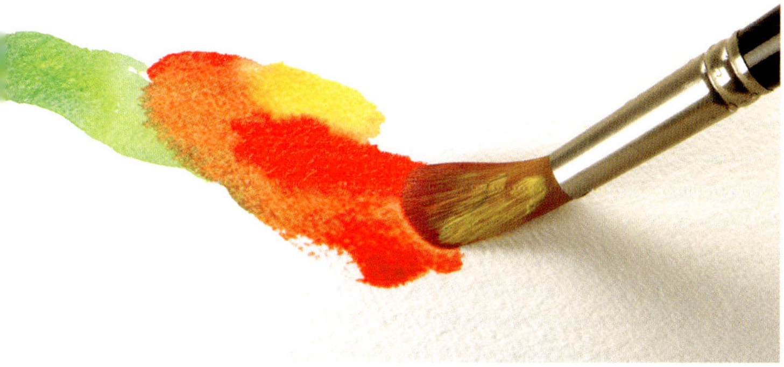

4 ADD MORE COLOR
Rinse your brush with water and then repeat the process. This time double load the brush with Aureolin Yellow and Scarlet Lake. Add these colors to the ones already on the paper, twisting the brush to disperse both colors and let them mingle on their own. Alternate the colors for better results.

Mingling Yellows

Yellow lights up a subject like no other color. It attracts the eye like a magnet and has been used successfully for years in advertising (think of how yellow signs jump out at you). However, yellow is also one of the most difficult colors to paint with, as it muddies easily and is not easy to darken.

By painting warmer yellows next to cooler ones, you can get wonderful effects that can help you define one area from another and add excitement to any passage. I primarily use New Gamboge, a warm yellow, next to Aureolin Yellow, a cool yellow. Yellow Ochre, a warm yellow, is perfect for dropping a bit of sunshine into a shadow.

Yellow is a potent color. You can create a glow by underpainting with yellow or dropping it into other pigments. Yellow can easily lose its integrity, though, when mixed on the palette with other colors. It's best to use the yellows as brilliantly and as cleanly as possible—one yellow hue next to the other.

LIGHTENING AND DARKENING YELLOWS

TO LIGHTEN	TUBE COLOR	TO DARKEN
add water	*Naples Yellow*	*add New Gamboge*
add water	*Aureolin Yellow*	*add New Gamboge*
add water	*New Gamboge*	*add Yellow Ochre*
add water	*Yellow Ochre*	*add Quinacridone Gold*

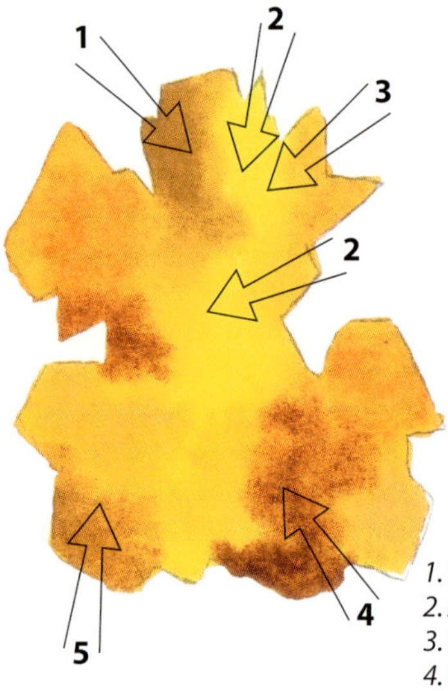

1. Yellow Ochre
2. Aureolin Yellow
3. New Gamboge
4. Quinacridone Gold
5. Naples Yellow

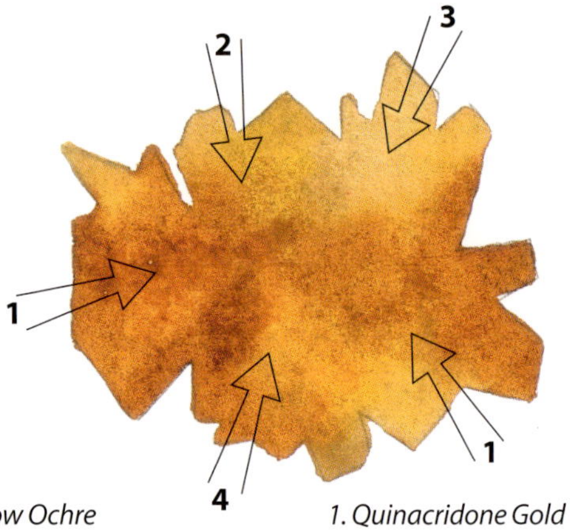

1. Quinacridone Gold
2. Yellow Ochre
3. Naples Yellow
4. New Gamboge

Mingled Yellows
These swatches show how different yellows look when dropped and mingled into each other. Use less water and less Aureolin Yellow to make mingled yellows look darker.

Characteristics of Yellows

1 **Aureolin Yellow**—a cool, lemony yellow that's very easy to lighten.

2 **New Gamboge**—a warm, intense yellow. It's great to use as an underpainting for reds. It's my favorite yellow to use when I want give an object a sunlit appearance.

3 **Naples Yellow**—this is the only opaque yellow I use. Dilute it with lots of water or it will look very heavy on the paper.

4 **Yellow Ochre**—this pigment stays where it's dropped. A little is all you need to add glow to any color.

5 **Quinacridone Gold**—a very powerful yellow that is great for darkening other yellows without muddying them.

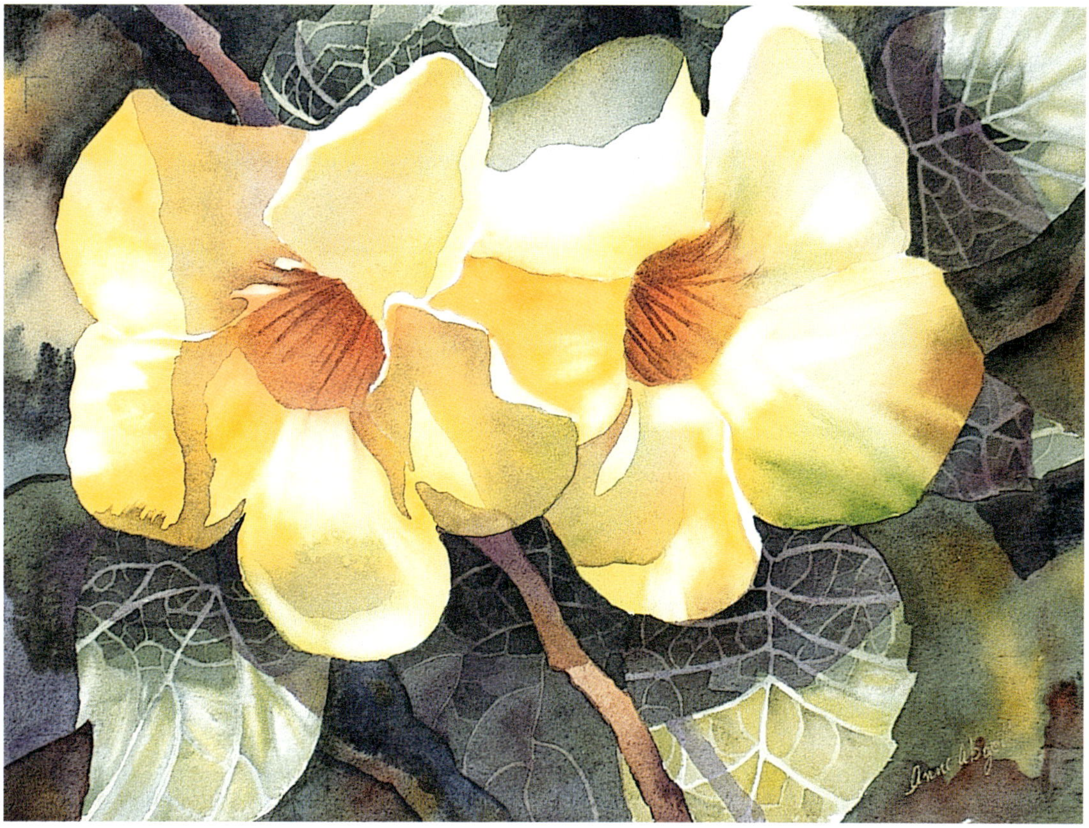

Mingle Warm Yellows Next to Cool Yellows

This sunny yellow flower is a perfect example of mingling all of the yellows on my palette. I created yellow-green shadows to indicate the reflections from the surrounding leaves.

Knowing how to use warm next to cool is an important technique. In these yellow flowers I have used warms and cools across the petals. It makes for lively, interesting passages. When you have petals side by side and close in value, use a warm against a cool to differentiate between the petals without a great value change.

OFF GULF OF MEXICO DRIVE
16" × 20" (41cm × 51cm)
Transparent watercolor on cold-pressed paper
Collection of Marcelle Forbes

SUGGESTIONS FOR USING YELLOWS

- *Mingle Aureolin Yellow or Yellow Ochre with Brown Madder and Mineral Violet for yellowish dirt, wood, concrete or dead grass in sunlight.*
- *Mingle Aureolin Yellow with Verditer Blue and Mineral Violet or Permanent Rose for foliage or grass in shadow.*
- *Mingle Naples Yellow and New Gamboge with Greenish Yellow for yellow objects in strong sunlight such as buildings or marsh grass in autumn.*
- *Mingle Yellow Ochre with New Gamboge and Mineral Violet for brilliant yellow-brown objects in foregrounds.*
- *Mingle New Gamboge with Antwerp Blue for midground foliage.*

ERASING PENCIL LINES

I find that graphite disappears under most pigments except yellow. Carefully lift pencil lines with a soft eraser before you lay down that yellow pigment!

Mingling Reds

For centuries, bold, bright red has been an important color on artists' palettes. It's one of the most exuberant colors an artist can add to a painting, creating excitement and warmth.

There is an amazing variety of reds. Just think about common vegetables and fruits: Say *cherry* or *onion*, and you instantly conjure up a certain red. Try this: Line up all the red vegetables and fruits you can find and paint a study. Try rhubarb, tomatoes, apples, raspberries, red onions, peppers, peaches, pears, cherries, strawberries—capturing all of the subtle distinctions among the reds will really challenge you!

Warm reds come forward and cool reds recede. For instance, using a warm red on the petal of a flower will make that petal appear closer than a petal painted with a cool magenta. The magenta will recede. This concept is a great help when composing any painting.

Red is a very important color in painting flesh tones as it adds pink tones. I use both Permanent Rose and Brown Madder in my skin tones. Lighten some reds with water to change the color somewhat when you use another pigment.

LIGHTENING AND DARKENING REDS		
TO LIGHTEN	TUBE COLOR	TO DARKEN
add water	*Scarlet Lake*	*add Quinacridone Magenta*
add water	*Permanent Rose*	*add Mineral Violet*
add water or Scarlet Lake	*Brown Madder*	*add Mineral Violet*
add water or Aureolin	*Quinacridone Red Orange*	*add Quinacridone Magenta*

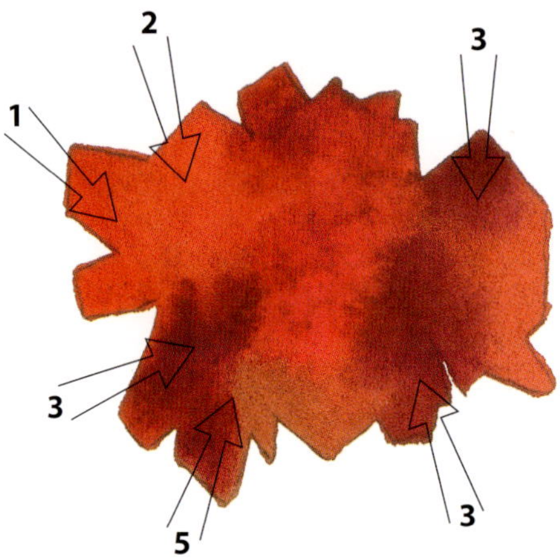

1. Scarlet Lake
2. Quinacridone Red Orange
3. Quinacridone Magenta
4. Brown Madder
5. Permanent Rose

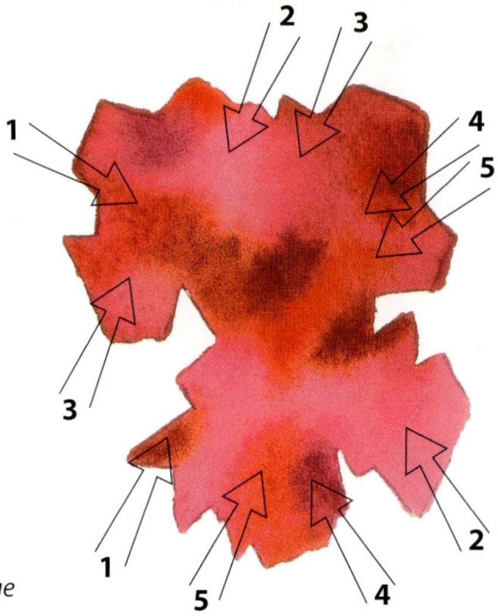

1. Brown Madder
2. Opera
3. Permanent Rose
4. Quinacridone Magenta
5. Quinacridone Red Orange

Mingled Reds
These swatches show how different reds look when mingled into each other. For lighter reds, use more water and more Opera.

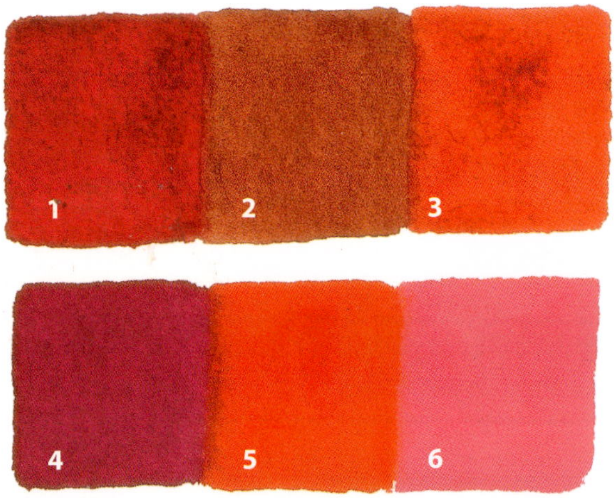

Characteristics of Reds

1 **Permanent Rose**—I use this instead of Alizarin Crimson because it isn't a fugitive and it's easy to lift. It mingles well with blues to make violets.

2 **Brown Madder**—I can't live without this color. I use it in dark backgrounds to suggest light and warmth. Mingle it with blues for gorgeous grays.

3 **Scarlet Lake**—my most intense red. I use it along with Indigo to make black.

4 **Quinacridone Magenta**—another intense red. Use it to mingle dark shadow on red objects and for dark backgrounds.

5 **Quinacridone Red Orange**—I drop this in when I want to make an object pop. Use this to make peach by mingling it with Naples Yellow.

6 **Opera**—I use this one sparingly as it tends to push other colors away. I use Opera when I see it in reds and to add excitement.

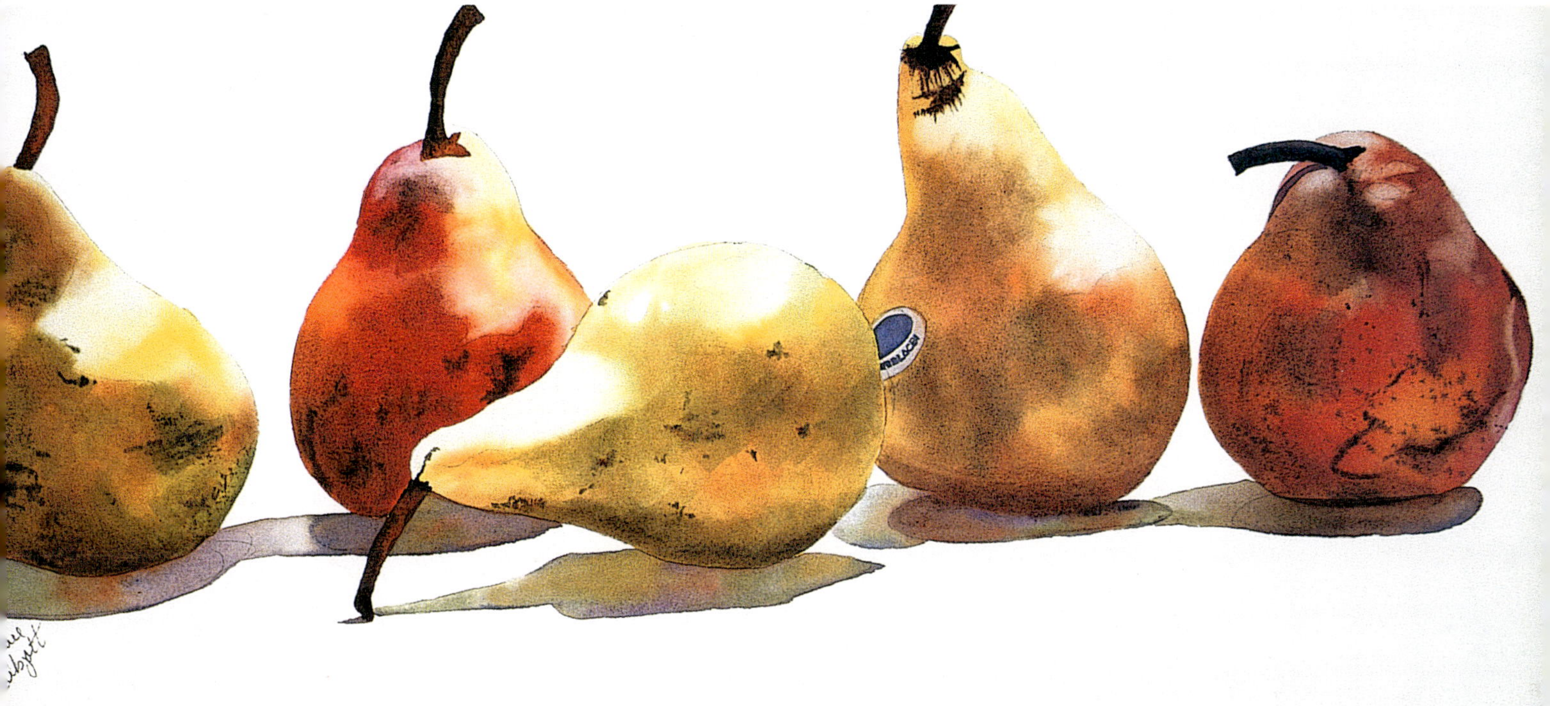

A Yellow Underpainting Adds Vibrancy to Mingled Reds

Mingling my palette's reds and yellows was essential for this painting of pears. I used all of the reds on my palette. The red pears were underpainted in some areas with New Gamboge. These areas appear closer to the viewer. I used Scarlet Lake and Quinacridone Red Orange over the yellow, and the cooler reds, Permanent Rose and Quinacridone Magenta, in the areas that recede.

NOT FOR SALE
11" × 24" (28cm × 61cm)
Transparent watercolor on cold-pressed paper
Collection of Mr. and Mrs. L. McGaughy

SUGGESTIONS FOR USING REDS

- *Mingle Scarlet Lake with Mineral Violet for red roofs in shadow or the side of brickwork.*
- *Mingle Brown Madder with Yellow Ochre or New Gamboge for light, warm-colored buildings in late afternoon sun or for autumn foliage.*
- *Mingle Brown Madder with Ultramarine Blue for rocks or old buildings.*
- *Mingle Permanent Rose with Cobalt Blue for clouds or shadows on objects light in color.*
- *Use Quinacridone Red Orange for bright, glowing beaks on birds.*

Mingling Blues

Blue surrounds us: It is the sky and the water. I think of blue as a strong yet peaceful color. Blue is essential for mingling grays (which we'll talk about on page 45).

When I lived in the northeastern United States near the Great Lakes, Ultramarine Blue was a very important color on my palette because it seemed a suitable color in the cool climate. Since I moved to the warm south, I use it less and have added different blues to my palette, such as Cobalt Teal Blue and Verditer Blue, to capture the spectacular warm and cool blues of the water where I live. I still use Ultramarine Blue for mingling and painting rocks, tree bark and stone.

Verditer Blue has replaced Cerulean on my palette. It is the color I used most and "cannot do without." I find it more transparent than Cerulean; it has much less white in it. Verditer Blue is the number one essential color on my palette.

LIGHTENING AND DARKENING BLUES		
TO LIGHTEN	TUBE COLOR	TO DARKEN
add water & P. Rose	*Verditer Blue*	*add Cobalt Blue*
add water	*Cobalt Teal Blue*	*add Antwerp Blue*
add water	*Cobalt Blue*	*add Ultramarine Blue*
add water	*Antwerp Blue*	*add Brown Madder*

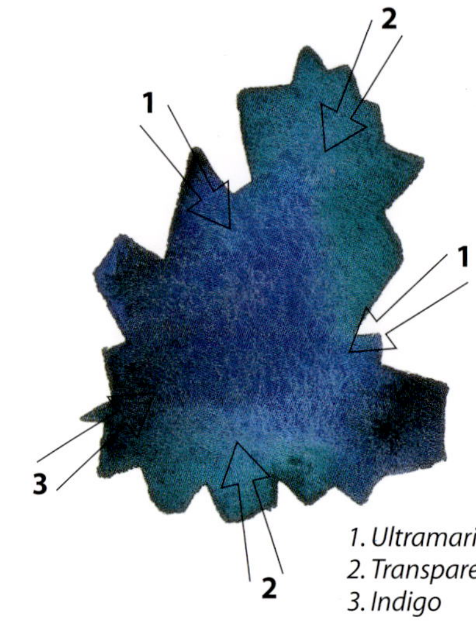

1. Ultramarine Blue
2. Transparent Turquoise
3. Indigo

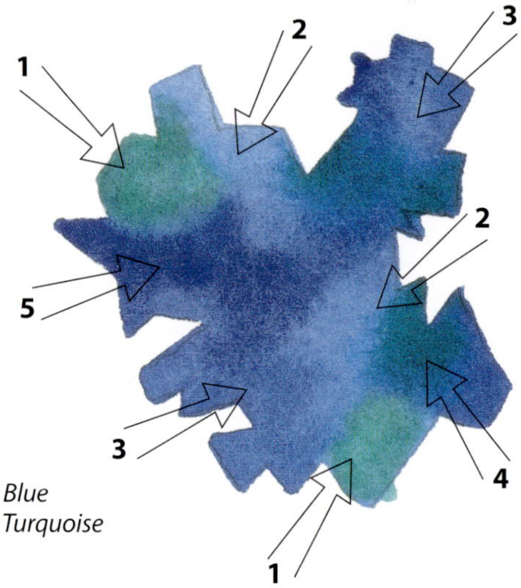

1. Cobalt Teal Blue
2. Verditer Blue
3. Cobalt Blue
4. Transparent Turquoise
5. Ultramarine Blue

Mingled Blues
Here you can see how different blues look when mingled into each other. Use more water with your pigments for lighter blues.

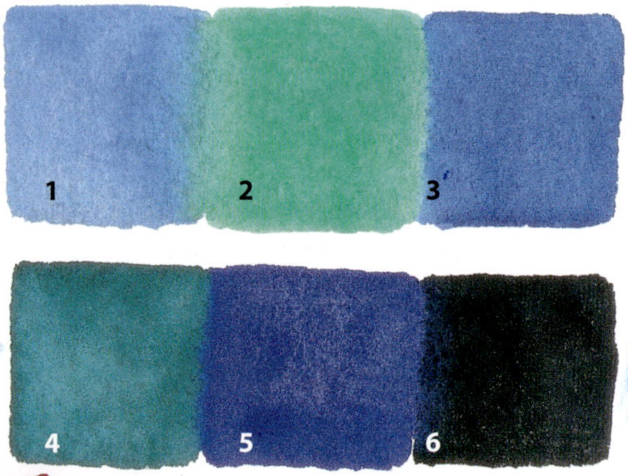

Characteristics of Blues

1 **Verditer Blue**—I use this instead of Cerulean Blue because it's a better mingler. It can push back entire areas of a painting and you can adjust its value without losing any of the integrity of the painting beneath.

2 **Cobalt Teal Blue**—this is highly opaque but I water it down and drop it into wet mingled pigment to create excitement.

3 **Cobalt Blue**—an essential blue for painting shadows. Drop it along the edges of wet mingled pigments and watch it creep into the other paints.

4 **Transparent Turquoise**—my favorite color to use when painting water.

5 **Ultramarine Blue**—a granular pigment that I use with Burnt Sienna to create wood.

6 **Indigo**—use this for dark backgrounds or mingle it with Scarlet Lake for an intense black.

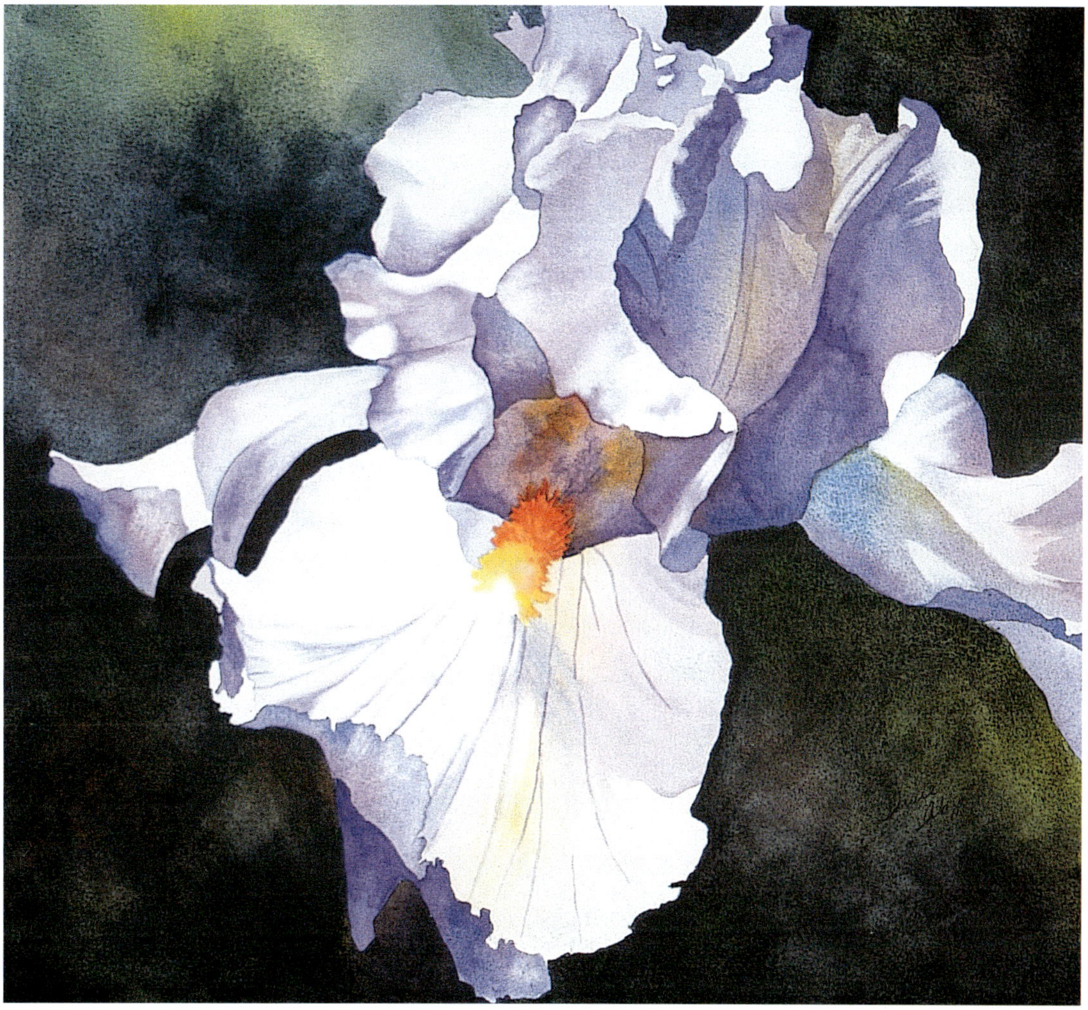

Mingled Blues Lightened With Water

I used several of my blues in this iris painting: Verditer Blue, Cobalt Blue and Cobalt Teal Blue. The upper far-right petal is Cobalt Teal Blue. I mingled Verditer Blue and Cobalt Blue with some light Cobalt Teal Blue for the other petals. I used lots of water as I mingled the colors to give the blues a light and airy feeling.

HEAVEN AT THE GATE
16" × 20" (41cm × 51cm)
Transparent watercolor on cold-pressed paper
Collection of Mr. and Mrs. Russell Beckwith

SUGGESTIONS FOR USING BLUES

- *Mingle Verditer Blue with Cobalt Blue for skies and shadows.*
- *Mingle Antwerp Blue with New Gamboge for orangish green foliage in the midground of autumn scenes.*
- *Mingle Cobalt Blue with Yellow Ochre to create pale greenish blue areas.*
- *Mingle Indigo with Scarlet Lake for dark blacks.*
- *Mingle Ultramarine Blue with Brown Madder for a black with a hint of warmth.*

Mingling Greens

The color green is everywhere in the environment. It's truly "nature's color." Greens can be dazzling or deadly. There are "tube greens," detested by some and loved by others because they can be bright and overpowering. I often tell my students that they would be better off mingling yellow and blues to get the greens that they want. But you can have it both ways. You can learn how to control tube greens by using the chart on this page.

LIGHTENING AND DARKENING GREENS

TO LIGHTEN	TUBE COLOR	TO DARKEN
add water and Aureolin	*Permanent Sap Green*	*add Antwerp Blue*
add water and Aureolin	*Olive Green*	*add Ultramarine Blue*
add water	*Undersea Green*	*add Indigo*
add water	*Greenish Yellow*	*add Permanent Sap Green*

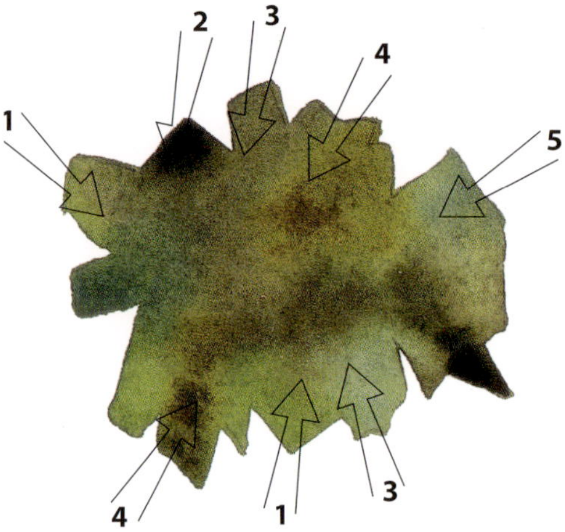

1. Permanent Sap Green
2. Undersea Green
3. Olive Green
4. Greenish Yellow
5. Verditer Blue

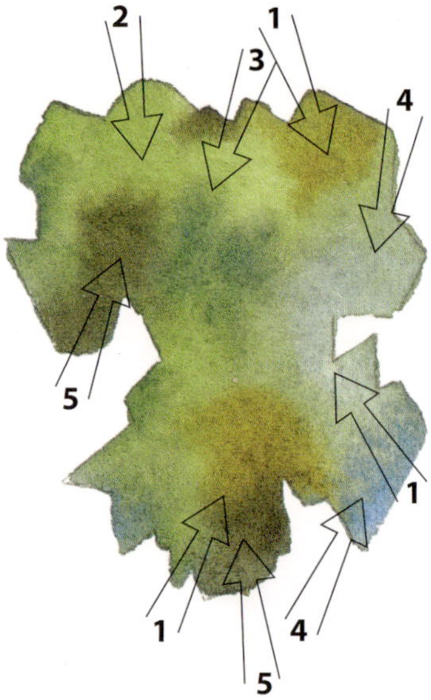

1. Greenish Yellow
2. Olive Green
3. Permanent Sap Green
4. Verditer Blue
5. Undersea Green

Mingled Greens
These swatches show how different greens look when mingled into each other. Using more water with your greens make them significantly lighter.

MINGLE PERMANENT SAP GREEN WITH OTHER COLORS FOR A RANGE OF GREENS

Mingle Permanent Sap Green with other colors and you will be able to create almost any green in nature. Here I've taken Permanent Sap Green out of the tube and mingled it with different colors to create yellowish greens, reddish greens and bluish greens.

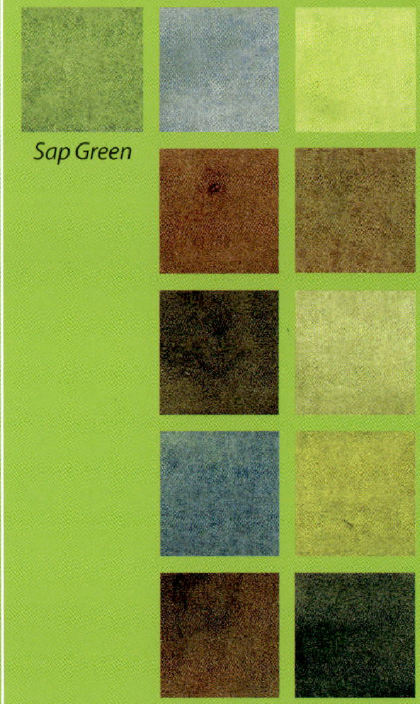

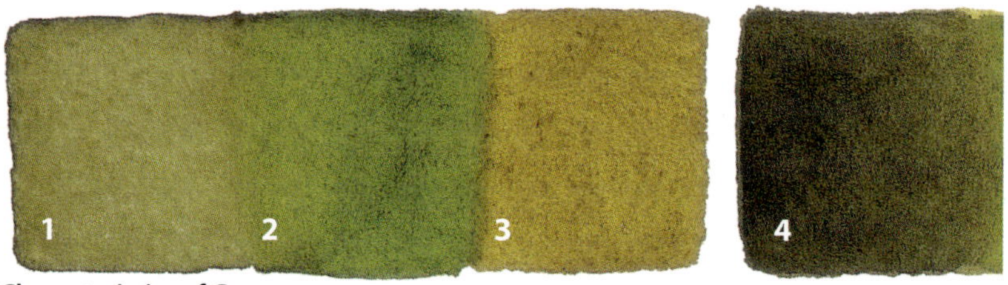

Characteristics of Greens

1 **Olive Green**—a quiet green that's less jarring on the paper than Permanent Sap Green can be.

2 **Permanent Sap Green**—a warm green but can be garish on the page. However, it mingles well with other colors to create interesting greens.

3 **Greenish Yellow**—very warm and pushes away other colors, so use it sparingly.

4 **Undersea Green**—a deep, intense green that mingles well with almost all colors. Use this to darken the value of other tube greens.

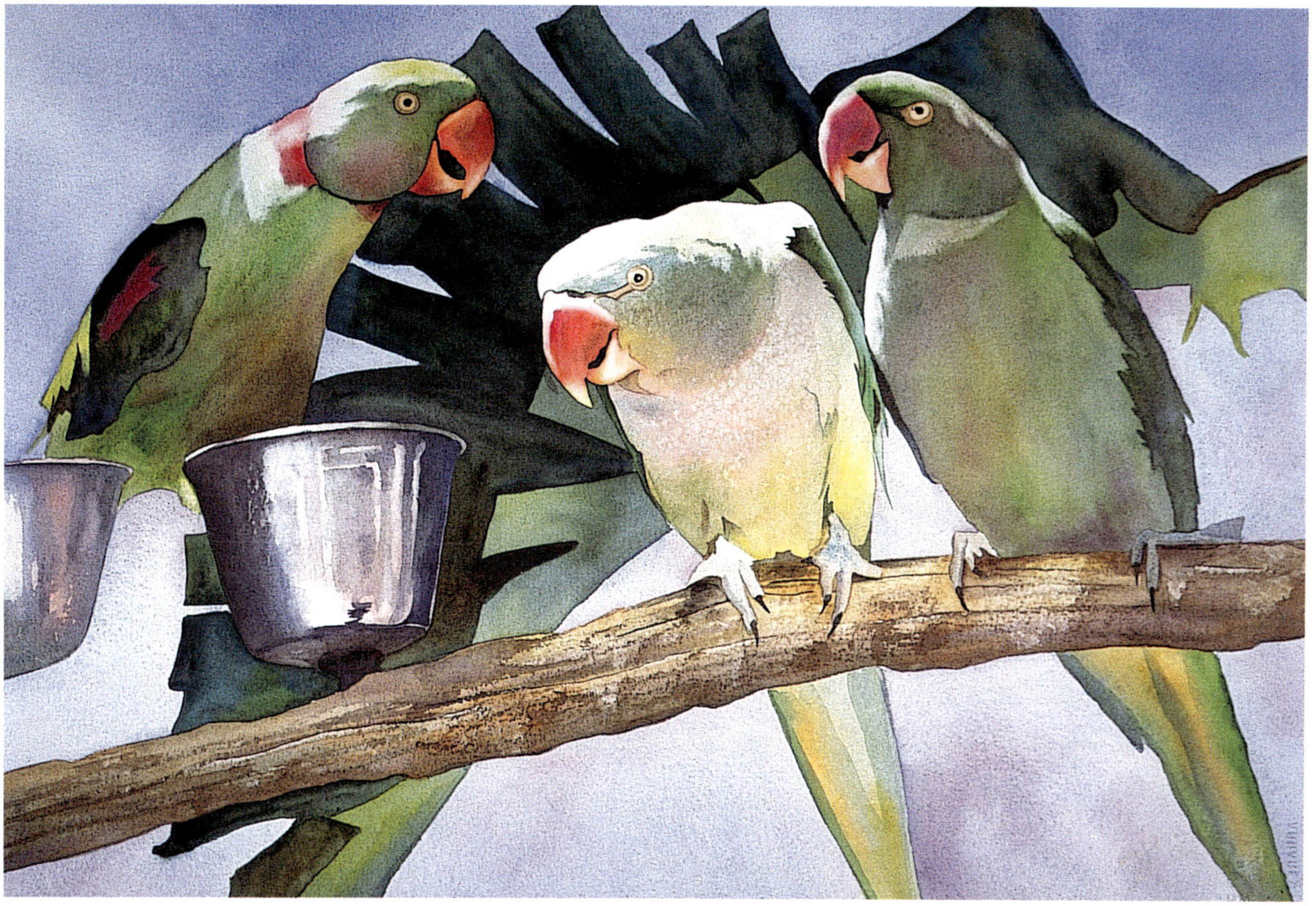

Mingling Tube Greens Can Create Brilliant Results

In this painting of parrots, I mingled all of the greens on my palette. I used Compose Green 1 in a few places; it's a lovely green but very opaque, so I use it sparingly and water it down a great deal.

BUSY BODIES
15" × 22" (38cm × 56cm)
Transparent watercolor on cold-pressed paper
Collection of Mr. and Mrs. S. Gregory

SUGGESTIONS FOR USING GREENS

- *Mingle Permanent Sap Green with Antwerp Blue for middle value foliage or foliage in shadow.*
- *Mingle Permanent Sap Green with Permanent Rose to gray down foliage.*
- *Mingle Olive Green with Verditer Blue for grass in sunlight.*
- *Mingle Undersea Green with Indigo for an intense dark green.*
- *Mingle Compose Green 1 with Verditer Blue and a lot of water for a gray green.*

Mingling Violets

Violet is the preferred name for colors composed of any red or blue; however, I don't like the way mixed violets look once dry—they're too dull. I prefer to use violets from the tube because they seem to radiate joy and lift the spirit—even when dry.

Winter scenes provide a great opportunity to use violets. Shadows on snow have shades of pinks and blues in them, depending on the time of day. A rainy day can have a blue-violet tinge—even a sky can look purple.

Of all the violets on my palette, Mineral Violet is the one I use the most. It's an unobtrusive color that I use for all shadows and for darkening reds.

LIGHTENING AND DARKENING VIOLETS

TO LIGHTEN	TUBE COLOR	TO DARKEN
add water	*Cobalt Violet*	*add Quinacridone Magenta*
add water	*Cobalt Violet Light*	*add Mineral Violet*
add water	*Mineral Violet*	*add Scarlet Lake*
add water	*Permanent Violet Reddish*	*add Permanent Rose*
add water	*Permanent Violet*	*add Alizarin Crimson*

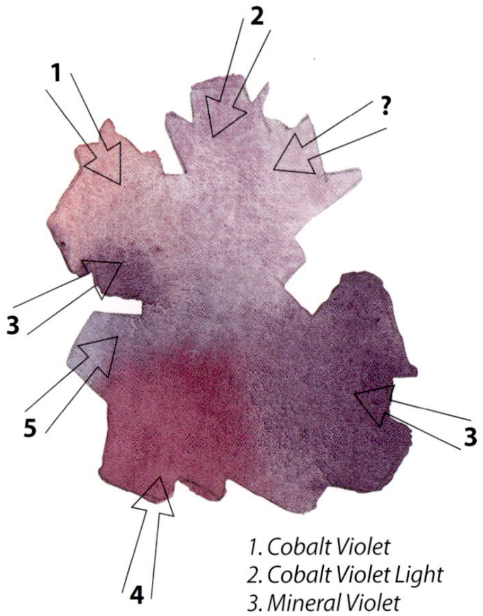

1. Cobalt Violet
2. Cobalt Violet Light
3. Mineral Violet
4. Permanent Violet Reddish
5. Permanent Violet

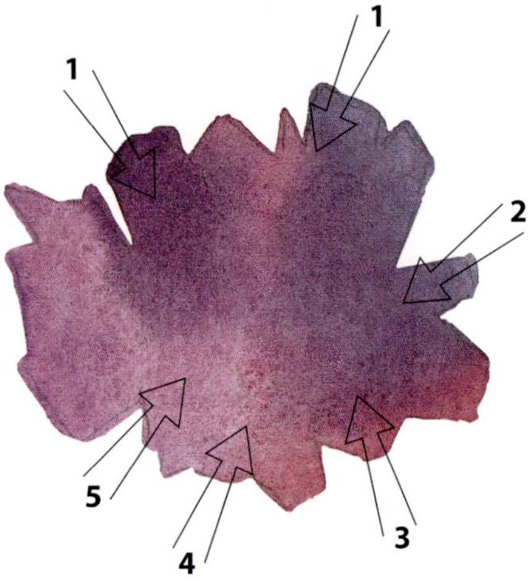

1. Mineral Violet
2. Permanent Violet
3. Permanent Violet Reddish
4. Cobalt Violet
5. Cobalt Violet Light

Mingled Violets
These swatches show how different violets look when mingled into each other. For darker violets, use less water with your pigments.

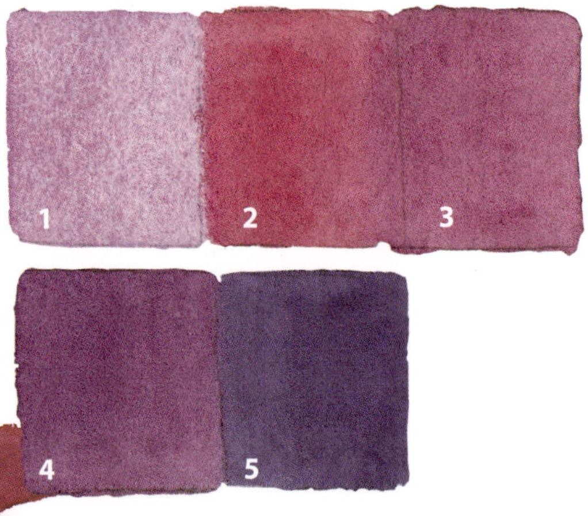

Characteristics of Violets

1 **Cobalt Violet**—a warm, nongranular violet (the only one I can find). It's very useful in skin tones.

2 **Cobalt Violet Light**—a cool violet.

3 **Mineral Violet**—one of my "can't do without" colors—somewhat granular; adds tension to greens; good in all shadows and darkens all reds.

4 **Permanent Violet Reddish**—an intense dark purple that mingles well in dark backgrounds using Permanent Sap Green and Mineral Violet.

5 **Permanent Violet**—another intense dark purple good for mingling dark passages.

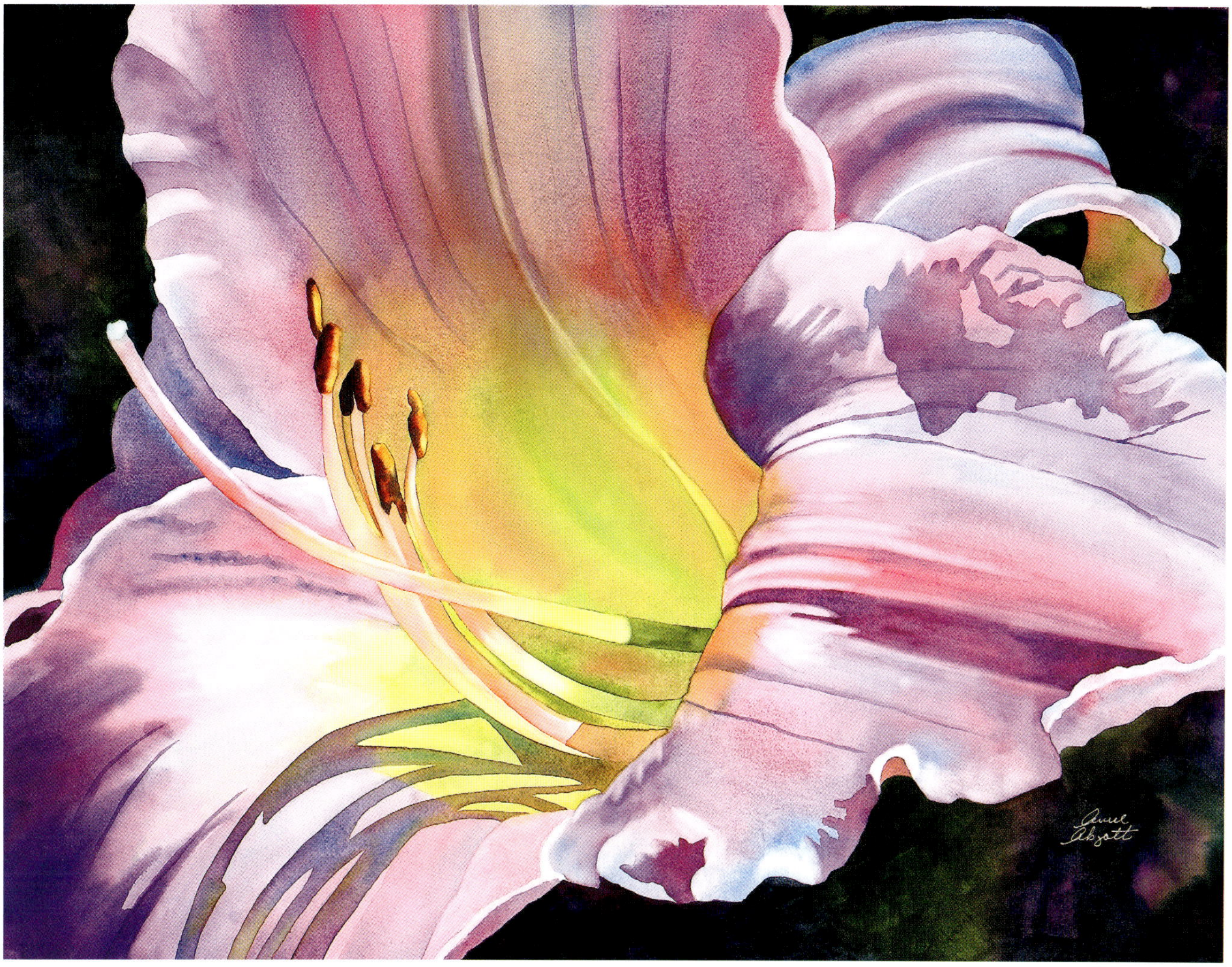

A Range of Mingled Violets
This daylily grew in my garden in North Carolina this summer. I was entranced by the lime green center and the light violet colors. I wanted to paint some up-close, "in-your-face" flowers, and this was a perfect subject. Notice that several violets are used in all sections of the painting. The lower-left petal combines Permanent Violet Reddish and Permanent Violet to create a darker lower edge. The right-middle petal shows (above the dark stripe center) the warm Cobalt Violet mingled up to the cool Cobalt Violet Light.

VIOLET DAZE
22" × 30" (56cm × 76cm)
Transparent watercolor on cold-pressed paper
Collection of the artist

SUGGESTIONS FOR USING VIOLET

- *Violets, especially Mineral Violet, add tension to foliage and leaves.*
- *Mingle Mineral Violet with any transparent green to create a nice granulated color.*
- *Drop Permanent Violet Reddish into the stems of flowers or leaves to give form to the dark side of the stem.*

Mingling Primary Colors

MATERIALS

BRUSHES
Nos. 4, 6, 12 and 16 rounds • ¾-inch (19mm) flat • no. 6 scrubber

COLORS
Aureolin Yellow • Brown Madder • Burnt Sienna • Cobalt Teal Blue • Mineral Violet • New Gamboge • Olive Green • Permanent Rose • Quinacridone Magenta • Scarlet Lake • Ultramarine Blue • Verditer Blue • Yellow Ochre

SURFACE
300-lb. (640gsm) Arches cold-pressed paper

OTHER
Razor blade

The challenge of this painting was keeping the reds, blues and yellows clean and bright. By mingling the paint side by side in a direct manner, I was able to keep the reds interesting—warm in some places, cool in others. Underpainting with New Gamboge on part of the breast of the bird creates the illusion of warmth and pushes the chest forward. I used cooler reds under the wings in areas that recede. I applied blues directly, side by side, to give the effect of several feathers without having to define them.

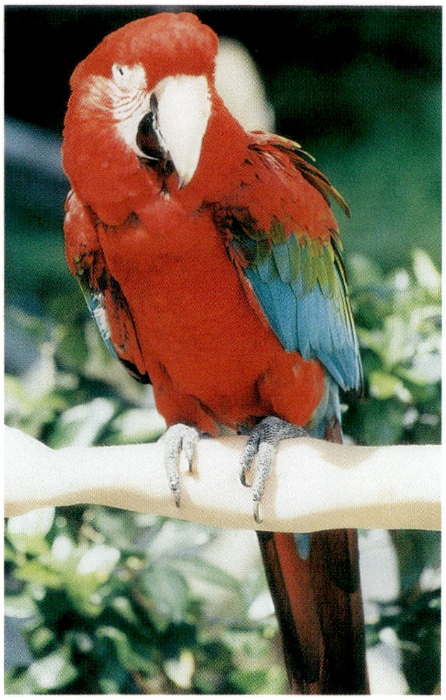

Reference Photo
I loved this bird's quizzical look as well as the good lights and shadows in this scene. The parrot was sitting on someone's arm, which I knew wouldn't make the most attractive painting, so I took artistic license and put him on a branch surrounded by leaves.

1 INTENSIFY THE VALUES, USE THE PAINT ON THE PAPER
Draw or trace the composition onto the watercolor paper. Wet the lightest area on the top of the bird's head with water using a no. 12 round. With a no. 16 round, begin to mingle Permanent Rose and Quinacridone Magenta on dry paper, working on the right side of the head across the forehead to the far left edge of the head. Let the paint touch the areas of water. While this is wet, pick up thick Scarlet Lake and Brown Madder paint on a ¾-inch (19mm) flat and drop this into the areas you want to darken.

Use a no. 4 round to pull small lines of red around the bird's eye while the paint is still wet. Switch to a no. 12 round and mingle New Gamboge with Scarlet Lake along the left side of the head and around and under the beak. Clean the round and mingle Quinacridone Magenta and Permanent Rose along and under the beak, going back to the right side of the bird. Drop in some Brown Madder to darken. Mingle New Gamboge into the paint for a push of yellow in the brighter area.

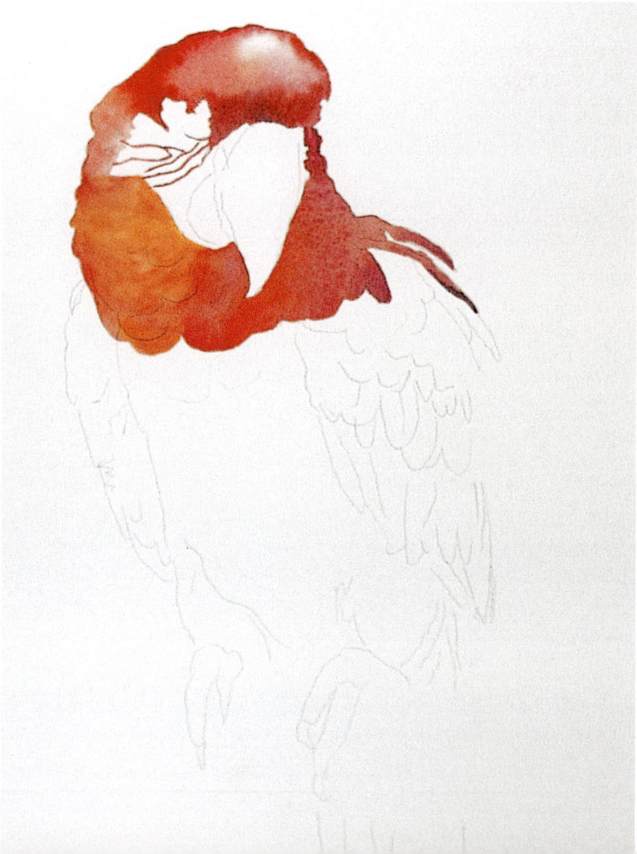

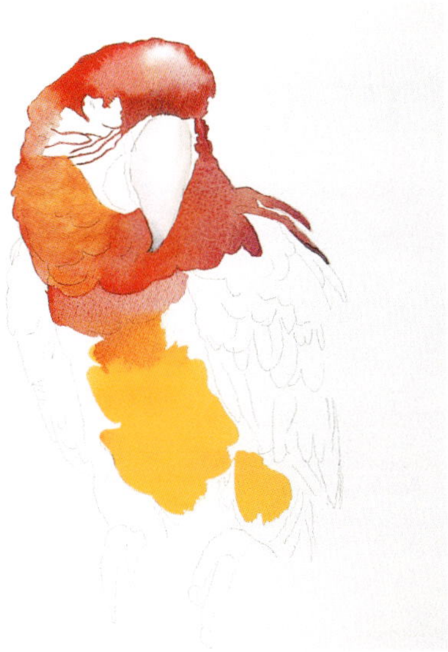

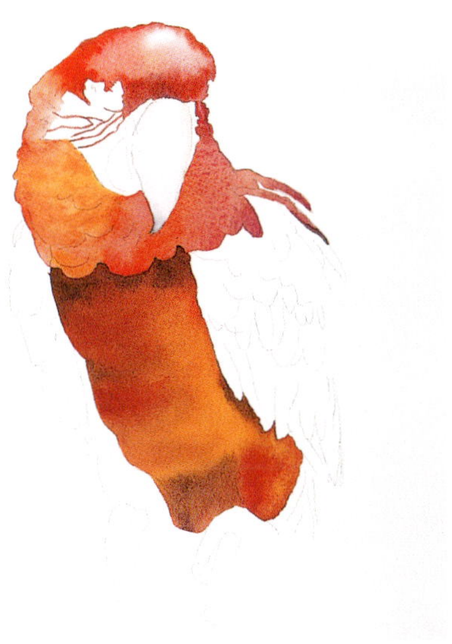

2 ADD A YELLOW UNDERPAINTING
Mingle a little Verditer Blue and Burnt Sienna and paint the left side of the beak, pulling the paint away with water. Add a light glaze of Aureolin Yellow to the right side of the beak. While this is wet, take a no. 4 round and drop in Brown Madder and Ultramarine Blue to create the dark tip of the beak. Cover the bird's breast with a no. 16 round loaded with lots of thick New Gamboge.

3 DARKEN THE BIRD'S BREAST WITH REDS
While the bird's breast is damp, paint over the yellow underpainting by mingling Scarlet Lake, Permanent Rose and Brown Madder with a no. 16 round. While this is wet, use a ¾-inch (19mm) flat and darken the paint with Mineral Violet and some Brown Madder. Do not add more water to these pigments; just use thick paint to darken the areas.

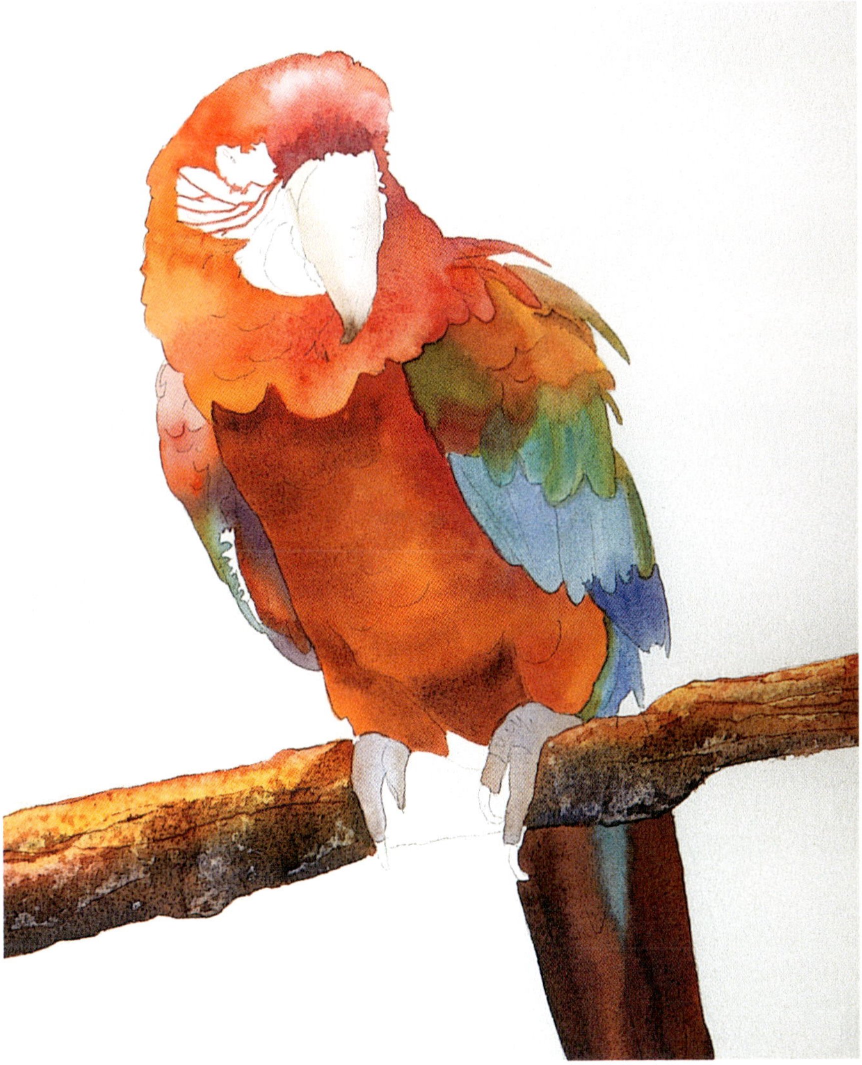

4 COMPLETE THE FEATHERS AND BRANCH
Starting at the top-right section of the bird's wing, mingle New Gamboge into Scarlet Lake then into Olive Green, Cobalt Teal Blue and Verditer Blue. Use a no. 12 round brush. While wet, drop in thick Ultramarine Blue for the darker areas. Mingle Scarlet Lake, Yellow Ochre and Cobalt Teal Blue for the tail. Darken these colors with Brown Madder and Mineral Violet using a no. 16 round.

Cover the branch with New Gamboge on a no. 12 round. With a ¾-inch (19mm) flat loaded with lots of pigment, begin to cover over the New Gamboge with Brown Madder and Burnt Sienna. On the underside of the branch drop in Ultramarine Blue and Mineral Violet. When the shine is off the paint, scratch in some texture with a razor blade. Use the whole blade in some places and just the tip of the blade in others.

Using a no. 6 round, mingle Verditer Blue and Burnt Sienna to paint the bird's feet.

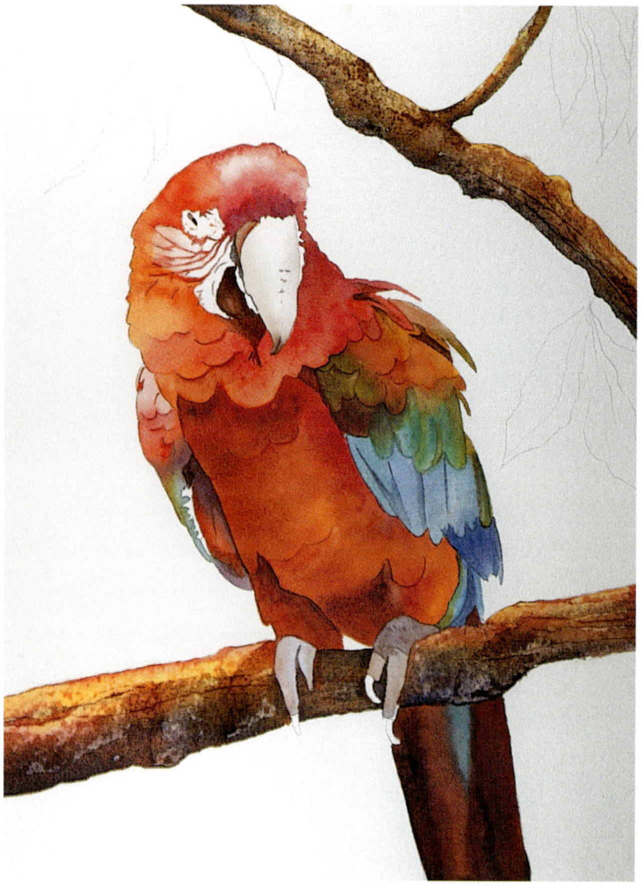

5 **DARKEN THE BEAK AND ADD MORE BRANCHES**
Mingle Brown Madder and Ultramarine Blue to darken areas on and under the beak with a no. 12 round. Develop the branch above the bird's head using the same techniques and colors you used in the previous step. Pay attention to the light areas on these branches and lift them out with a razor blade as before. Pull a little red into the eye and add Ultramarine Blue to create a pupil.

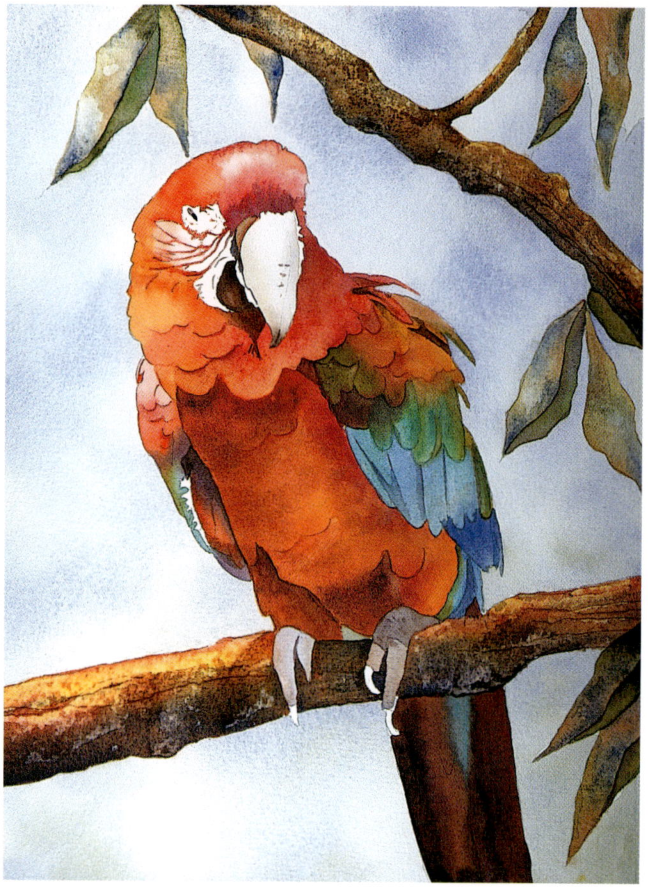

6 **PUT IN THE LEAVES AND SKY**
Paint the leaves by mingling Olive Green, Aureolin Yellow and Brown Madder with a no. 16 round.

When the leaves, branches and parrot are all dry, use a no. 16 round to wet some areas of the background with clean water. Load a no. 16 round with Verditer Blue and paint from dry areas of the paper to wet areas, letting the blues mingle with the water to create the sky. By applying the water first, you will keep the paint lighter in some areas, giving the eye a place to rest.

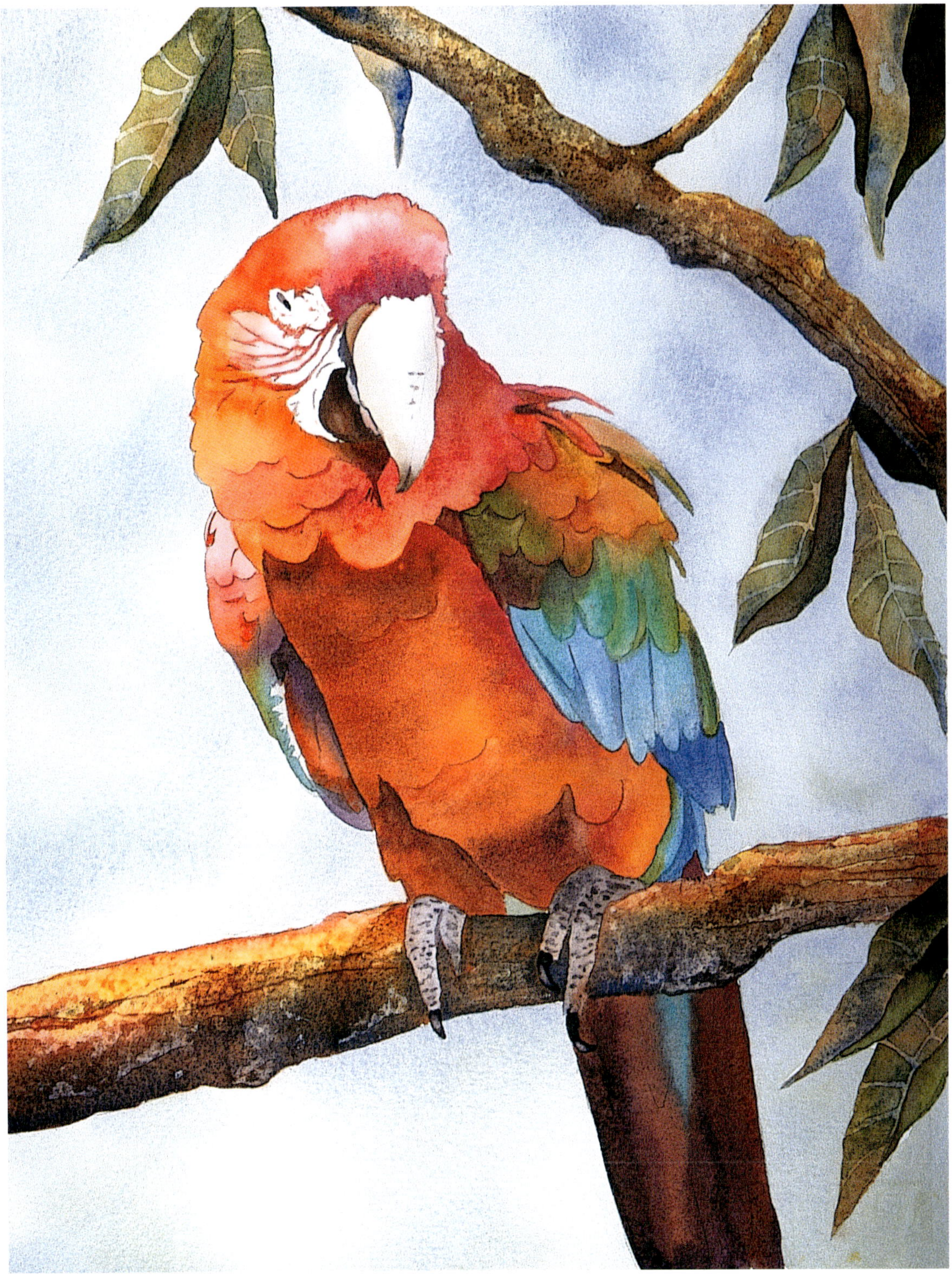

7 FINISH THE PAINTING
Finish the toenails and add some texture to the feet by mingling Brown Madder and Ultramarine Blue with a no. 4 round. Lift and adjust a few feathers using your no. 6 scrubber.

PARROT WITH ATTITUDE
16" × 20" (51cm × 41cm)
Transparent watercolor on cold-pressed paper
Collection of Mr. and Mrs. S. Gregory

The Importance of Grays

Most traditional paintings contain not only clean, vibrant, unmixed colors, but also an abundance of gray. Grays comprise a lot more of your paintings than you would think, so it's important to know how to make them. Why are grays so important? They are a quiet place where the eye can rest, and they can be great way to connect your shapes and unify a painting.

I really dislike tube grays because they make my colors appear dead, flat and uninteresting. There is nothing worse than a lovely shadow shape painted with a dead color. Also, most tube grays are opaque and chalky.

Tube Gray and Tube Black

These swatches show Payne's Gray and Peachy Black with water added to show the progressive values of lightness that can be achieved. As you can see, the results are very dull and monochromatic.

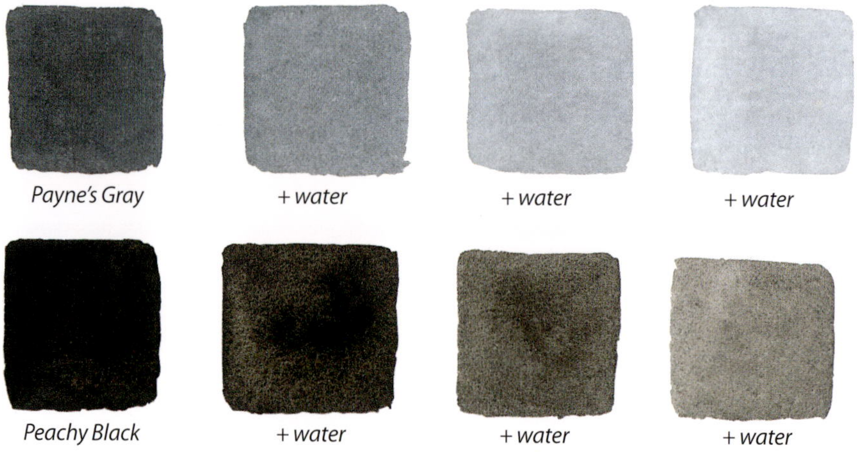

Grays From Mixed Colors

Many traditional blacks are created by mixing colors on the palette. By adding water to any of these black mixtures, you create various shades of gray. Notice how the mixed colors have more color variation.

The first black mixture is created with equal parts Alizarin Crimson and Winsor Green.

The second black consists of Scarlet Lake and Indigo mixed in equal parts. If I need to use black, this is the mixture I prefer because it is more colorful.

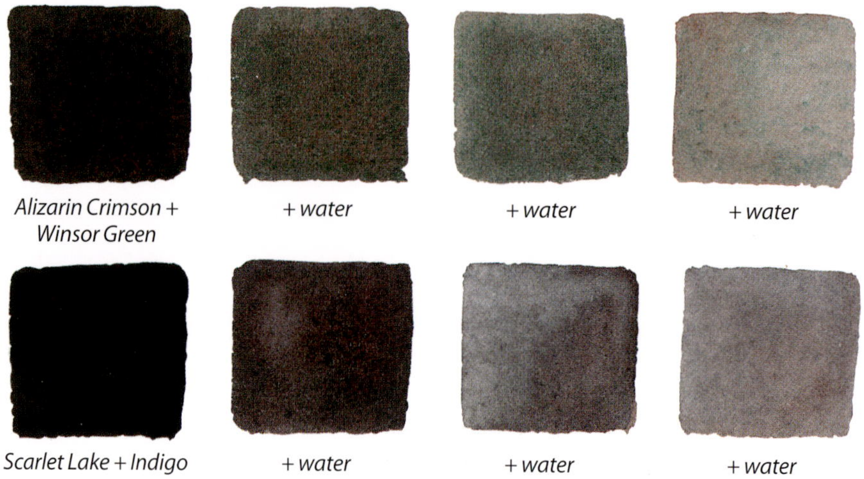

Mixing vs. Mingling Grays

The simplest way of neutralizing a color and reducing its intensity is to mix it with its complement (the color opposite to it on the color wheel) or a near complement (a color that sits on either side of the direct complement). This tones down areas, giving the eye a place to rest.

I have a favorite triad of colors that I have used in many of my paintings: Verditer Blue, Burnt Sienna and Brown Madder. Mingling them instead of mixing them produces a livelier result.

Mixing Colors on the Palette
Here are some colors mixed on the palette. I call them *homogenized* mixtures, because they look dull and boring. The top row of swatches are mixtures of Verditer Blue and Brown Madder, a blue and a red. This results in a flat and uninteresting gray. The bottom row of grays are mixed from Verditer Blue and Burnt Sienna. One of the colors is warm and one is cool, but mixed on the palette, they still turn into a flat gray because they were mixed rather than being allowed to mingle!

Verditer Blue + Brown Madder — *+ water* — *+ water*

Verditer Blue + Burnt Sienna — *+ water* — *+ water*

Mingling Colors on the Paper
Here I mingled Verditer Blue, Burnt Sienna and Brown Madder. Allowing the colors to mingle on the paper, rather than homogenizing them, makes the resulting grays exciting. No dull grays here.

Paintings Using Mingled Grays

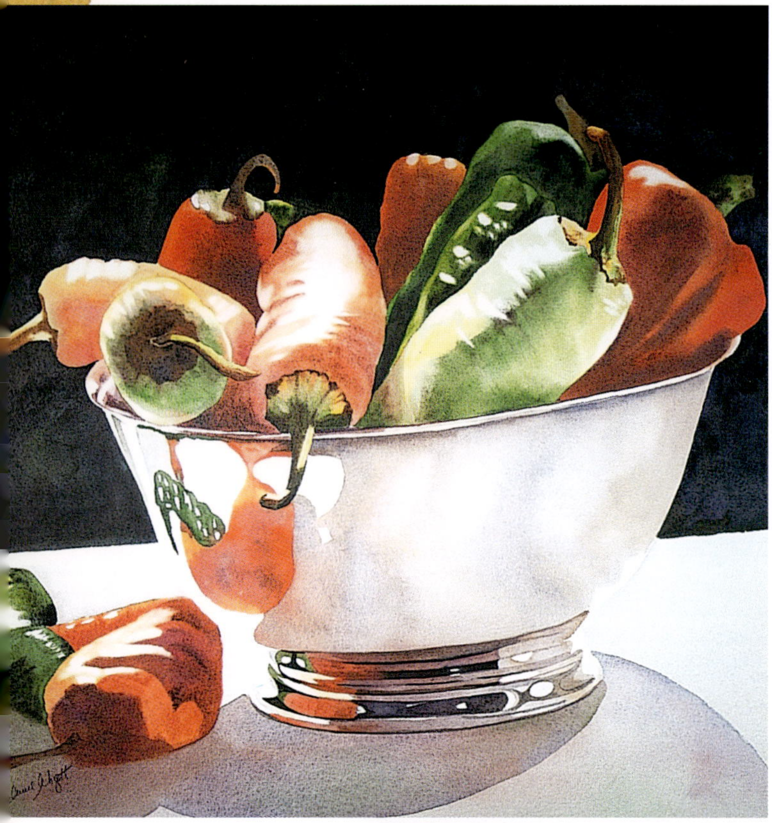

Mingle an Object's Color Into Its Shadow

Here I mingled Verditer Blue, Burnt Sienna and Brown Madder on the paper for the silver bowl. I covered only the areas of the bowl in shadow with paint and left the light-struck areas the white of the paper. I created darker areas of the bowl with Brown Madder, Indigo and Scarlet Lake. I used Verditer Blue, Burnt Sienna and Brown Madder for the light shadow on the table. Then I dropped in Mineral Violet and some Greenish Yellow to reflect the color of the yellow-green pepper. As the shadows got closer to the red pepper, I added Scarlet Lake, Brown Madder, Mineral Violet and Indigo.

OLÉ
22" × 22" (56cm x 56cm)
Transparent watercolor on cold-pressed paper
Collection of the artist

Make Your Grays Sparkle With Saved Whites

Grays are everywhere in this painting—they're part of the silver bowl, in the shadows and even part of the background. I mingled Verditer Blue, Brown Madder and a little Permanent Sap Green for the background. For the light gray areas, I mingled Verditer Blue, Brown Madder and Burnt Sienna. For the dark areas of the silver bowl I mingled Brown Madder and Indigo. With all this gray, the saved white of the highlights really plays an important role in making the silver seem to shine.

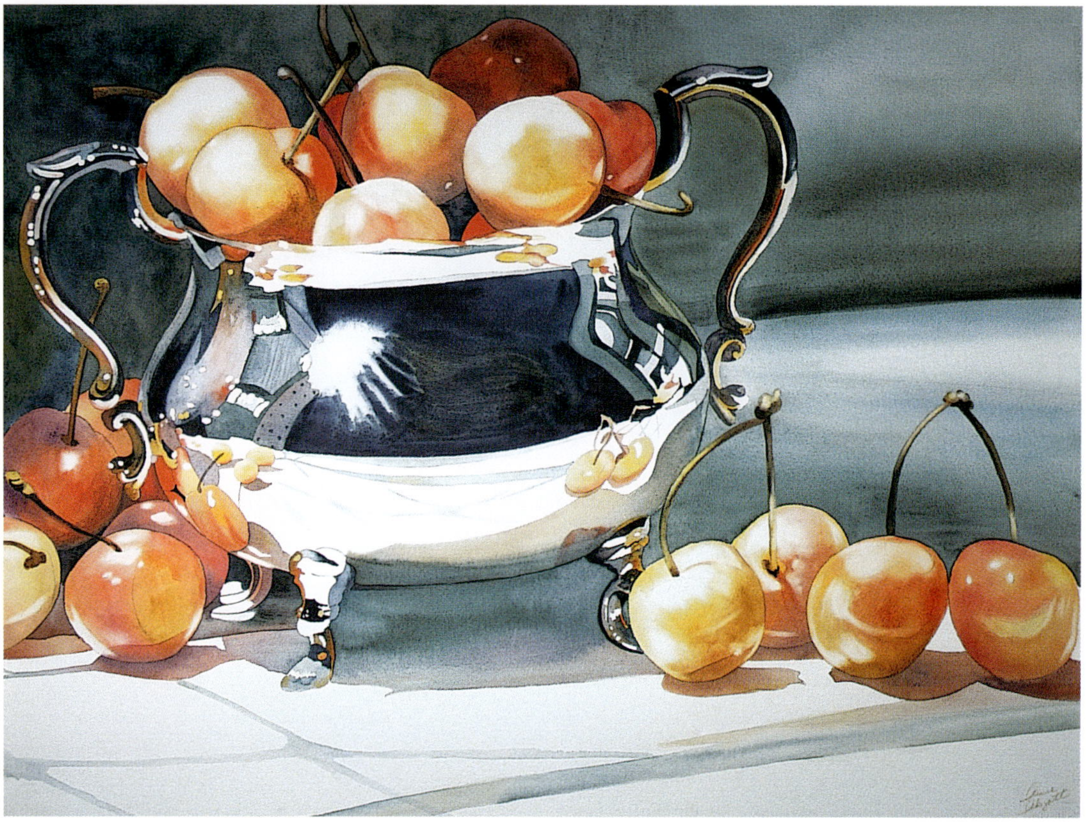

RAINIER REFLECTIONS
22" × 30" (56cm x 76cm)
Transparent watercolor on cold-pressed paper
Collection of the artist

Mingling Grays

MATERIALS

BRUSHES
Nos. 4, 6, 12, and 16 round • ¾-inch (19mm) and 1-inch (25m) flats • no. 6 scrubber

COLORS
Aureolin Yellow • Brown Madder • Burnt Sienna • Cobalt Blue • Cobalt Teal Blue • Greenish Yellow • Indigo • Mineral Violet • New Gamboge • Olive Green • Permanent Rose • Permanent Sap Green • Quinacridone Gold • Quinacridone Magenta • Quinacridone Red Orange • Scarlet Lake • Ultramarine Blue • Verditer Blue • Yellow Ochre

SURFACE
300-lb. (640gsm) Arches cold-pressed paper

OTHER
Absorbing pad • masking fluid • old no. 4 round • paper towels • soapy water

I found this sculpted silver bowl at a flea market. The lacy cutouts attracted me and I knew that they would make great, interesting shadows.

Besides making an interesting shadow pattern, you'll also practice using some colors in an object's shadow that you didn't use to paint the object itself. Instead of using Verditer Blue as part of the silver bowl's shadow, you'll use Cobalt Teal Blue instead. Why? Because it jazzes up the painting and I like it! Artistic license!

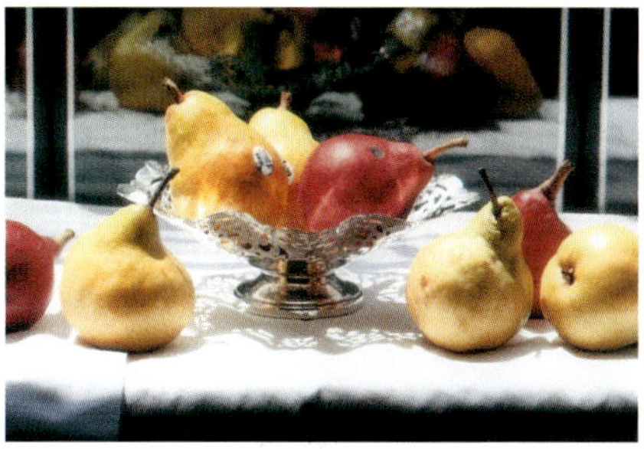

Reference Photo
I like this composition but I'm going to change the colors of some of the pears, making one of the yellow pears red and adding a green pear.

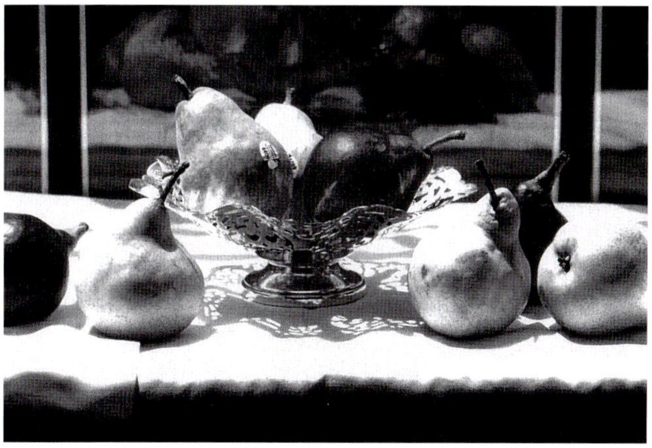

Black-and-White Photocopy

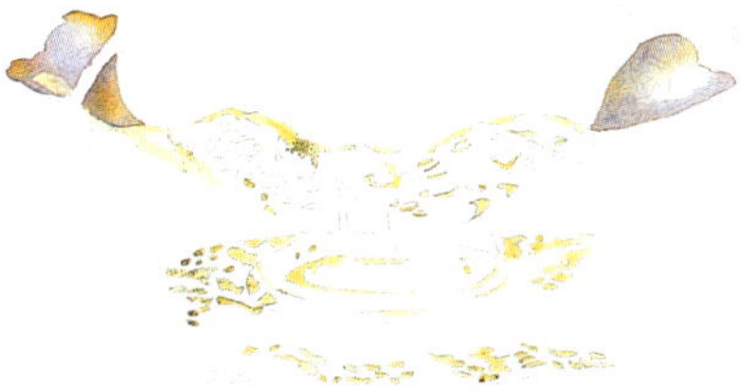

1 APPLY MASKING FLUID AND BEGIN TO PAINT THE BOWL

Draw or trace your composition onto the watercolor paper. Mask the holes in the shadows and in the reflections on the table using an old no. 4 round coated with soapy water. Repeat the coating every five or six strokes to preserve the bristles of your brush. Let the masking fluid dry completely.

With a no. 12 round, mingle Verditer Blue, Brown Madder and some Mineral Violet to paint the inside edges of the bowl. Following the value pattern (see pages 72–74) in your black-and-white photocopy, keep the light areas light by using more water and less pigment in those areas.

2 COMPLETE THE SILVER BOWL

Start in the upper-left corner. With a no. 12 round, apply Verditer Blue and drop in a little Brown Madder, painting right over the holes that seem dark and over the masking fluid. Don't worry about preserving darks. They go in last! Mingle and join Verditer Blue, Brown Madder, Burnt Sienna and Mineral Violet to create a rich gray. Repeat these colors over the whole surface of the bowl.

While this is wet, drop in Quinacridone Gold, Quinacridone Red Orange and Cobalt Teal Blue for the dark bottom of the bowl. This will also suggest the reflected colors of the pears.

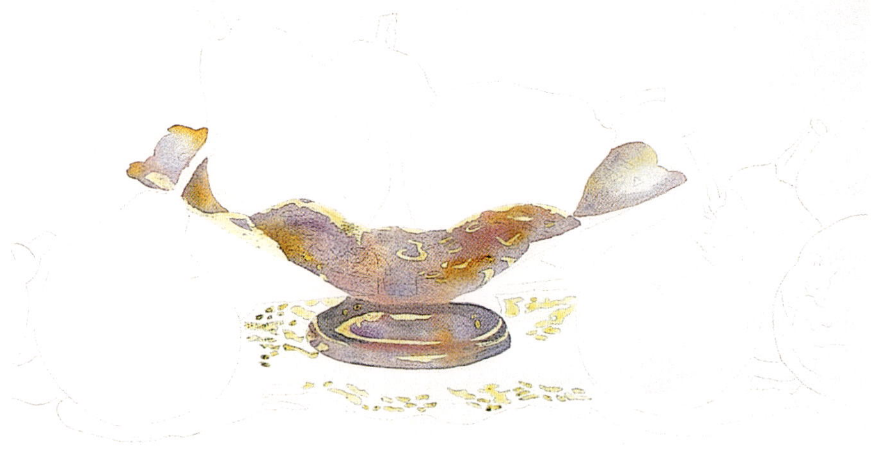

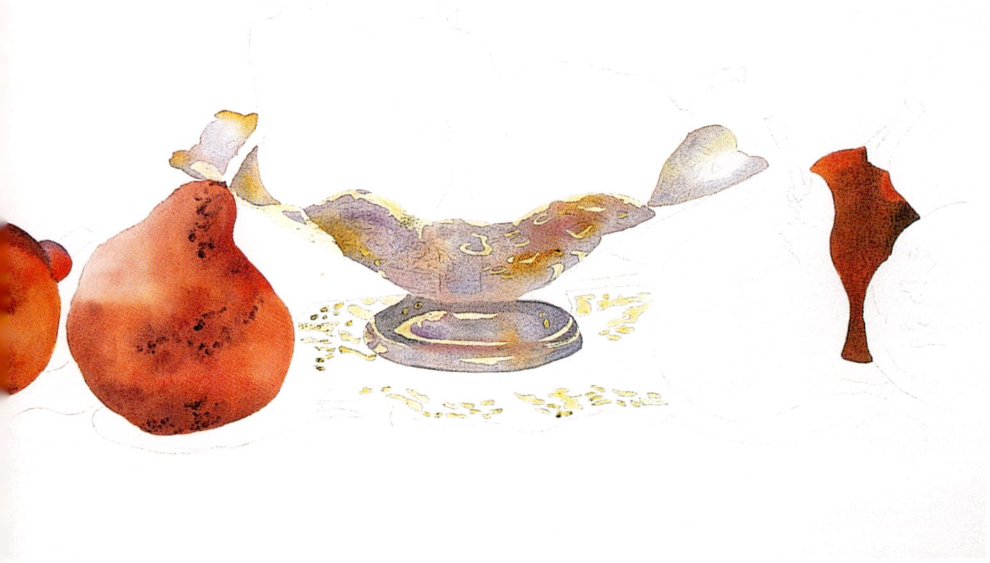

3 PAINT THE RED PEARS

Wet the lightest areas of the red pears. On dry areas of the paper, underpaint with a no. 16 round loaded with New Gamboge. Let the paint touch the damp areas and move into them. When the whole pear is wet with water and pigment, drop in Quinacridone Red Orange, Permanent Rose, Brown Madder and Scarlet Lake to the New Gamboge. Switch to a ¾-inch (19mm) flat and add Quinacridone Magenta and Mineral Violet to the darker areas of the pear. Let this dry slightly. Use a 1-inch (25mm) flat and a piece of paper towel to lift the light reflections off the pear. Lift the paint with the brush and deposit it onto a paper towel. Clean your brush, lift, and deposit again. Do this until you get the effect you want.

Paint the red pear in the right side of the background with more Mineral Violet and Quinacridone Magenta to darken and push it back.

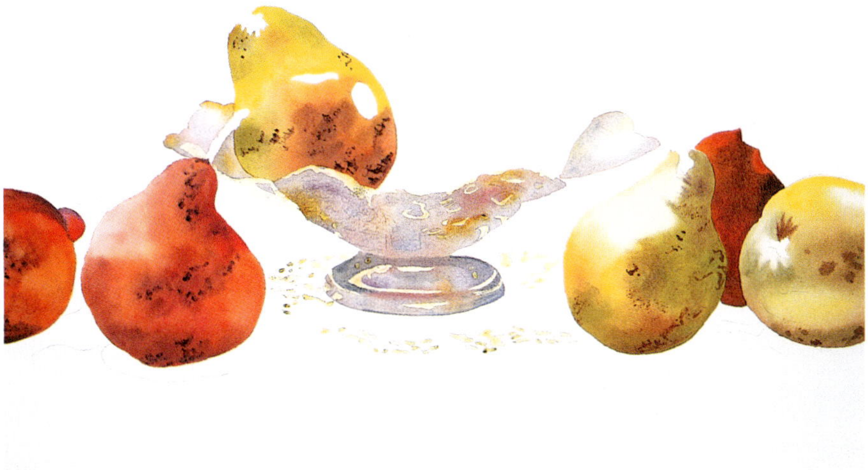

4 PAINT THE YELLOW PEARS
Wet the lightest areas of the yellow pears with a no. 12 round. Mingle Aureolin Yellow, Greenish Yellow, New Gamboge and Yellow Ochre. Mingle Olive Green, Permanent Sap Green and Brown Madder for value changes. Be sure to reflect the surrounding colors into all of the subject matter by dropping in neighboring colors while the areas are wet using a ¾-inch (19mm) flat. Use lots of pigment, no water.

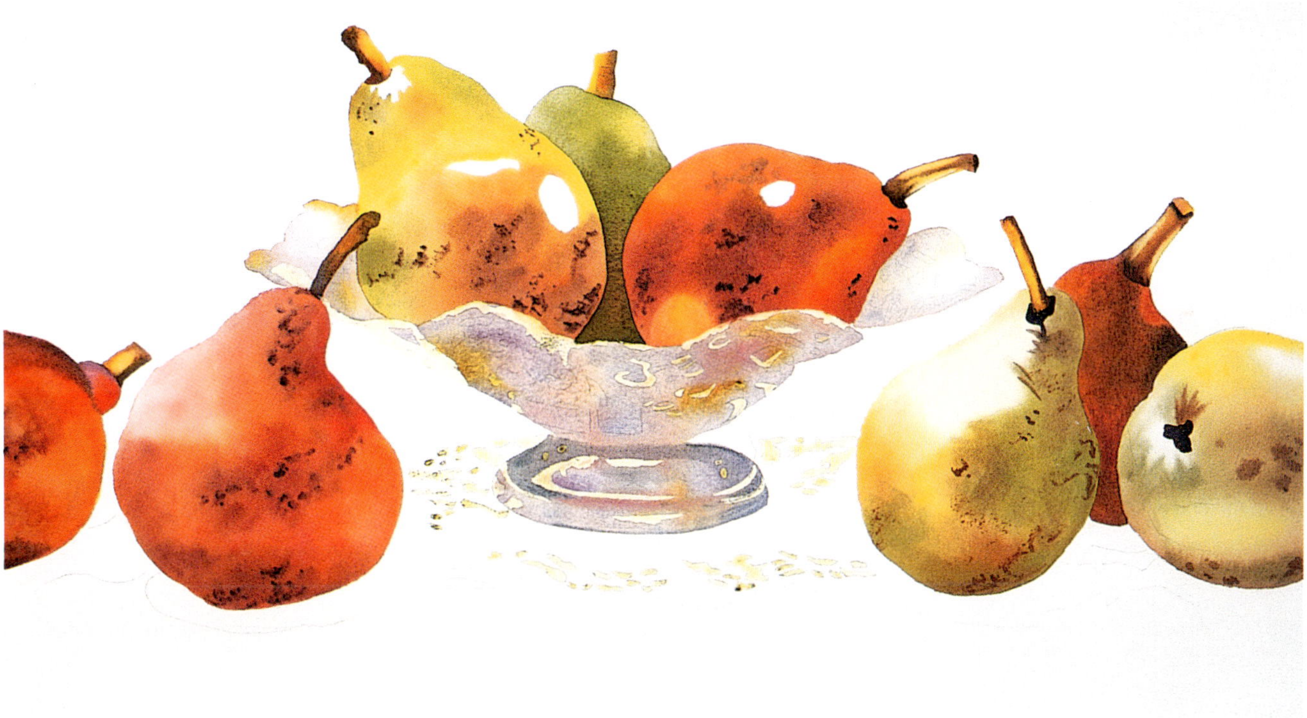

5 PAINT THE STEMS
Underpaint the stems with New Gamboge and a no. 6 round. Mingle Brown Madder and Burnt Sienna for the lights and midtones and Ultramarine Blue for the dark tones. Darken the area of the stem where it comes out of the fruit with Brown Madder and a touch of Mineral Violet.

To anchor the pears to the surface, darken the value of the pears' undersides by adding more pigment to those areas if necessary.

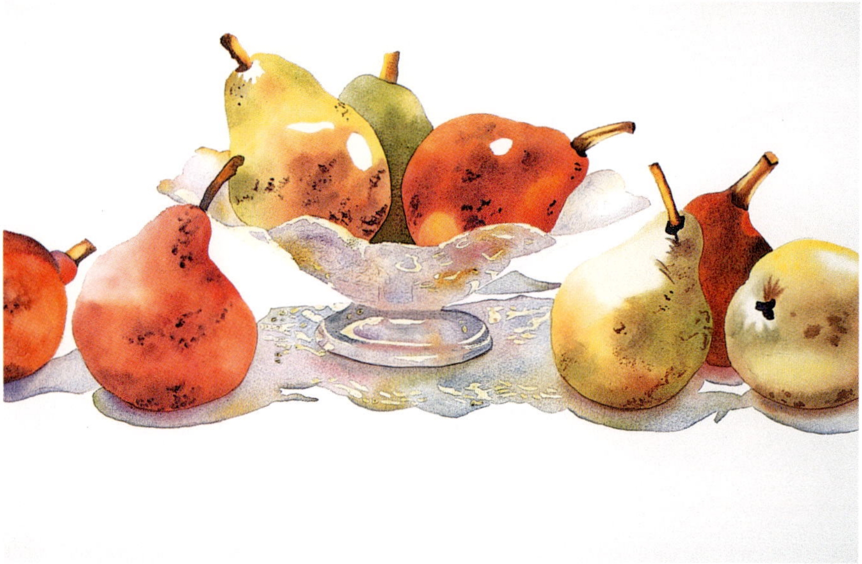

6 PAINT THE SHADOWS

Working left to right with a no. 16 round, mingle the following colors side by side to create the shadow shapes: Verditer Blue, Brown Madder, Mineral Violet, Burnt Sienna and Cobalt Teal Blue. Clean your brush each time you change colors and change the colors every three to four strokes. Paint right over the masking fluid if necessary. Vary and change the colors. Add more Brown Madder under the red pears and mingle in some Yellow Ochre and Brown Madder under the yellow pears to reflect the color of the pears into the shadows. Add more pigment in the darkest areas of the shadows. Use the absorbing pad to control the water on your brush and add more pigment than water to these areas.

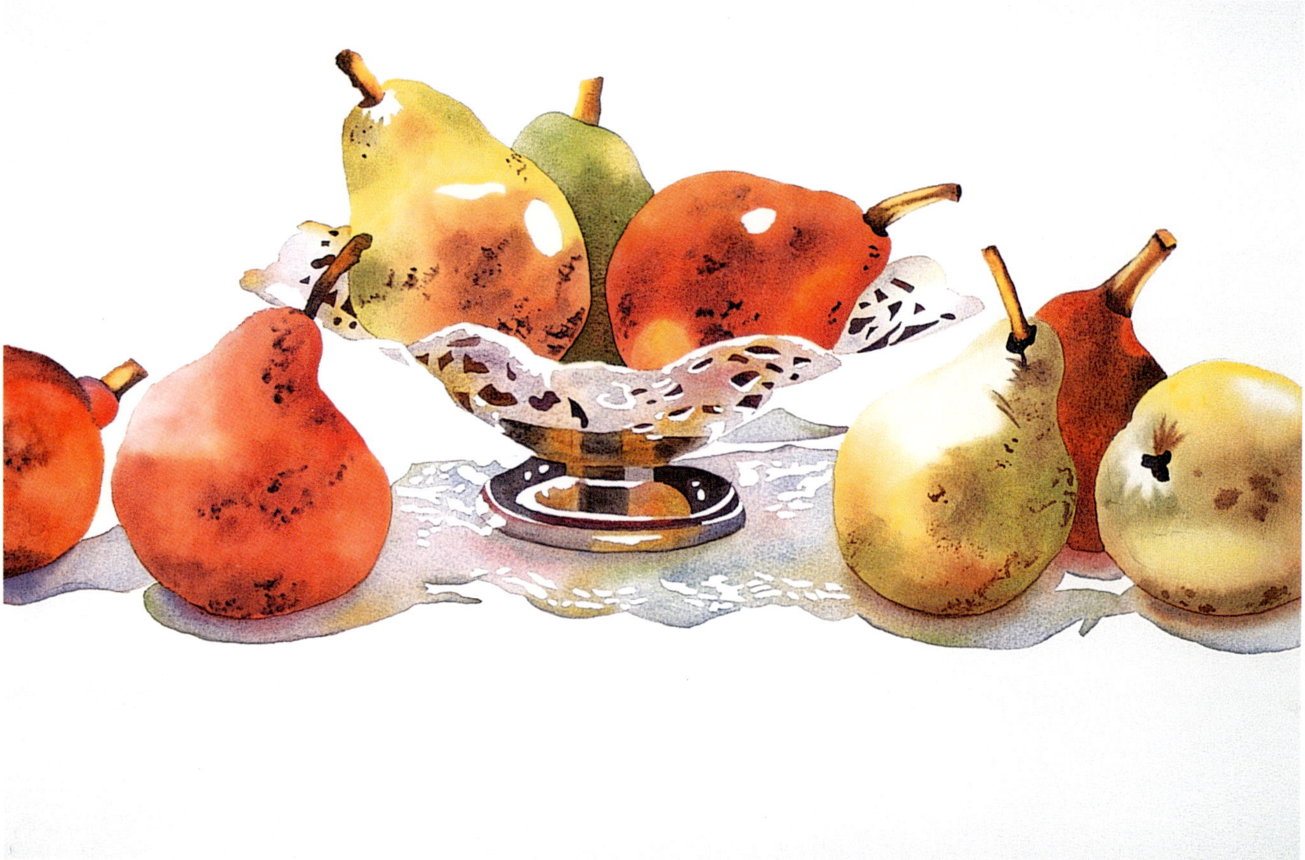

7 REMOVE THE MASKING FLUID AND ADD DARKS TO THE BOWL

Once the painting is dry, remove the masking fluid using your finger, an eraser or a commercial masking remover.

Use the no. 6 round and Brown Madder to carefully paint the dark shapes on the bowl's surface. Apply Ultramarine Blue to the darkest shapes of the bowl. Glaze some Indigo and Quinacridone Gold onto the bowl's bottom to suggest the pears' reflections.

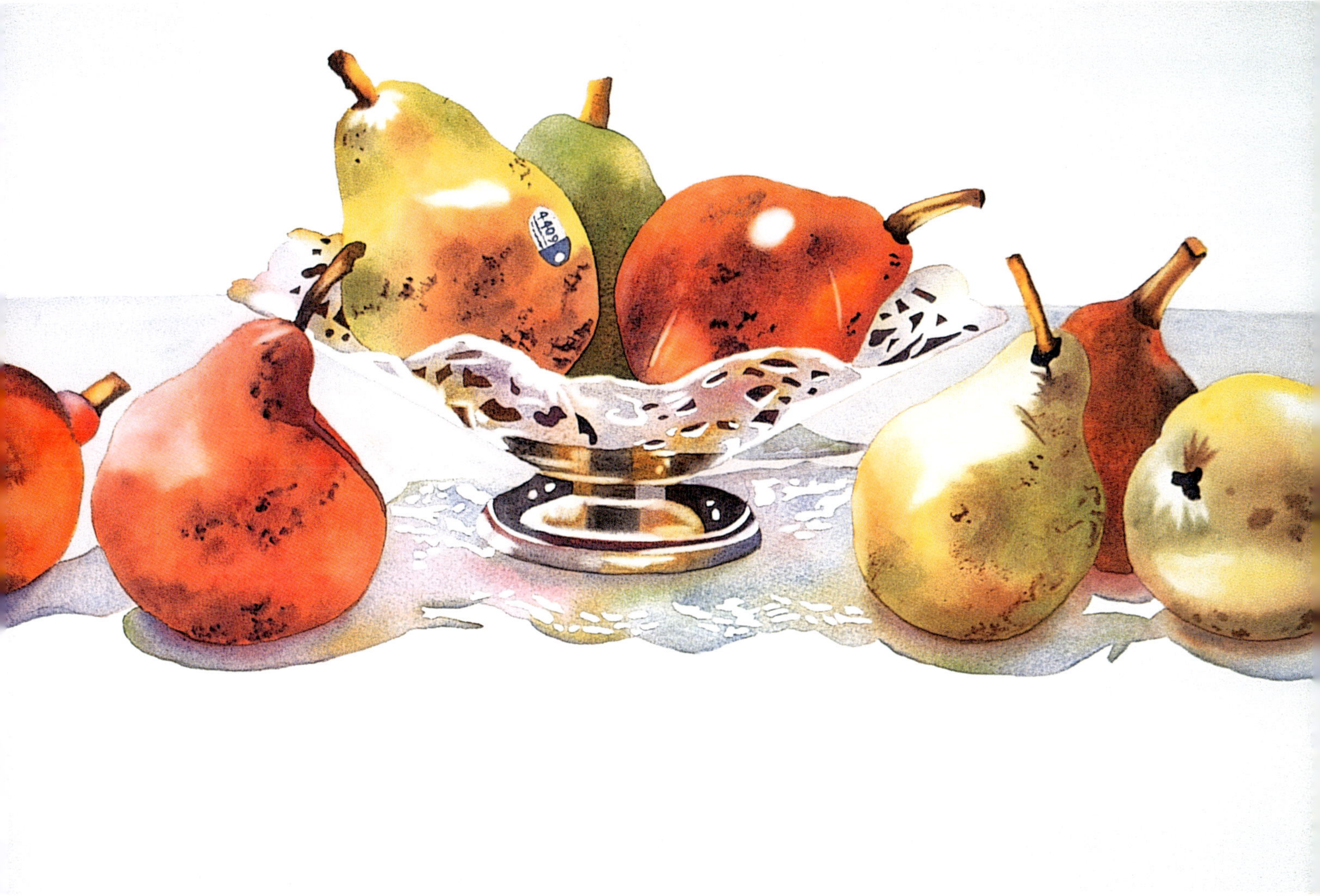

8 ADD THE FINISHING TOUCHES

I thought including the sales sticker on the yellow pear would be a fun thing to do. Paint the sticker with a no. 4 round and Verditer Blue to tone down the white of the paper. Let this dry. Use Cobalt Blue and the no. 4 round for the lettering. Use your no. 6 scrubber to lift and soften the edges of the highlights in the bowl and the silver reflections on the pears. Try adding a table line by mingling Verditer Blue, Brown Madder and Burnt Sienna. Leave the background white.

PICK A PEAR
22" × 28" (56cm × 71cm)
Transparent watercolor on cold-pressed paper
Collection of Mr. and Mrs. Ben Johnson

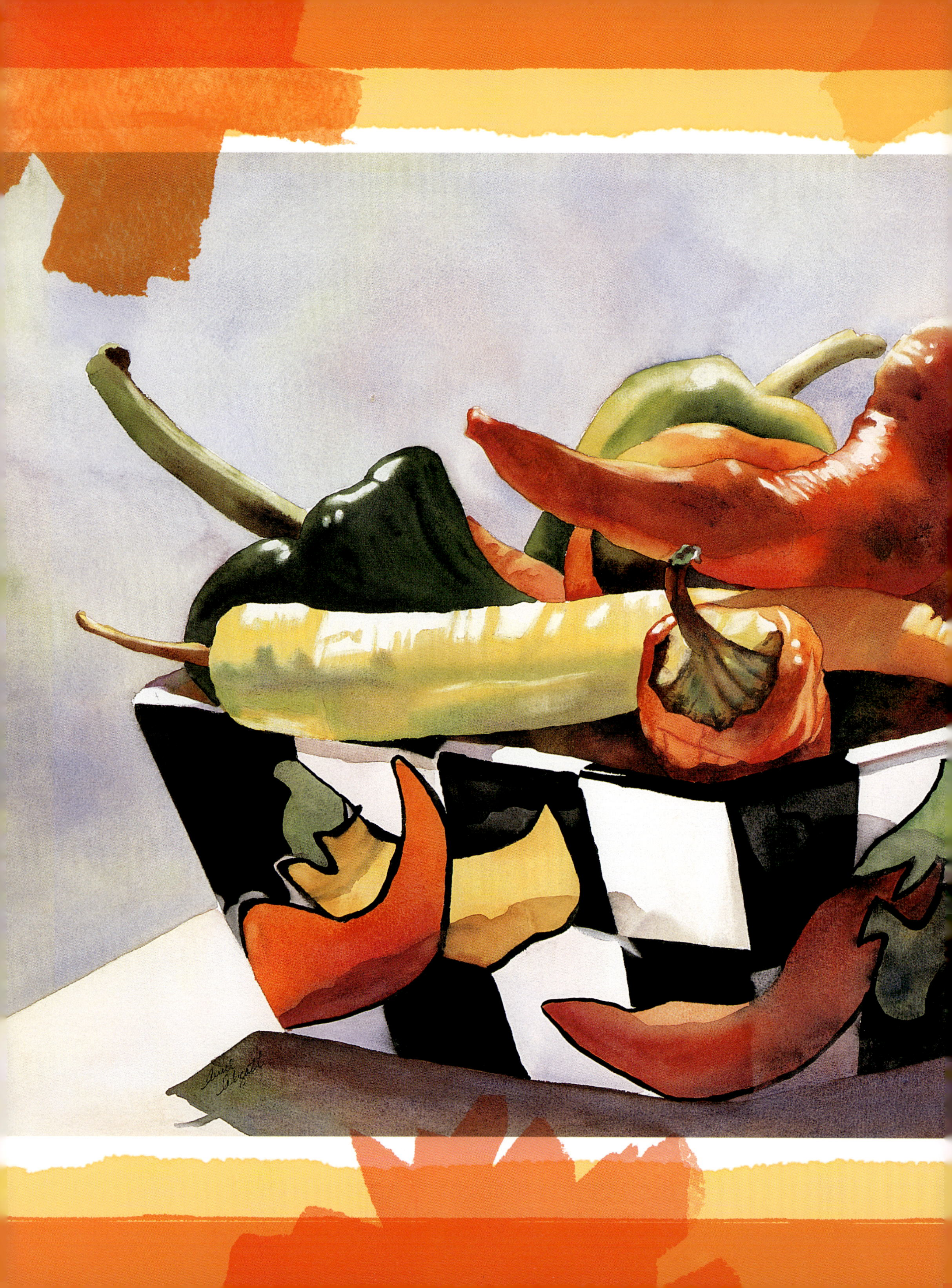

3 Composition: Constructing a Painting Using Photographs

I work exclusively from reference photos that I have taken myself. I find that this creates an emotional connection between me and the image. Composing paintings this way can be tricky, but in this chapter I'll show you some of my favorite tricks and shortcuts for creating good compositions from photographs. You'll soon discover the artistic freedom afforded by working from reference photos.

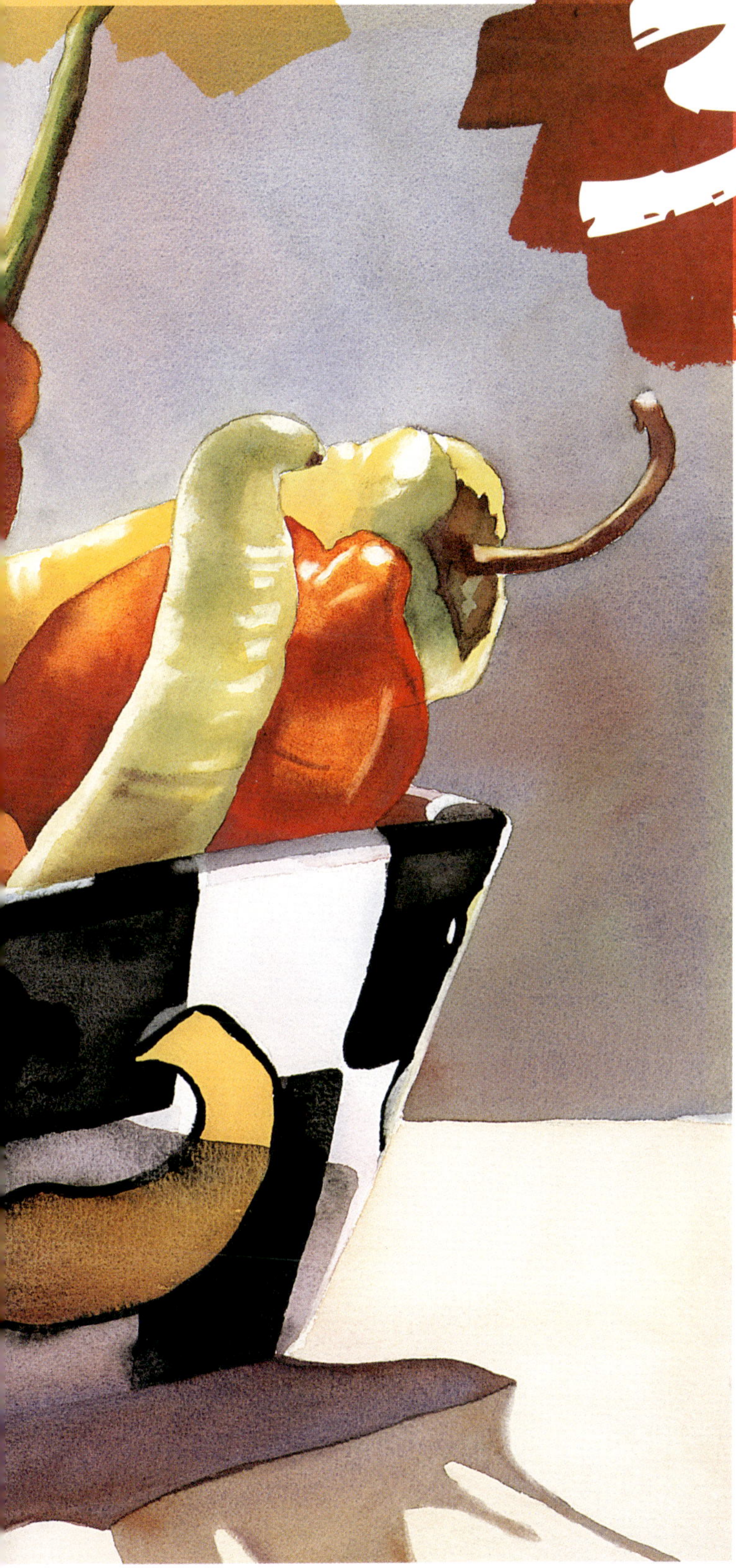

HOT IN ANY COLOR
22" × 30" (56cm × 76cm)
Transparent watercolor on cold-pressed paper
Collection of the artist

Taking Good Reference Photos

A camera allows you to instantly capture a fleeting moment of light, a moving figure, or a flash of emotion. I like to capture the natural light, so, because it is moving and changing all the time, I need that instant imaging that photographs provide. I also like to paint indoors where wind and dust don't affect my painting and where I have more time to think and plan. So painting from reference photos works well for me.

It's important to paint what you love, but that doesn't mean you should copy a reference photo exactly. Part of being an artist is interpreting the world around you into an interesting composition. Often, reference photos don't have the elements of good design or may be too busy for a good composition.

Before you paint from a photo, analyze its composition to see if it has the elements of good design. If it's lacking in one or more areas, don't hesitate to move, change or eliminate objects in the photograph to make a better painting. Once you become conscious of these issues, you'll be able to make design decisions even before you snap the shutter—by adjusting your distance from your subject or the angle at which you are photographing it—so that more of your reference photos will be great ones.

Shape. Your photograph should contain interesting positive shapes (the actual objects) and negative shapes (the spaces around the objects). Get close to your subject so that it fills the frame. Otherwise you'll be left with a lot of unappealing negative space to paint.

Size. Repeated shapes in a photograph should be varied in size. This kind of variety adds interest and depth to a painting, especially when shapes overlap.

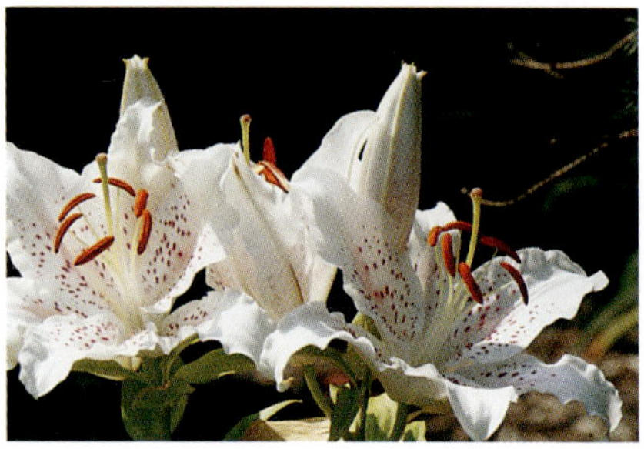

Poor Use of Space
The flowers are positioned in the lower half of the image, dividing the space of the photograph nearly in half. The large background area constitutes an uninteresting negative shape.

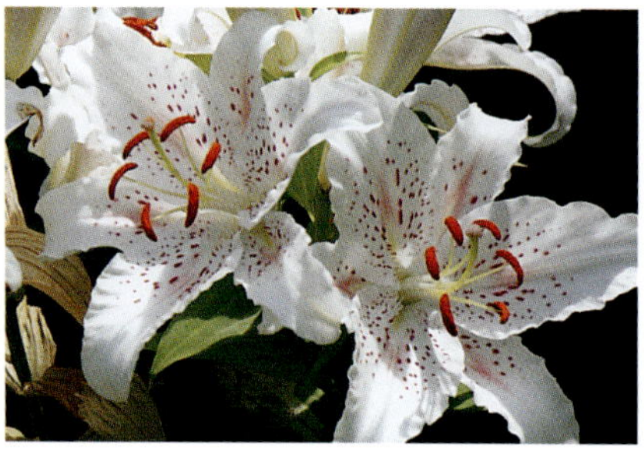

Better Use of Space
When the same flowers are photographed from a different angle, they fill the picture area nicely and create better negative shapes.

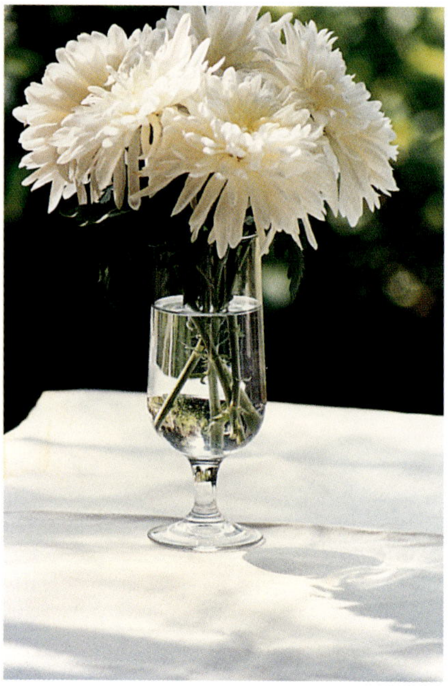

Poor Placement of Focal Point and Color
The focal point—the blossoms—is way up at the top of the image. The vertical line of the tall glass sends the viewer's eye straight up, merely emphasizing the imbalance. The white tablecloth mutes the image.

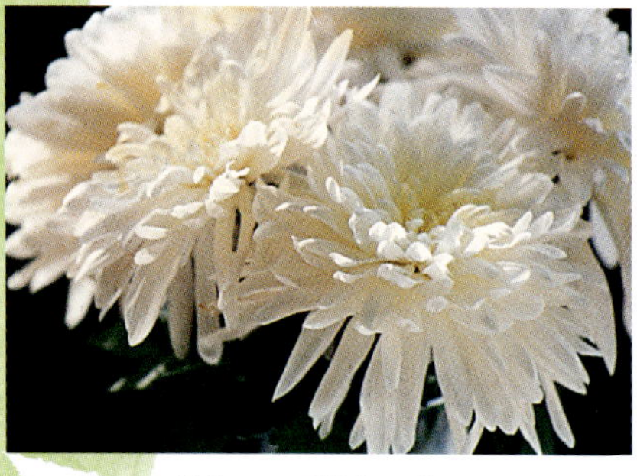

Good Use of Line and Value Contrast
In this close-up of the same flowers, the area of interest nicely fills the frame without leaving large areas of uninteresting space. The white flowers are a nice contrast to the dark background.

ORGANIZE YOUR PHOTOS BY SUBJECT

Store your reference photos in plastic boxes, shoe boxes—whatever works for you—and sort by subject. If you find the perfect house to paint but it's surrounded by boring trees, you can reach for your envelope of tree photographs and quickly find some trees that will work better for the composition.

Color. The colors you use in a painting help convey a mood. Depending on the time of day your reference photograph was taken and the quality of the light, the color in the photograph may or may not convey the mood you want. Also consider whether the color in the photo directs the eye to the focal point. Generally the focal point should have the most intense color notes. Side-by-side complementary colors also attract the eye.

Texture. The photograph should show more than one texture. When shooting reference photos, take shots of the overall scene, but also shoot several close-ups for texture. For example, don't just shoot the lilac bush; also get close-ups of one flower, of the foliage, of closed buds and dead flowers.

Line. Check the lines in your photograph. Do they guide the viewer's eye into and around the painting? If a strong linear element goes right off the edge of the photograph, you'd be wise to modify your painting to interrupt that line. You want to keep the viewer's eye on your painting, not send it off to someone else's painting!

Value. Include a range of values to add interest and depth to your painting. Generally speaking, the focal point should have the greatest level of value contrast.

Consider your reference photo with those points in mind, then improve the composition for your actual painting. You can exaggerate, downplay or eliminate colors or objects; repeat important shapes, lines and patterns; or simplify the amount of detail in areas of the scene that are not the focal point. Always remember that, as the artist, you are the boss, and you can change anything at any time.

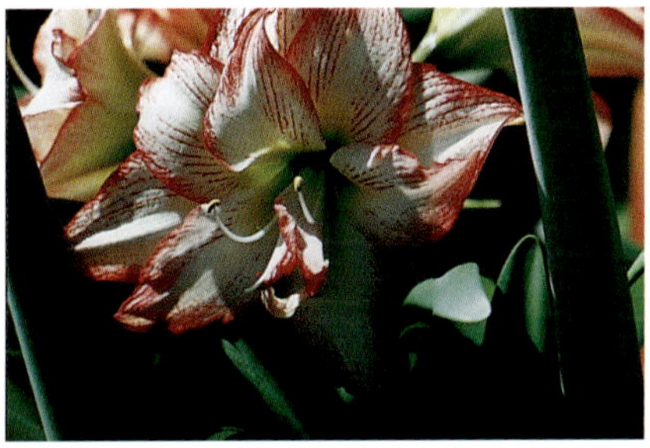

Full Sun

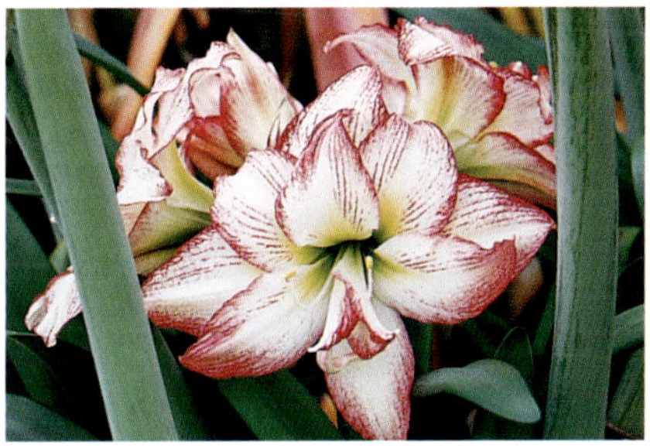

Overcast Day

The Right Sunlight Makes Rich Shadows

I never shoot on overcast days; direct sunlight is very important to me because it makes good shadows. The best time to photograph is early morning or late afternoon, when the light comes from a low angle and the shadows are long and colorful. Don't photograph at midday, when shadows are dark, harsh and lacking in detail.

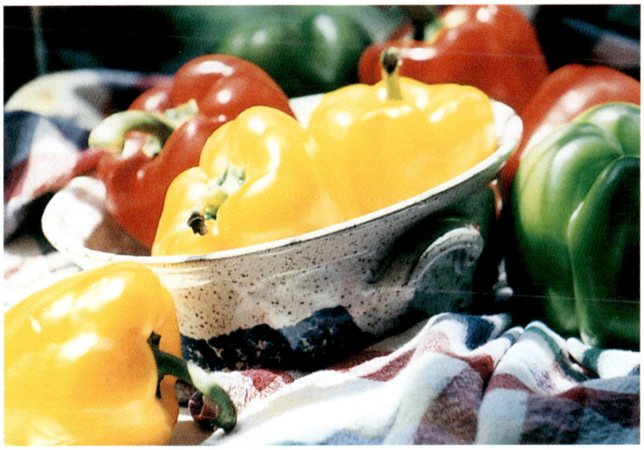

Good Use of Texture and Shape

The woven tablecloth is a nice contrast to the glossy peppers and bowl. The peppers overlap, filling the space back to front as well as left to right. These varied shapes and textures seem to speak to and introduce each other in this photograph.

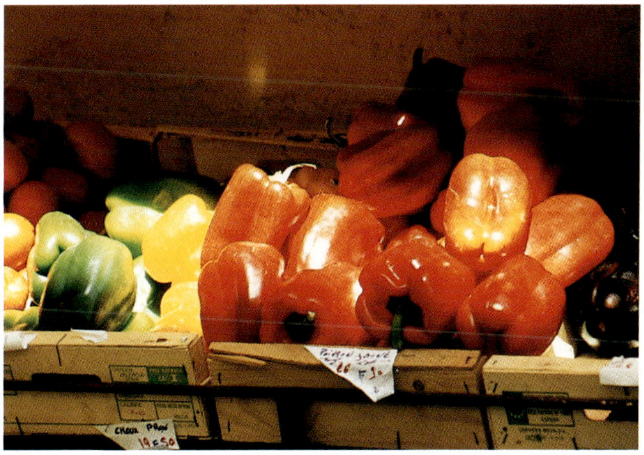

Poor Use of Texture and Shape

The glossy skins of the vegetables are the only texture really visible here. The arrangement is too linear to be interesting.

Cropping Photographs for the Best Composition

Croppers are a great tool for finding potential paintings within a photograph. They're simply windows in pieces of cardboard, and they are easy to make. As you move the cropper around and over different areas of the photograph, you will be amazed by the many wonderful compositions that present themselves.

MAKING YOUR OWN CROPPERS

Gather these simple materials:

- *Sturdy cardboard or paper*
- *Ruler*
- *Craft knife*
- *Acetate (available at art and craft supply stores)*
- *Scissors*
- *Masking tape*
- *Permanent marking pen*

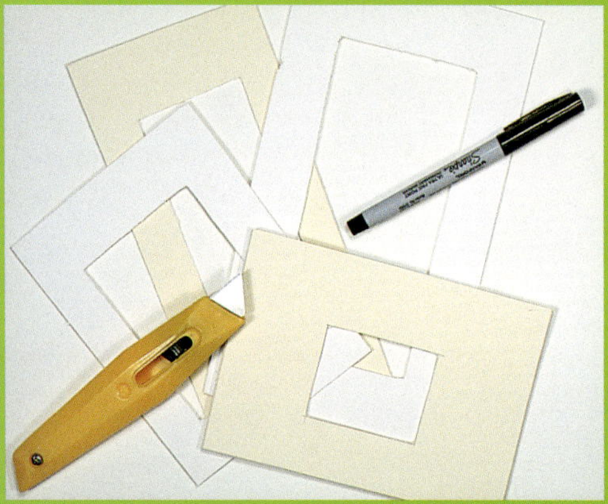

Measure the desired size of the window in the cardboard, then cut out the window using a craft knife. Start with windows in these sizes: 4" × 6" (10cm × 15cm), 3½" × 5" (9cm × 13cm), 3" × 6" (8cm × 15cm) and 3" × 3" (8cm × 8cm). These sizes work well with most photographs. Try moving a cropper around your reference photo and surprise yourself with new composition ideas.

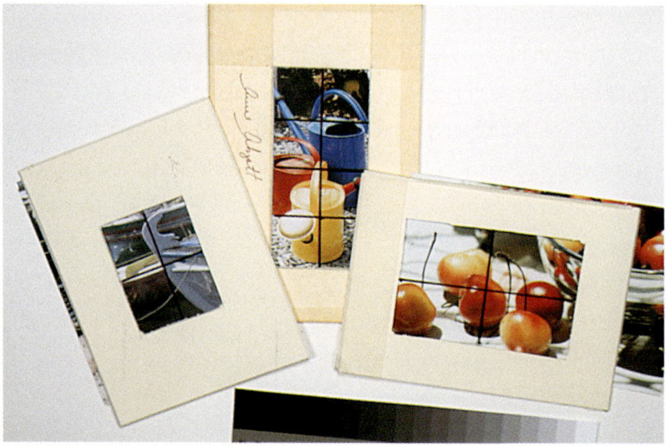

Croppers as Drawing Tools

If you want to use a cropper as a guide to help you draw more accurately, cover the window with acetate (available at art and craft supply stores), and secure the acetate with masking tape. Using a ruler and a permanent marker, mark lines on the acetate that divide each side of the window in half. You can divide the resulting squares or rectangles further if needed. Eight sections is probably the most you will need to provide drawing guidance for all the shapes in the photograph.

When you lay this graphed window over your reference photo, the lines divide the image into smaller shapes that are easier to copy freehand onto your watercolor paper. Lightly sketch a graph onto the paper that contains the same number of squares or rectangles of the same proportion as the acetate graph. (You can double the composition's size by doubling the size of the divisions on your cropped photo.) Then copy the shapes into the squares on your paper, one square at a time.

I find it especially helpful to do this with the photo and the watercolor paper upside down, because I am forced to see the image as shapes.

Creating Compositions Using Tracing Paper

Some reference photos don't always cooperate even when you use croppers. However, you may find elements in two or more reference photos that can be put together to create a good composition. Tracing paper makes it easy to combine elements from multiple reference photos.

Simply slide your reference photos into position under one piece of tracing paper, then lightly trace the basic shapes with a pencil. Or you can trace the desired portion of each photo on separate pieces of tracing paper, cut them out, and then arrange and rearrange them until you get a composition you like. Do three or more compositions, then choose the best one to transfer to your drawing paper. Transfer your chosen design to your watercolor paper by drawing with the grid method or by using a projector to help you trace the image onto your watercolor paper.

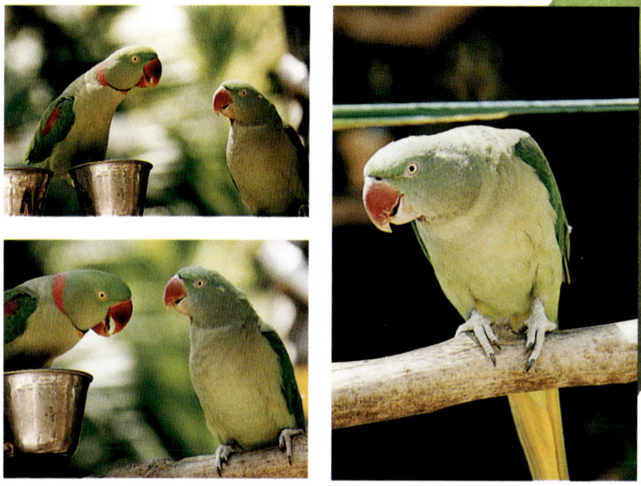

Reference Photos

I liked the parrots in each of these photographs, but I wanted my painting to show more interaction among the birds. I used the three reference photos to create one drawing for a possible painting. The more I looked at them, the more the birds appeared to be talking to each other.

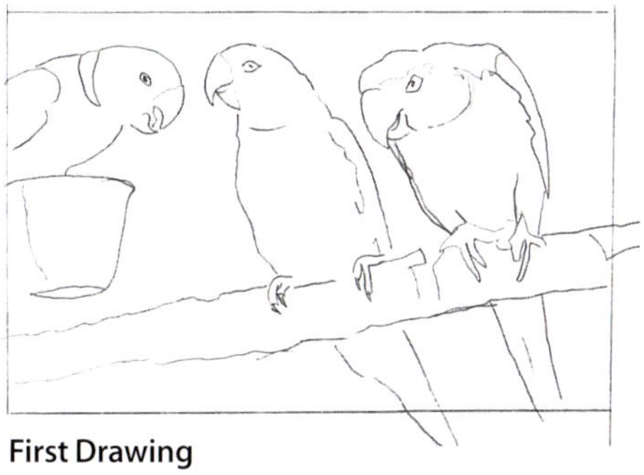

First Drawing

Here, I took two reference photos and combined them into one design by slipping one photo at a time under the tracing paper. I lightly traced around the image with a pencil. Notice that I did not add a lot of detail to my tracing. I just focused on the shapes.

Notice how this first drawing lacks interesting shapes. The birds are too evenly spaced and the center of interest isn't clear.

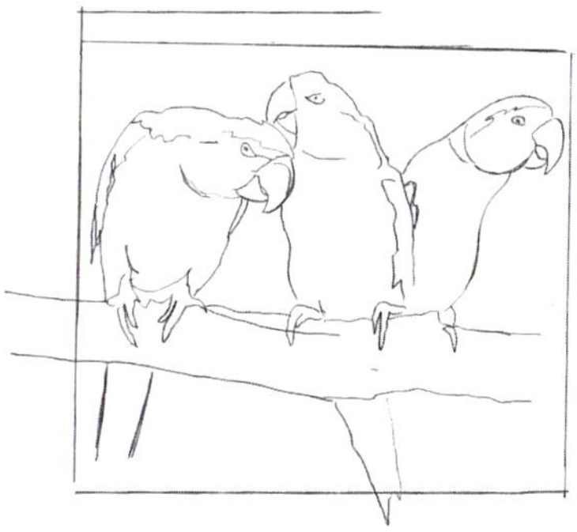

Second Drawing

Here I traced around the birds' shapes again, rearranging them for a different composition. If you do each drawing from scratch, then you have them all to compare and choose from.

This solved the spacing problem and made a more interesting shape. However, two birds face the same way, leading the viewer out of the picture.

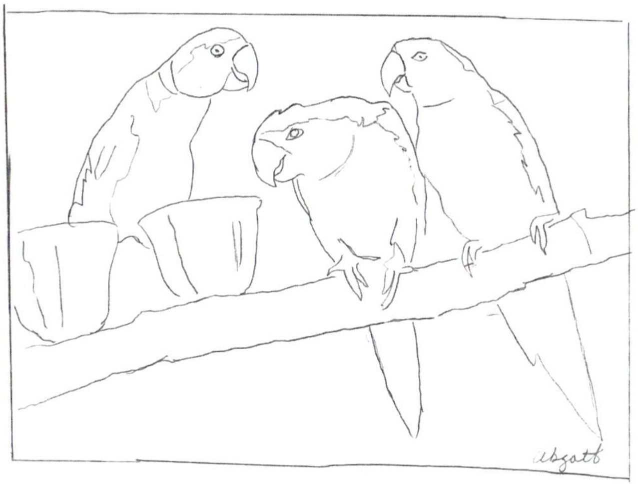

Final Drawing

Again, I rearranged the photos and started tracing over the birds in a different composition. This is the drawing I used to create the painting on page 37. Note that it has interesting shapes, a clear center of interest (the bird in the middle) and the interaction and character of the birds.

Eliminating Unnecessary Details

MATERIALS

BRUSHES
No. 12 round, no. 6 scrubber

WATERCOLORS
Aureolin Yellow • Brown Madder • Burnt Sienna • Cobalt Blue • Cobalt Teal Blue • Mineral Violet • New Gamboge • Olive Green • Opera • Permanent Rose • Scarlet Lake • Transparent Turquoise • Ultramarine Blue • Verditer Blue

SURFACE
300-lb. (640gsm) Arches cold-pressed paper

OTHER
Masking fluid • old no. 4 round (for applying masking fluid) • projector grid • soapy water • tracing paper

Photographs capture more detail than a painting will ever need. Great artists know what to eliminate from a photograph. Learn to take out the unnecessary details. Remember that you don't have to paint something just because it's in the reference photo.

Lay a piece of transparent tracing paper over your photo and lightly trace the subject and center of interest. Concentrate on eliminating the unnecessary and keeping your sketch as simple as possible. Simplicity catches the eye.

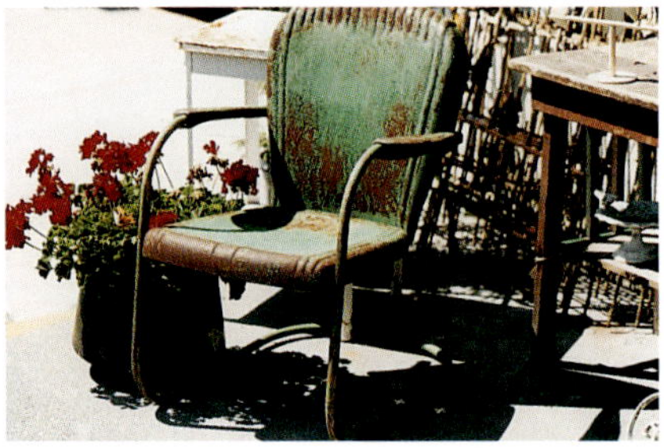

Reference Photo
My mother used to paint our old metal chairs a different color each summer. The layers of paint and the rust on this chair created a wonderful textural effect. The shadow of the chair on the driveway caught my eye, but I had to eliminate all of the junk behind the chair and concentrate on simplifying this photo.

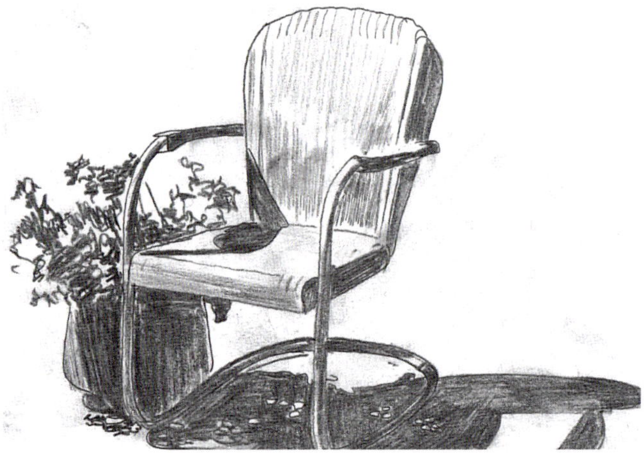

Composition Sketch
I used croppers to simplify the reference photo and made this compositional sketch on tracing paper.

1 PAINT THE CHAIR

Trace your composition onto watercolor paper using a projector or use the grid method discussed on page 56 to transfer the image. Take a no. 12 round and on dry paper mingle Transparent Turquoise, Cobalt Blue, Brown Madder and Burnt Sienna for the chair's seat and back. Indicate the light areas of the chair, such as the front of the armrests and seat, by using less paint and more water.

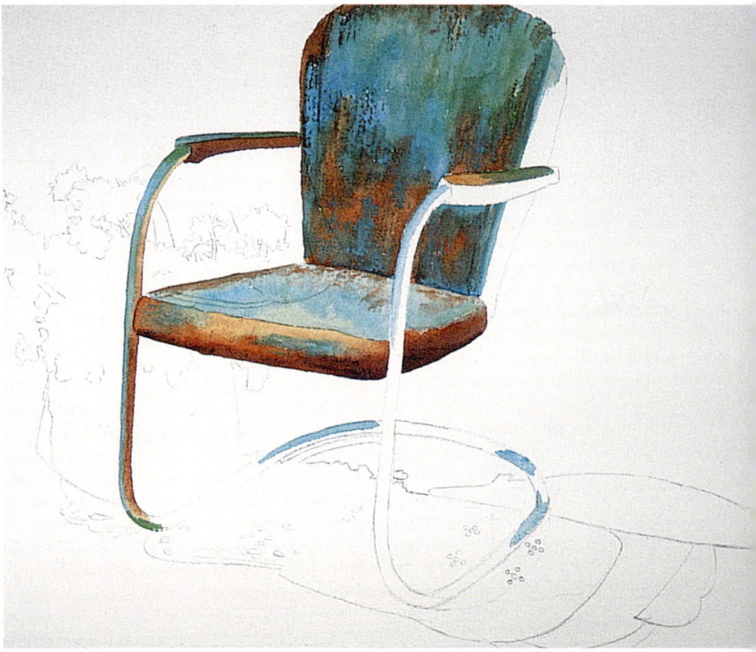

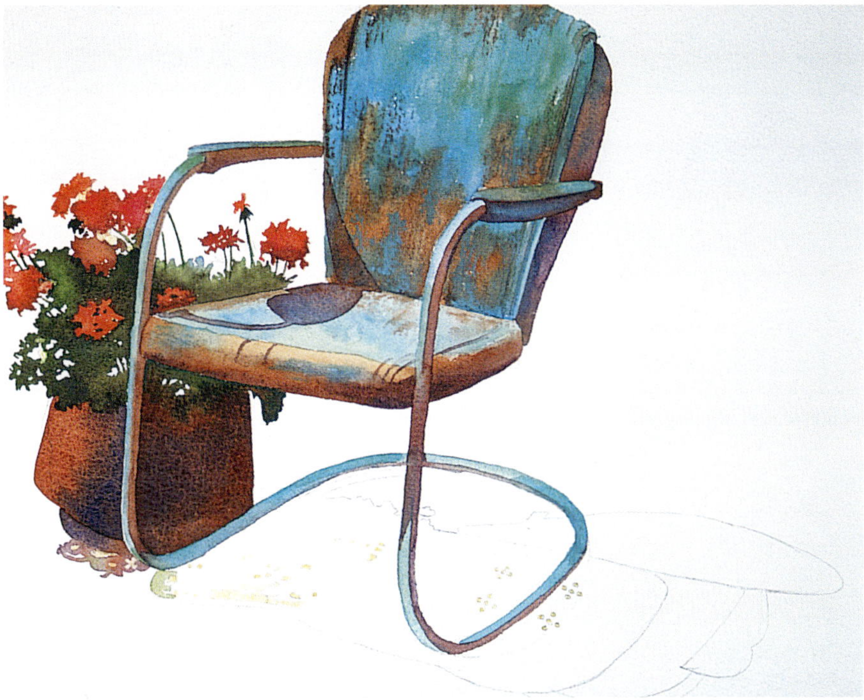

2 PAINT THE POT

Take a no. 12 round loaded with New Gamboge and, on dry paper, underpaint the left edge of the pot, then drop some Brown Madder into the New Gamboge. As you move into the shadow area, apply Brown Madder, then mingle Mineral Violet and Burnt Sienna into the Brown Madder to darken it. You can also add a little Ultramarine Blue. Paint the geraniums by mingling New Gamboge, Opera, Permanent Rose and Scarlet Lake. Paint the leaves with a combination of Olive Green, Aureolin Yellow and Mineral Violet.

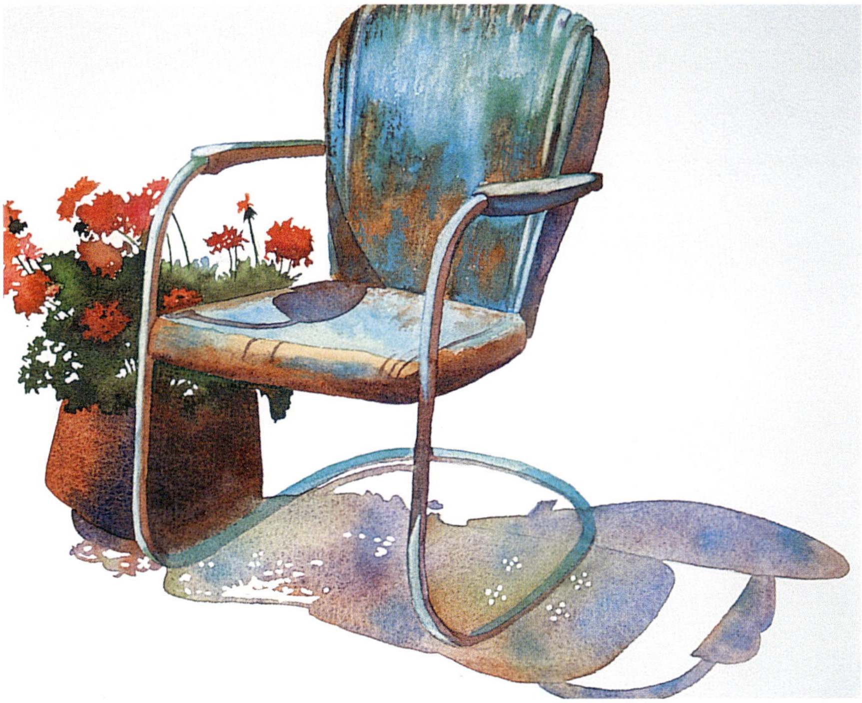

JUNKYARD CHAIR
11" × 14" (28cm × 36cm)
Transparent watercolor on cold-pressed paper
Collection of the artist

3 FINISH THE PAINTING

Use the tiny lights underneath the chair to add interest to the shadow. Mask the tiny lights underneath the chair with masking fluid and an old no. 4 round dipped in soapy water and let dry. With a no. 12 round, and starting at the edge of the pot, mingle Brown Madder, Verditer Blue, Mineral Violet and Cobalt Teal Blue. Work your way across the shadow, joining the colors. While this is wet, add more color into some areas. While the shadow is still damp, drop a little Cobalt Blue around the edges and watch how it creeps in and adds interest. You can see how the shadow under the chair is repeating some of the colors in the chair. Once the shadow area is dry, remove the masking fluid. Use the no. 6 scrubber to soften some of the shadows along the edges and lift out any lights on the chair.

Composing With Photographs and Sketches

MATERIALS

BRUSHES
Nos. 6, 8, 12, 16 and 36 round, no. 6 scrubber

WATERCOLORS
Aureolin Yellow • Brown Madder • Burnt Sienna • Cobalt Blue • Gamboge Nova • Mineral Violet • Permanent Blue • Permanent Rose • Permanent Sap Green • Ultramarine Blue • Verditer Blue •

SURFACE
300-lb. (640gsm) Arches cold-pressed paper

OTHER
Absorbing pad • commercial masking fluid remover • masking fluid • old no. 12 round • razor blade • soapy water

When nature doesn't provide you with the perfect photo, you need to know how to create a good composition. I keep files of sketches I do from life and photos. You never know when you will need an interesting tree shape for a landscape or an active person to add life to a street scene. I transfer these drawings to transparent tracing paper and lay them over my photos where I need to. They are a valuable source of material—just as important as the photo.

KEEPING REFERENCE PHOTOS ORGANIZED

I keep all my photographs in antique boxes that double as end tables. I have them divided into subject matter. I bind like subjects together with rubber bands. For instance, flowers are subcategorized by a specific flower type.

This is my system:

- *Things that breathe (people, animals)*
- *Things that don't breathe (still life)*
- *Architecture (buildings, chairs, etc.)*

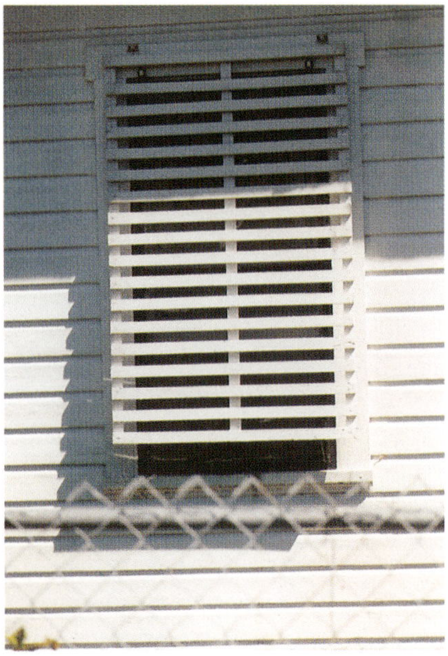

Reference Photo
I have many photos of the shutters in my neighborhood, but none of them had any exciting shadows. So I went to my file of shadow shapes, on transparent paper, found a shape I liked and laid it over the tracing of the shutter to create a composition I liked.

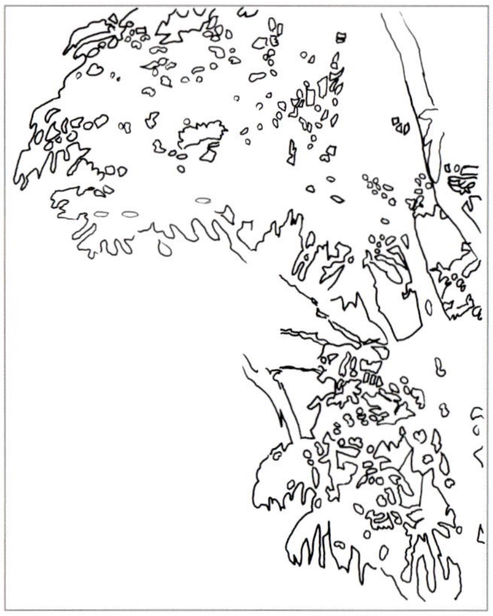

Shadow Shape
Here I tried another shadow shape over the shutter and drew it out on paper.

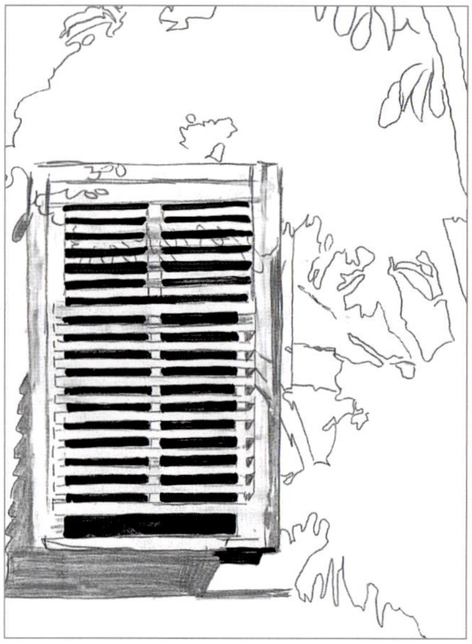

Final Composition
This is the composition I chose to paint. I drew the shutter and the shadow shape out on plain drawing paper about 5" × 7" (13cm × 18cm) in size. I placed this drawing in my projector and traced it onto my watercolor paper.

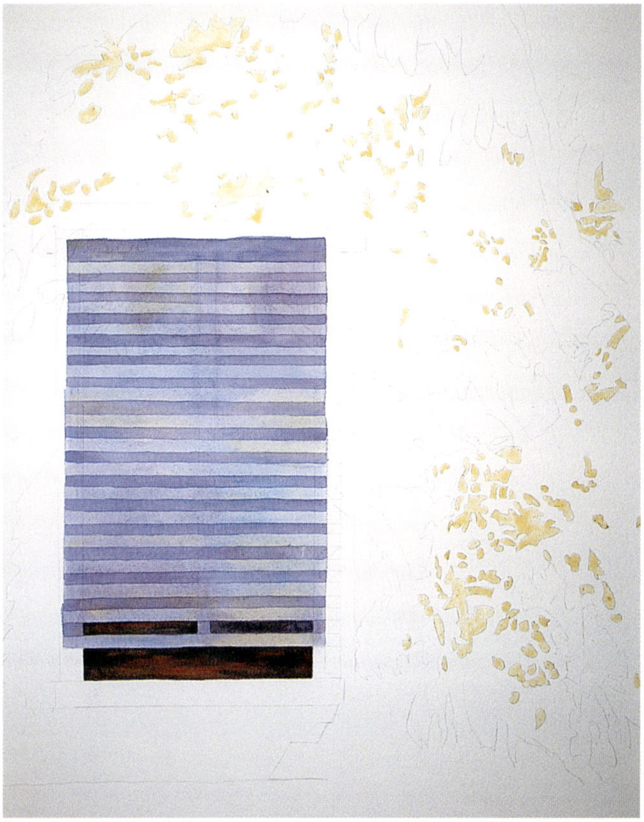

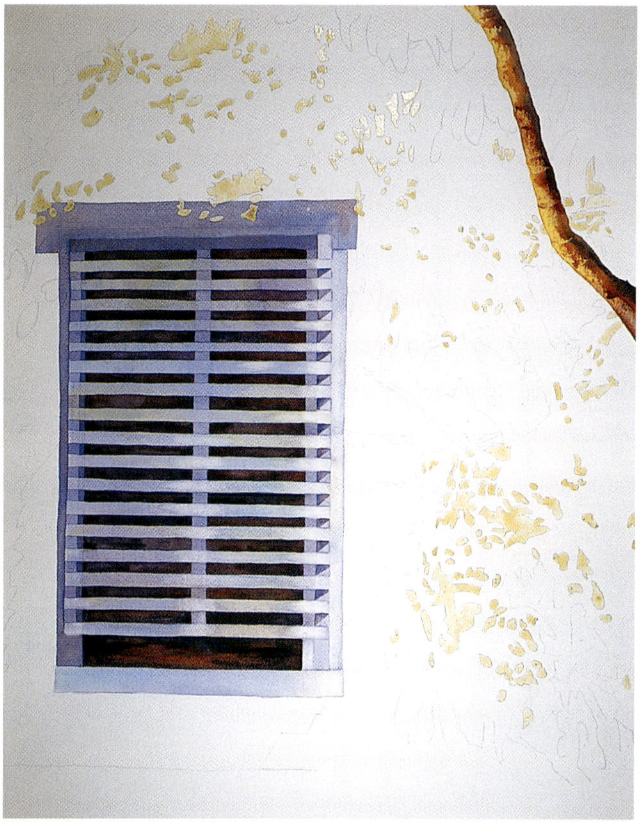

1 SKETCH THE COMPOSITION AND ADD SHUTTERS

Lightly pencil in the shadow and shutter design on watercolor paper. Dip an old no.12 round in soapy water and apply masking fluid to the shadows' negative spaces. Let this dry. With a no. 12 round, dampen some areas of the shutter. Mingle Verditer Blue, Permanent Blue and Cobalt Blue over the shutter area. While this is damp, pick up some Aureolin Yellow with a no. 16 round, touch the brush to the absorbing pad and gently drop the color into a few areas of the shutters to suggest sunlight hitting them. Let this dry, then use a no. 6 or 8 round to apply paint between the slats of the shutters, mingling Brown Madder and Ultramarine Blue to get these darks.

2 ADD SHADOWS AND A TREE BRANCH

Mingle Brown Madder and Ultramarine Blue to create dark slats. Paint two strokes of one color then two of the other, allowing the Brown Madder to show where the sun hits the subject. On dry paper with a no. 12 round, underpaint the branch with Gamboge Nova, then drop in a little Brown Madder. While this is wet, mingle Burnt Sienna, Ultramarine Blue and Mineral Violet on the shadow side of the branch. Once the wet glisten of the watercolor disappears, scratch off some paint with a razor blade to suggest the texture of wood.

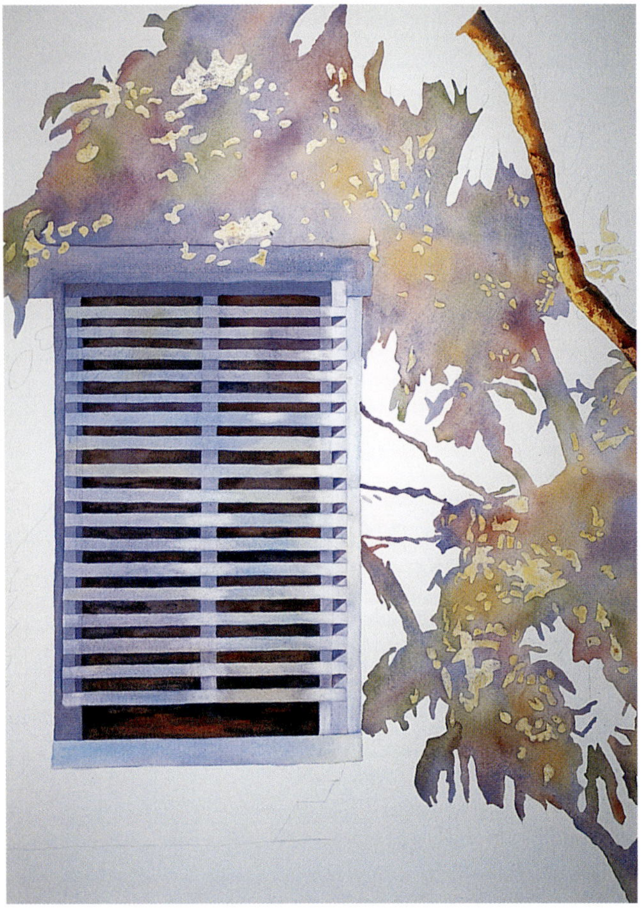

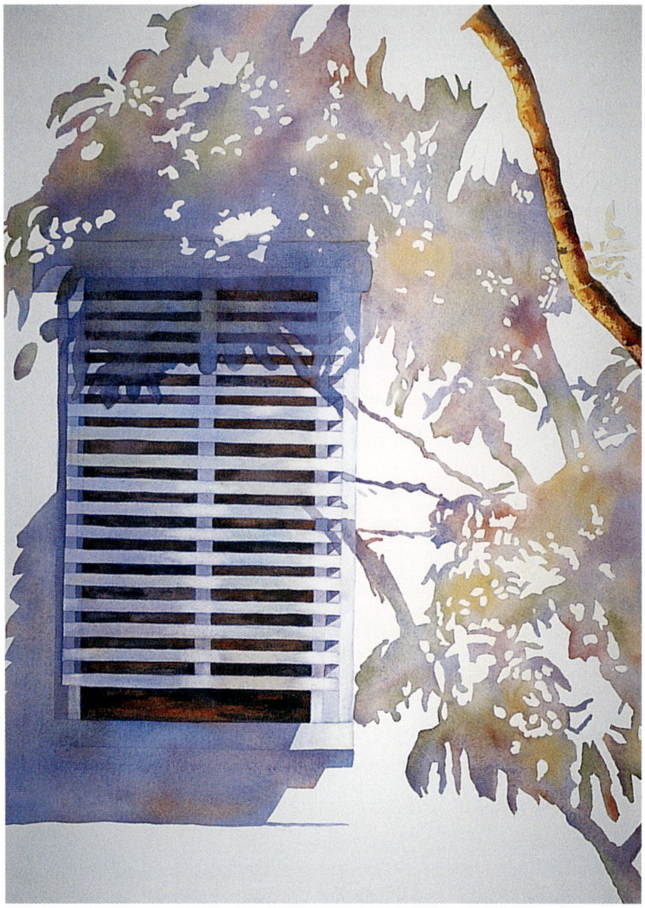

3 CREATE LEAF SHADOWS

Start at the left upper edge of the shadow area of the leaves. Use a no. 36 round loaded with Verditer Blue to cover a few inches of paper. Then clean your brush and pick up Permanent Rose. Join Permanent Rose to Ultramarine Blue. Let them mingle together. Paint over the dry masking fluid. Change and repeat the colors until the entire shadow shape is covered with mingled colors. Clean the brush each time you change colors. While the shadow shape is still damp, add Permanent Sap Green where the leaves reflect back into the painting. Add more Cobalt Blue to the areas of the shadow around the shutter. Let dry.

4 ADD TREE SHADOWS AND REMOVE THE MASKING

Paint the tree's shadow on the upper part of the shutter with a no. 12 round, mingling Verditer Blue, Cobalt Blue and Mineral Violet. Pull the wet paint up into the dry shadow shape on the wall and blend the paint with water. Complete the shadow under the shutter using the same colors. Let this dry and remove all of the masking fluid with a commercial masking remover. Run your fingers over the surface to be sure you have removed all the mask.

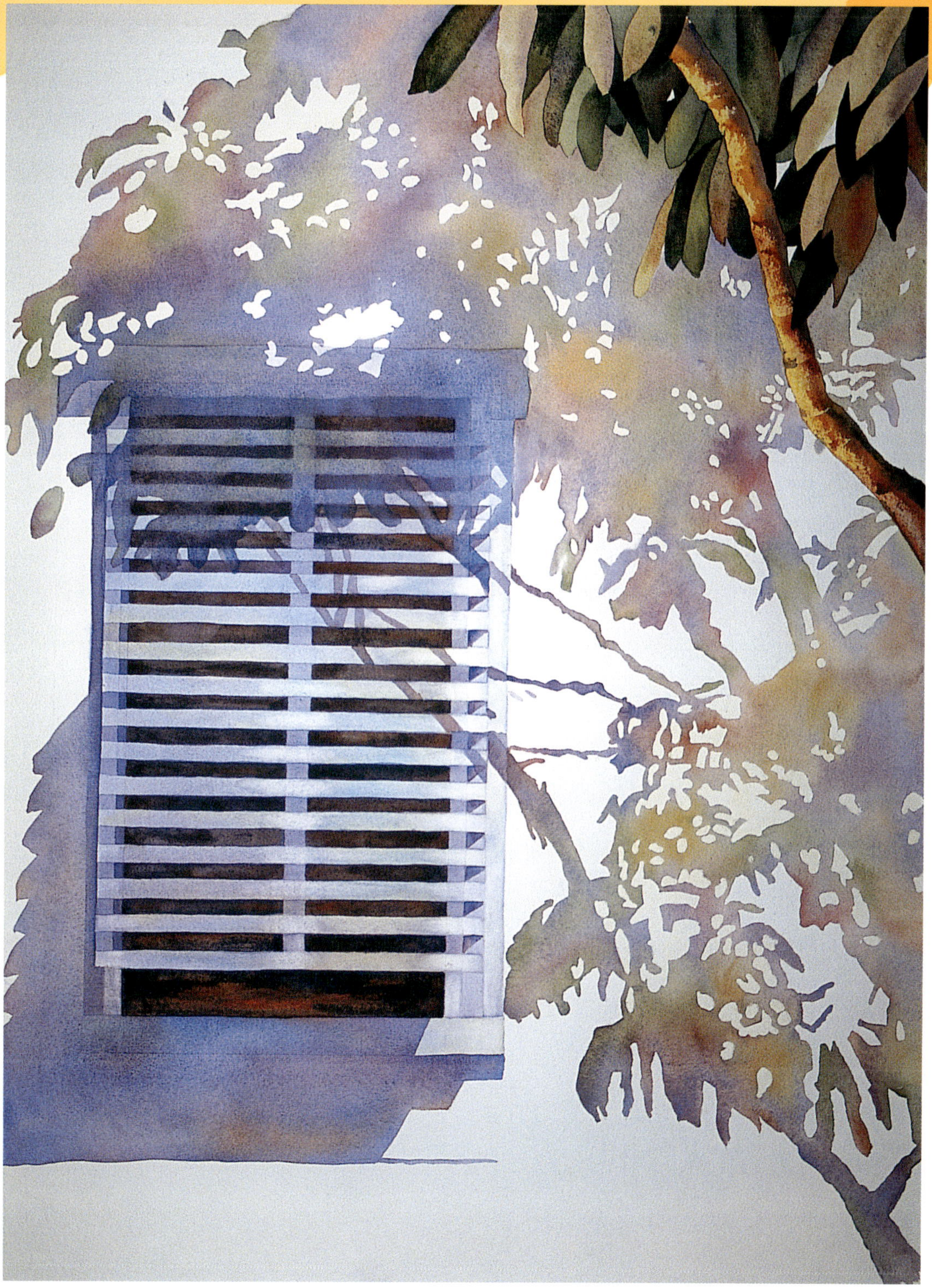

5 COMPLETE THE PAINTING
Paint the leaves on the tree using a no. 12 round, mingling Gamboge Nova, Permanent Sap Green, Brown Madder and Permanent Blue. To add more shadow shapes to the shutters, use a no. 8 round and mingle Cobalt Blue with Mineral Violet. Finish by cleaning up areas and softening ragged edges with a no. 6 scrubber.

CLOSED FOR THE SEASON
22" × 30" (56cm × 76cm)
Watercolor on cold-pressed paper
Collection of Mrs. Virginia Linscott

Creating a Tight Composition

MATERIALS

BRUSHES
Nos. 8, 12 and 16 round • ¾-inch (19mm) and 2-inch (51mm) flats • no. 6 scrubber

COLORS
Aureolin Yellow • Brown Madder • Burnt Sienna • Cobalt Blue • Cobalt Teal Blue • Naples Yellow • New Gamboge • Quinacridone Red Orange • Transparent Turquoise • Ultramarine Blue • Verditer Blue

SURFACE
300-lb. (640gsm) Arches cold-pressed paper

My son-in-law was dying from a terrible brain cancer at too young of an age. This book is dedicated to him. He was one of the bravest, kindest human beings I have ever known.

I did this painting for him from a photo of a boat taken in Corsica. For the painting, I zoomed in on the important aspects of the reference photo to make the composition more attractive.

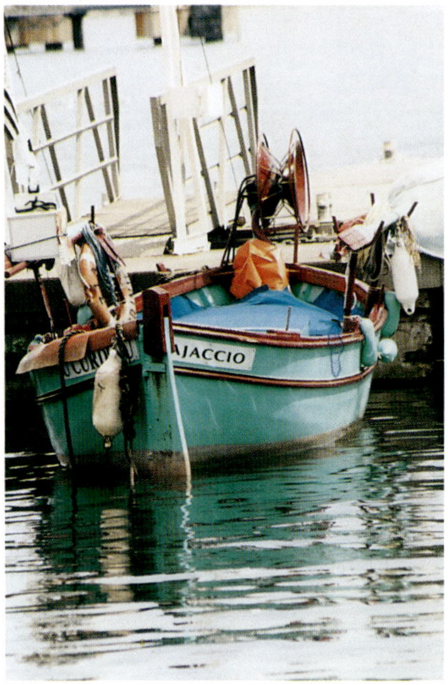

Reference Photo
The color of this boat, along with that of the orange life preservers is daring and exciting. The beautiful turquoise color reflecting into the water drew me to paint this photograph.

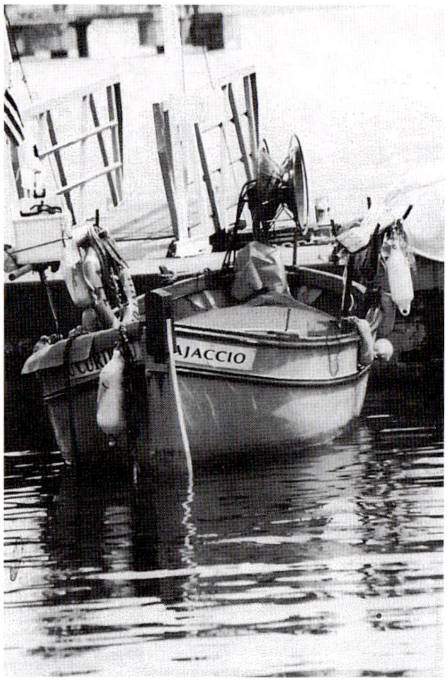

Black-and-White Photocopy

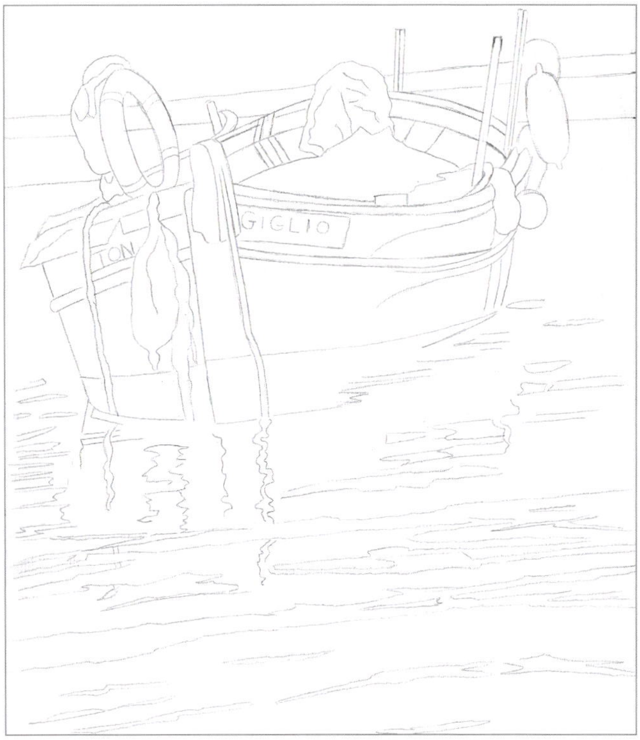

Final Composition
The reference photo is very busy, so I deleted most of the background and some of the things hanging off the boat. I anchored the composition to the sides of the painting by drawing a simple dock. I also moved the boat higher up on the surface to avoid dividing my paper in half with its shape. I chose to keep all aspects of the water in the composition.

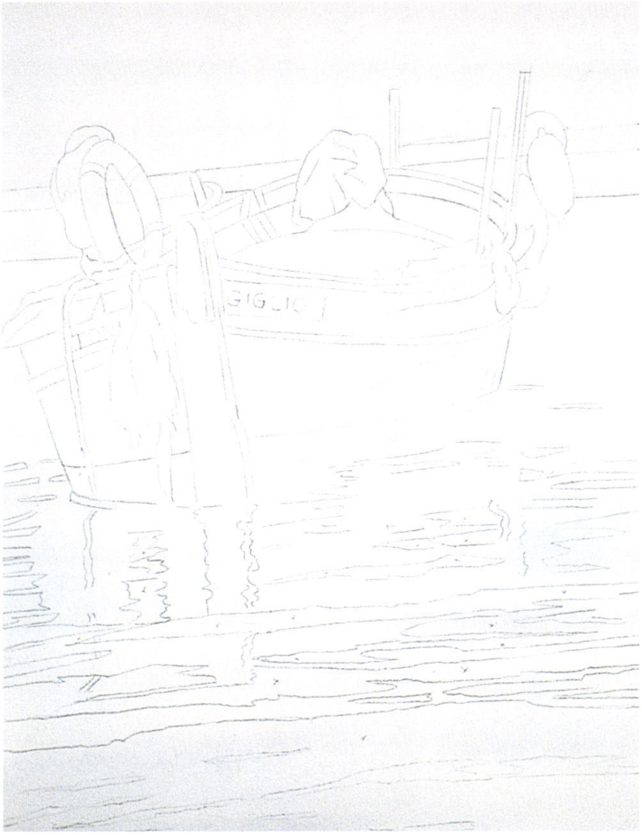

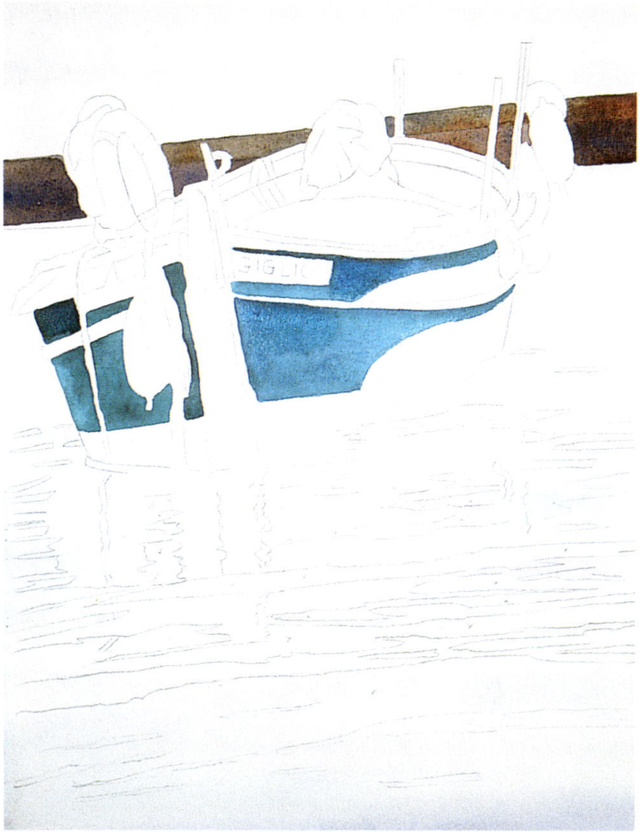

1 PUT IN THE LIGHTS OF THE WATER

Take your 2-inch (51mm) flat and wet the entire water area with clean water. With your paper flat on the table, mingle and drop Verditer Blue and Cobalt Teal Blue into some areas of the wet surface with a no. 16 round. Keep the values very light. These will become the lightest lights in the water. Let this dry thoroughly.

2 ADD THE BOAT

Use a no. 12 round to mingle Cobalt Teal Blue and Transparent Turquoise across the surface of the boat. Be sure to alternate the colors as you go. Paint the top of the dock with a mingling of Burnt Sienna and Cobalt Blue.

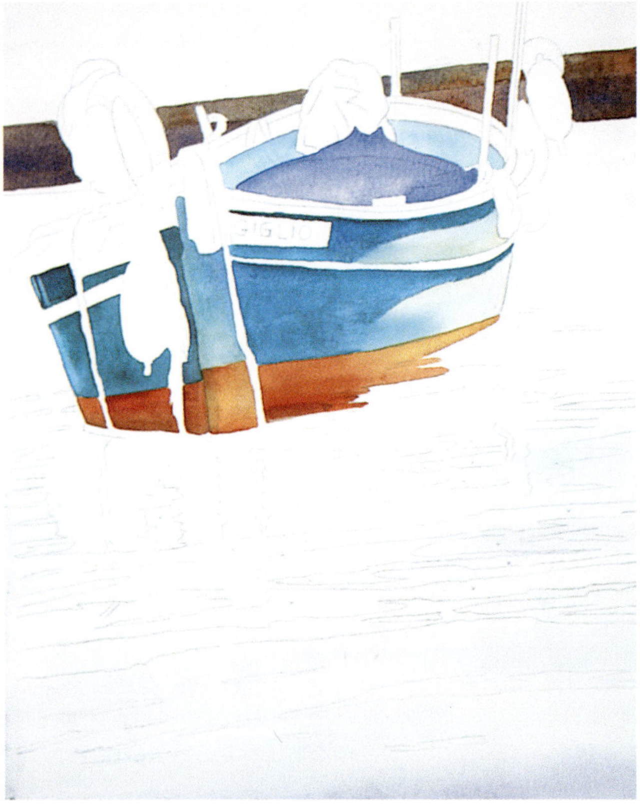

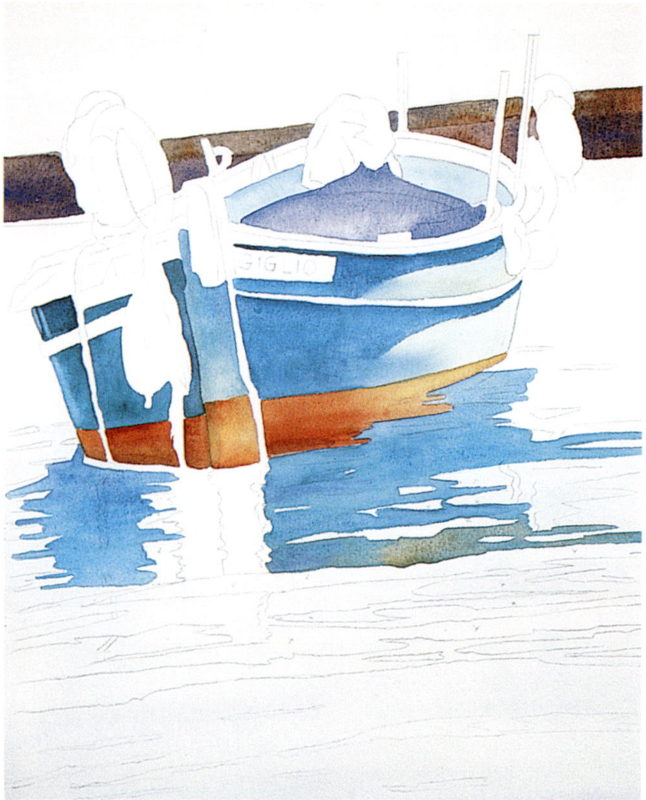

3 CREATE LIGHT AREAS ALONG THE BOAT'S SIDES
Let the paint on the sides of the boat dry thoroughly. With a ¾-inch (19mm) flat, drop in a little Aureolin Yellow and some Cobalt Teal Blue on the boat's sides. Pull the paint toward the dry areas and lightly blend with the ¾-inch (19mm) flat. Starting on the far left of the lower edge of the boat, Mingle New Gamboge and Burnt Sienna along the sides of the lower edge of the boat where it sits in the water. Work your way across the boat, dropping less yellow where you see less light and adding Burnt Sienna with some Ultramarine Blue where necessary in the dark areas. As you move across into the light areas, drop a little Brown Madder. Paint the inside canopy of the boat with Cobalt Blue and Ultramarine Blue. Let this dry completely.

4 PAINT THE BOAT'S SHADOWS IN THE WATER
Take a ¾-inch (19mm) flat and, following the value patterns in the black-and-white copy, mingle Cobalt Teal Blue and Transparent Turquoise across the shadow shape in the water area. You will be able to form the shape very easily with the flat edge of the brush. It may be easier if you turn your painting and black-and white photocopy upside down. You will see the shadows as a shape and as water. While the paint is wet, mingle in a little Brown Madder here and there to reflect the brown from the boat's bottom. I placed the Brown Madder far from the boat because I saw it in the photograph.

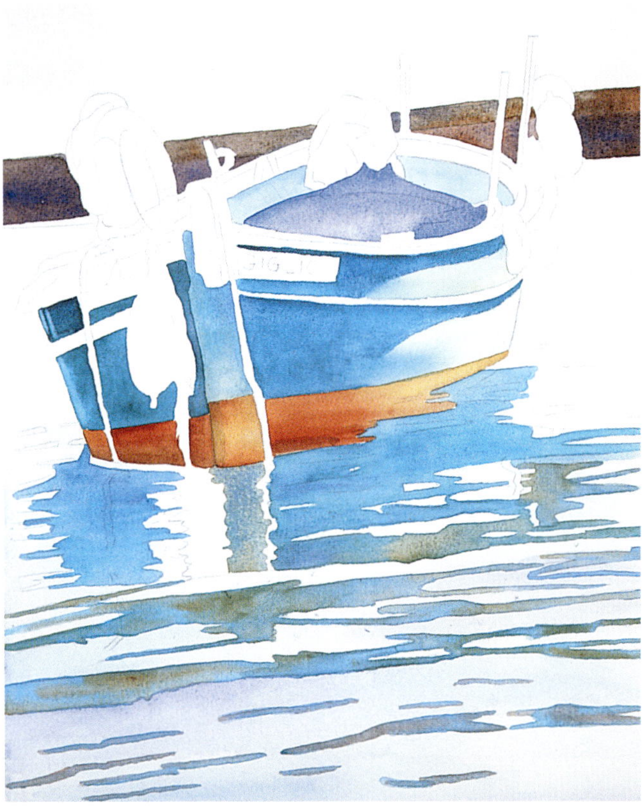

5 FINISH THE WATER

Using your ¾-inch (19mm) flat, continue to mingle Verditer Blue and Cobalt Teal Blue, using less Transparent Turquoise. As the shadows come out from the boat, they will absorb more light and become lighter in value, so you might use a little more water with your pigments in these areas. Remember, you are painting the reflections of the boat, so use some of the boat's colors in the blues of the water. Add Brown Madder to areas of water that show red reflections.

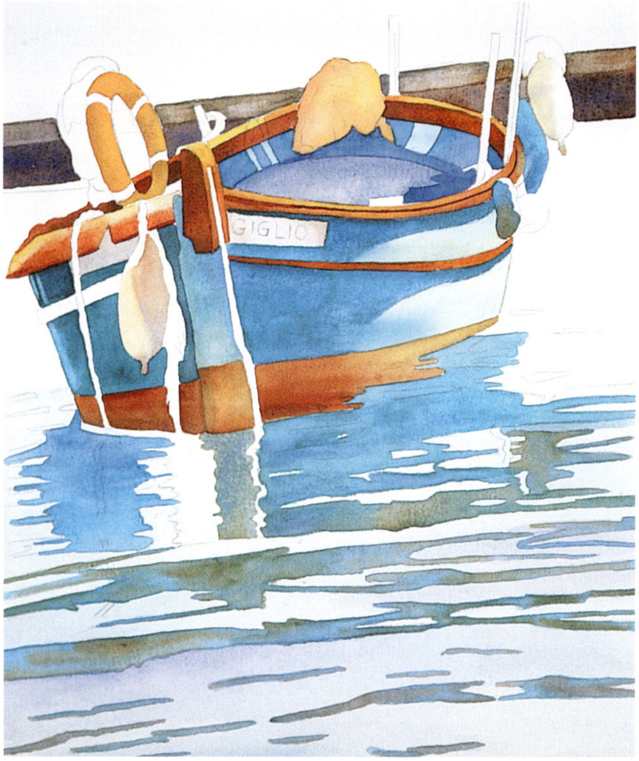

6 ADD DETAIL TO THE BOAT

Use a no. 8 round to put the red-brown details into the side of the boat with Brown Madder and New Gamboge. Remember to reflect the sun hitting some of these areas. The red-brown trim on the boat has areas that are light struck. I use more water and yellow to create this sun-struck area. Wet the paper first in the light areas and paint from dry to wet. Always refer to the black-and-white photocopy for these details. Use Naples Yellow and Quinacridone Red Orange to paint the life preserver and rags hanging on the boat. Mingle Verditer Blue and Burnt Sienna to paint the shadows on the white objects.

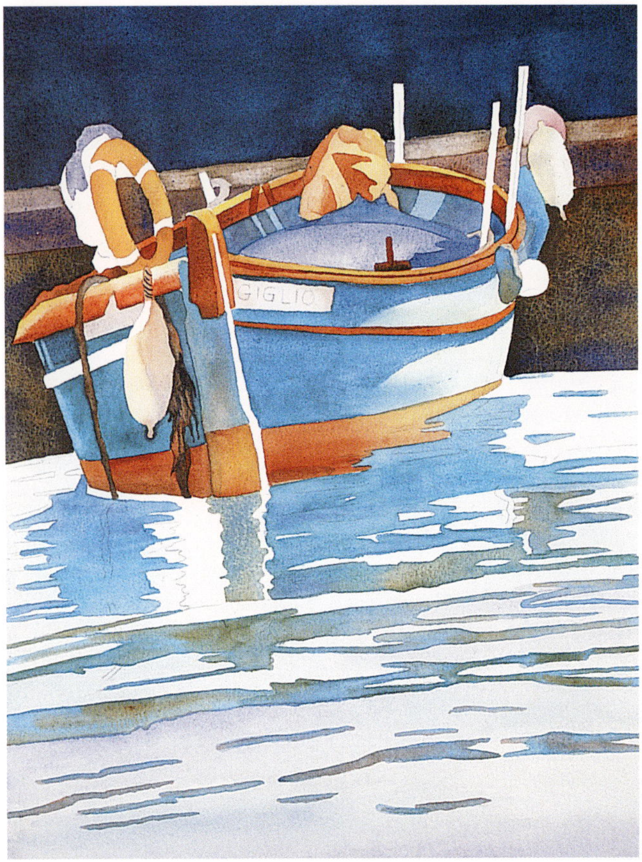

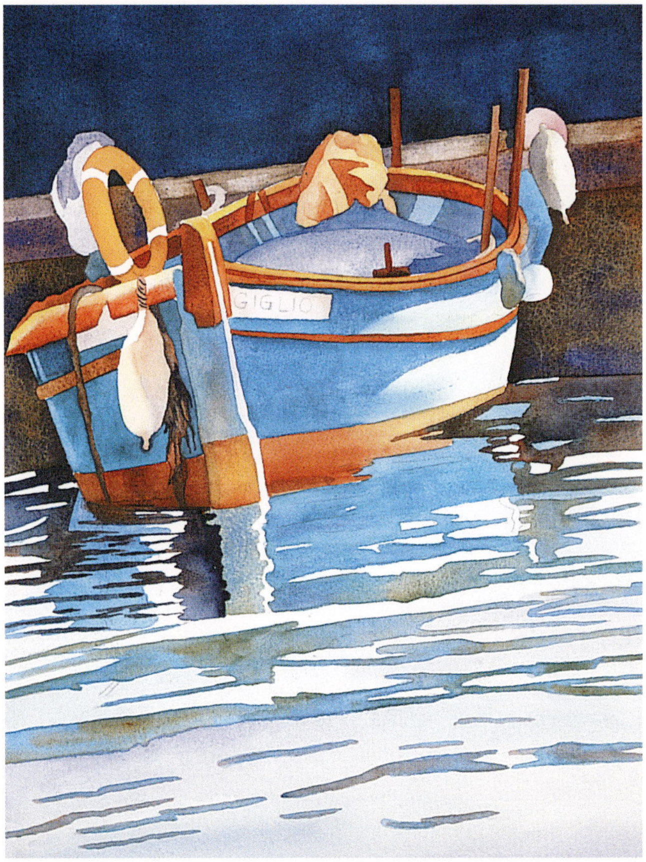

7 FINISH THE BACKGROUND
With the same no. 16 round, mingle Burnt Sienna, Ultramarine Blue and Brown Madder for the dock wall. Burnt Sienna and Ultramarine Blue are granular and will create a rough, textural effect.

8 PULL DARKS INTO THE WATER
While the paint on the dock wall is still damp, begin to pull the colors down into the water. Do this by mingling Brown Madder, Burnt Sienna and Cobalt Blue with a no. 12 round brush. The Cobalt Blue is less granular than the Ultramarine Blue and works to suggest water. Continue to paint in the dark shapes that you see.

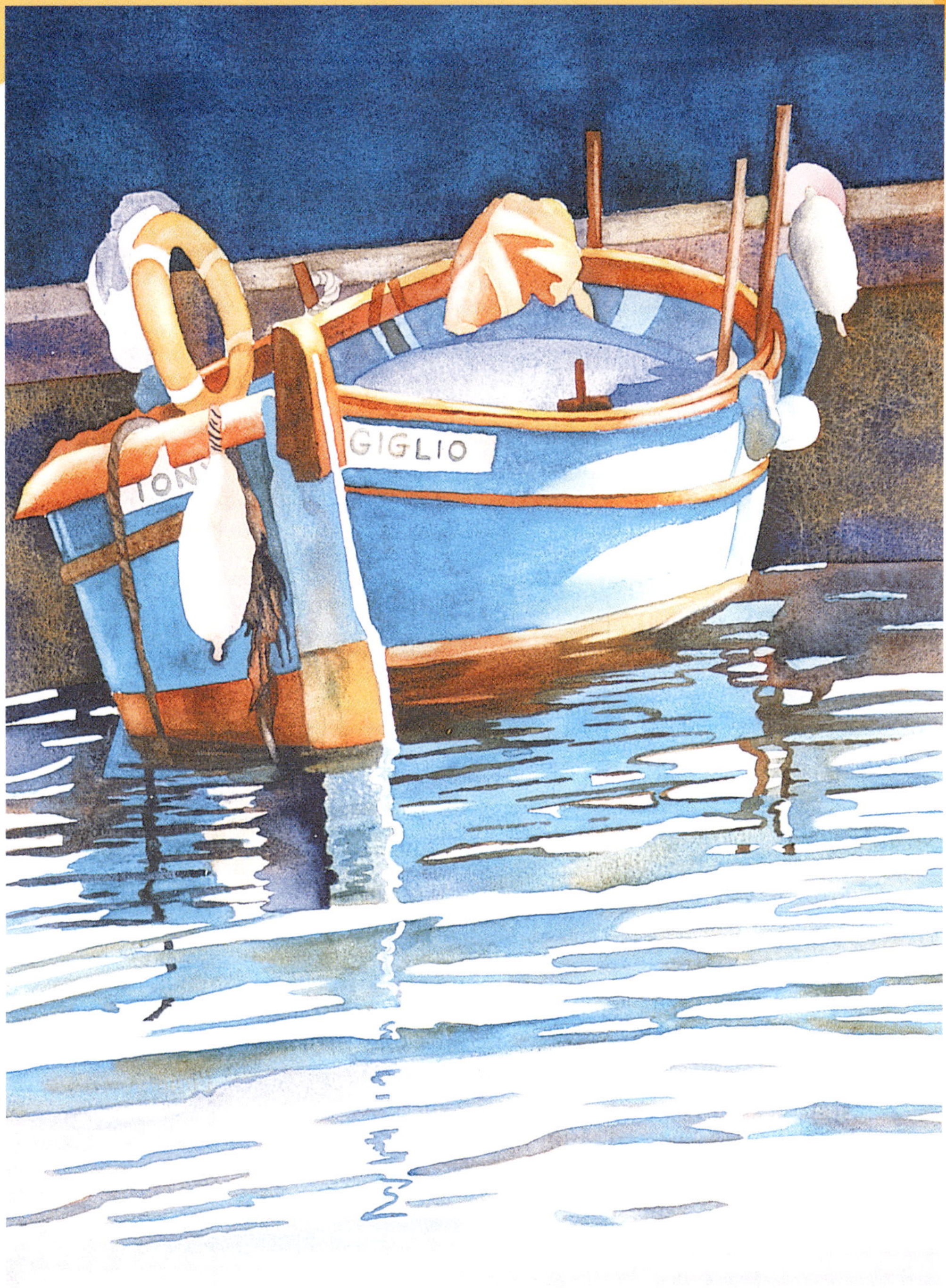

9 ADD THE FINISHING DETAILS

Using a no. 8 round, put the dark shapes and shadows you see in your black-and-white photocopy into the water. Paint the dark line across the bottom of the boat that sets it into the water. Mingle Burnt Sienna and Ultramarine Blue for a black. To do this, use a no. 12 round and mingle first Burnt Sienna and then Ultramarine Blue, joining them on the paper under the boat. Use lots of pigment here and then add water to fade out this dark. Add a little water and paint the text on the boat. You don't want this to be too vivid, just subtle. Finally, use a no. 6 scrubber to lift and soften any uneccessary hard edges once your painting is completely dry.

ANTHONY GIGLIO
20" × 16" (51cm × 41cm)
Transparent watercolor on cold-pressed paper
Collection of Tony Giglio Jr. and Annie Giglio

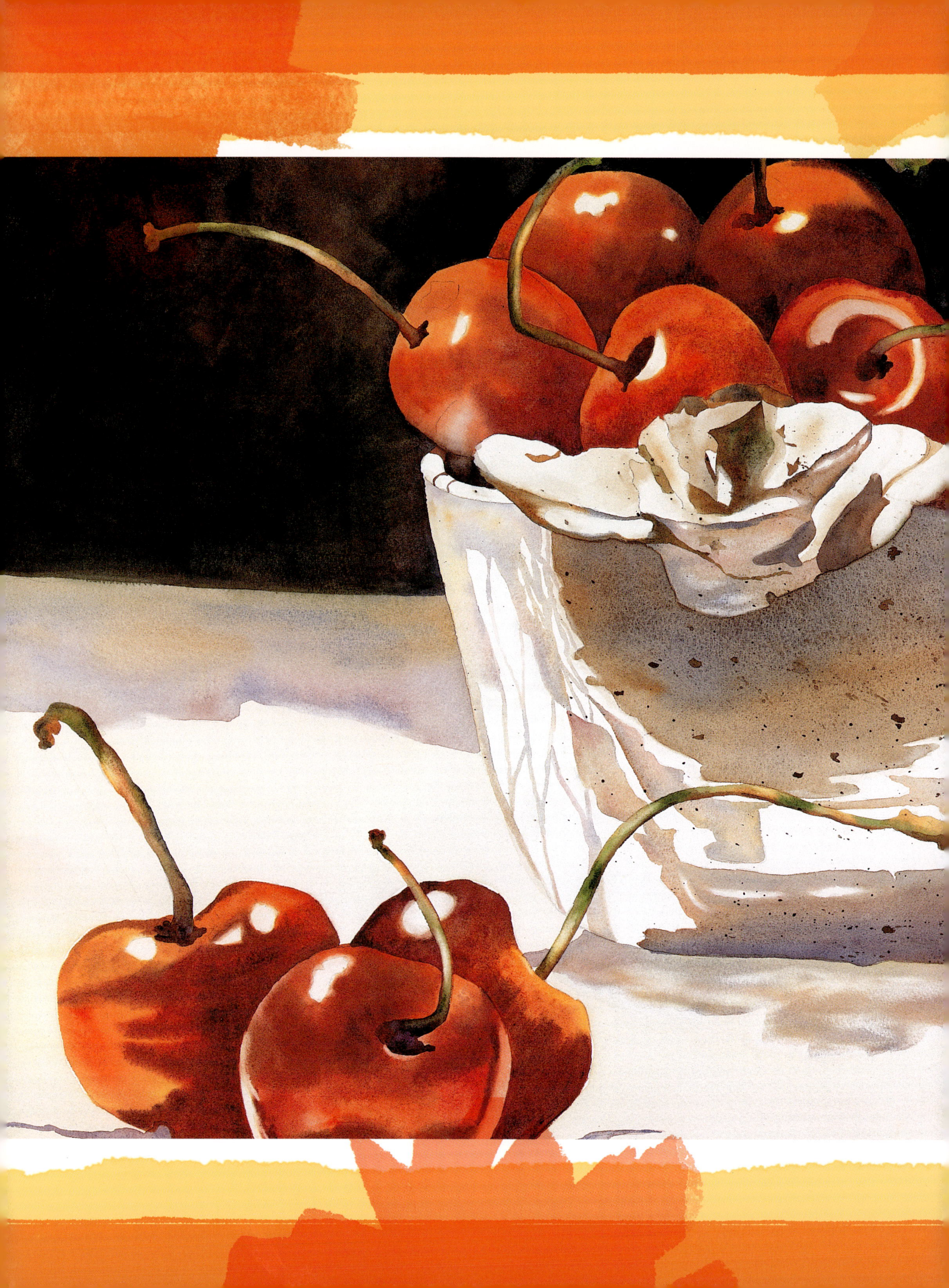

4

Value

A successful painting doesn't just have beautiful, juicy color; it uses the correct values. In this chapter I'll show you a simple way to achieve accurate values. All you have to do is make a black-and-white photocopy of your reference photo and you'll have a quick and easy way to determine the correct value to use in your artwork. I consider my black-and-white photocopy as my map to finding the right values—and I haven't gotten lost with it yet!

Value is the main means of creating dimension on a flat piece of paper and making a three-dimensional object look correct. The form of any object appears on the paper by the change of values seen in your black-and-white photocopy.

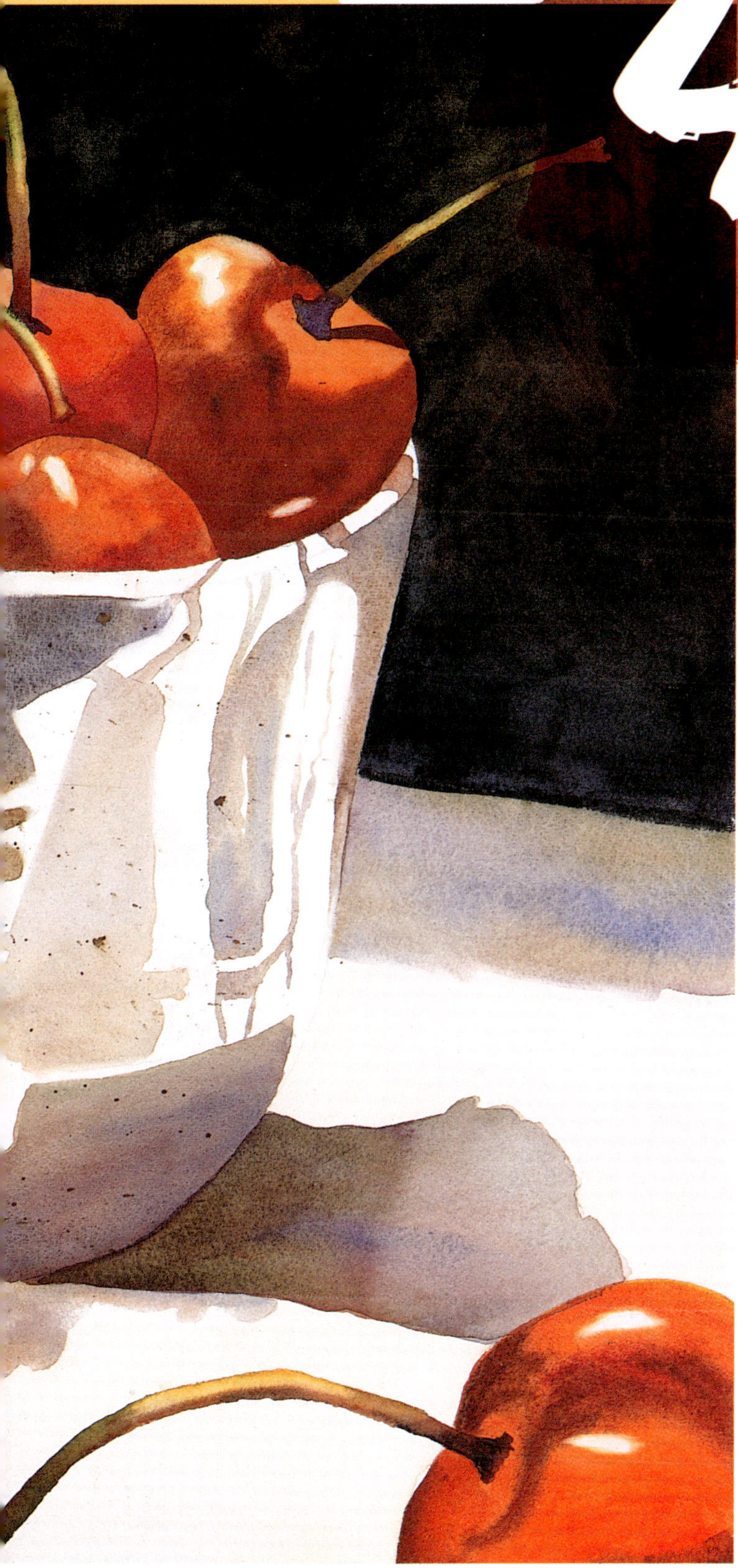

SOMETHING ABOUT LIFE AND A BOWL OF CHERRIES
22" × 30" (56cm × 76cm)
Transparent watercolor on cold-pressed paper
Collection of Mr. and Mrs. John Ramsey

Tools for Seeing Value

Value is the relative lightness or darkness of a color. Use value changes to establish an object's form or to suggest the direction of light in a painting. The ability to use the correct value is a painter's most important attribute. A perfect composition and dramatic color will not make a good painting if the values are wrong. The tools I use to accurately portray values in my paintings are black-and-white photocopies of my reference photos. However, value scales also are a useful way to see the range of values of a particular color.

VALUE SCALE

Using a value scale is one way to measure a color's range of light and dark values. A value scale is an organized linear scale of value swatches ranging from a color's darkest dark to its lightest light. In addition to using a value scale, you can check the contrasts and value patterns in your paintings by squinting your eyes. Squinting eliminates detail so you can focus on the value patterns. You can make your own value scales for the colors on your palette, starting with the pure pigment, then adding water to progressively dilute and lighten it. It's a good idea to produce five to ten values for each color.

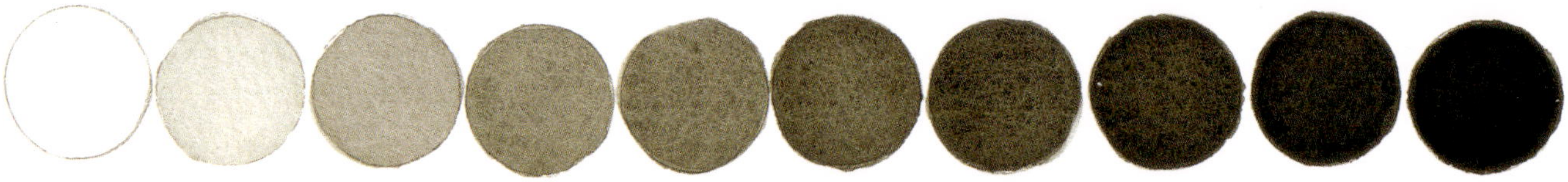

Black-and-White Value Scale
A black-and-white value scale like this can help you determine the value of the color you want to use. Use this with a black-and-white photocopy of your reference photo to help you achieve an effective value pattern.

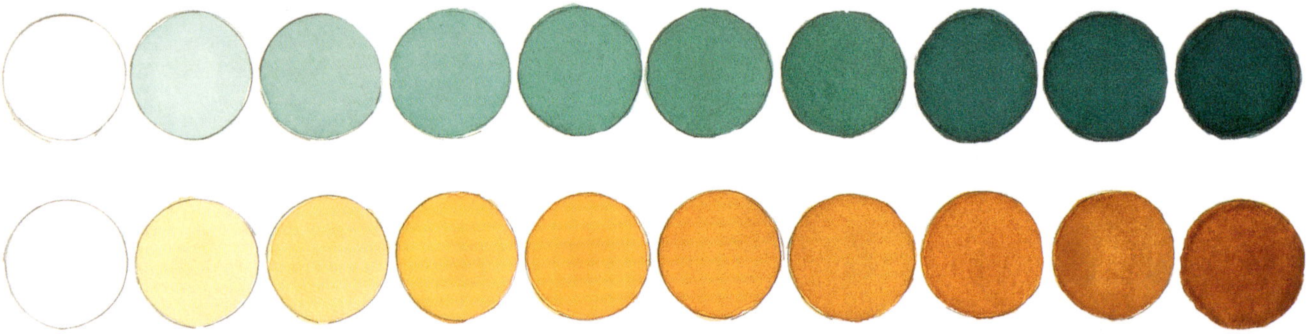

Value Scales of Yellow and Blue
Making value scales for the colors of your palette will give you a general idea of each color's value range. Notice the darkest value of blue isn't as dark as black but is darker than the darkest yellow value.

BLACK-AND-WHITE PHOTOCOPY

I have found that a black-and-white photocopy of my reference photo is a quick and useful way to interpret value. It can help you recognize the overall key for the subject you're painting. A *high-key* painting uses the lighter values on a value scale; while a *low-key* painting uses the values on the lower end of the scale. The photocopy helps me see the white areas, the midtones and the darks. The simplicity of black and white emphasizes the strong contrasts that direct attention to the important areas of the composition.

If you start with a good value pattern, any color you paint with will be correct as long as its value matches the value pattern. A red flower can become blue by just following the map that the black-and-white photocopy provides. I can paint without my color photo, but not without my black-and-white photocopy.

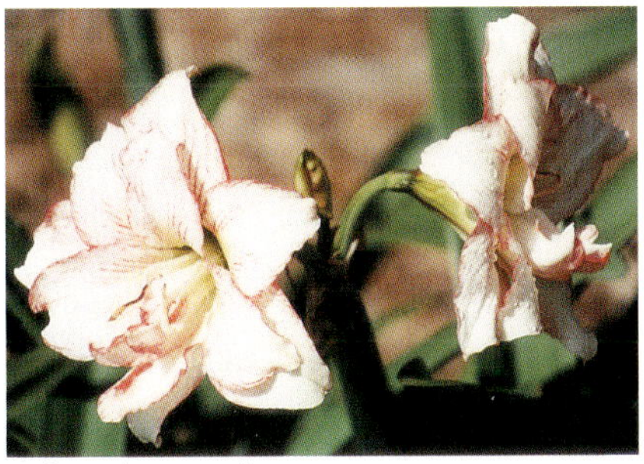

Color reference photo

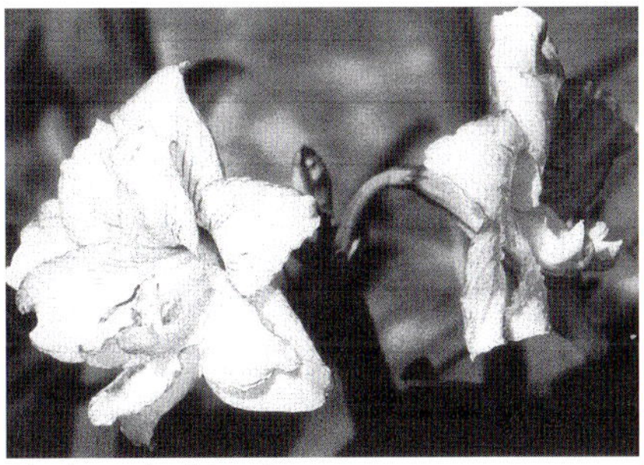

Black-and-white photocopy

High-Key Value Pattern

Because of the predominantly light values of the black-and-white photocopy, you can tell that this is a high-key value pattern.

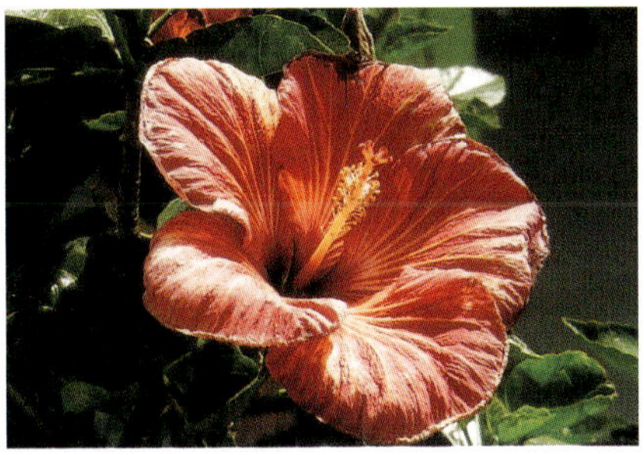

Color reference photo

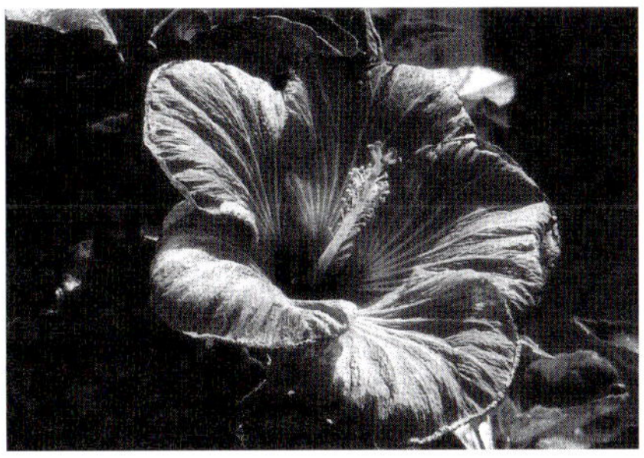

Black-and-white photocopy

Low Key Value Pattern

Here the predominately dark values in this black-and-white photocopy indicate this composition is a low key value pattern.

ADJUSTING THE BRIGHTNESS OF PHOTOCOPIES

Depending on the photograph you're copying, you may need to tweak the brightness setting to get a useful value pattern. You may need to darken light objects like vases, fabric and flowers so the details are visible in the copy. The same is true for dark objects. Lighten them so you can see them better. Simply use the appropriate controls on the photocopier.

Simplify Values

Our eyes see an almost infinite number of values, or shades, between white and dark. However, it wouldn't be practical to paint that way. Part of the artist's task is to simplify the values of a scene into a manageable number. If your painting is based on a good value pattern, you are free to use color any way you want. A successful value plan will contain whites, midvalues and darks. Remember that value sketches and black-and-white photocopies are even more simplified representation of the values in a scene. A photocopy, for example, probably shows three or four values, at most, that appear in any given painting. So although you may see a single dark value section in your photocopy, it doesn't mean that section should be painted a single dark value. It does mean that the values you use in that section should be within a dark range of values.

A painting should have a value pattern that can be seen easily from across the room. Check the value pattern in a painting by blowing up your black-and-white photocopy to the same size as your painting. Place them beside each other across the room from you. This will help you see where you need to adjust the values in the painting.

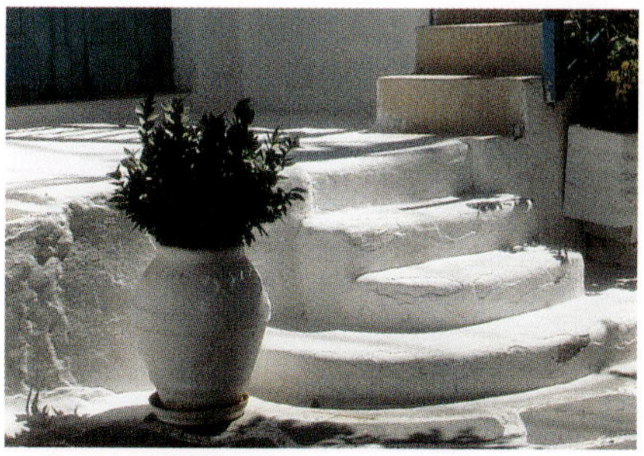

Reference Photo

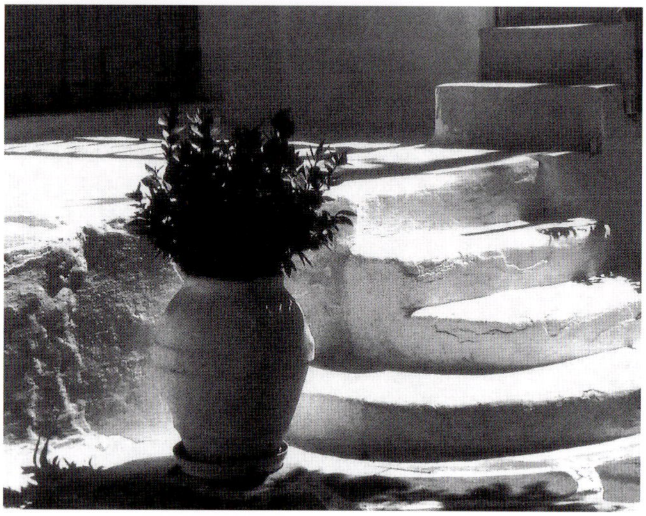

Black-and-White Photocopy
The black-and-white photocopy easily simplifies the values into lights, midtones and darks. Let the white of the paper be your lightest light and use a lot of pigment with just enough water for flow in your darkest darks.

Painting With a Simplified Value System
This is a painting of steps in an old Greek town, done with a simplified, three-value system using only the white of the paper, the midtones and the darks. Notice, however, that there is a range of values even within the three simplified values. Keep this in mind as you paint for a more interesting composition.

ANDALE
16" × 20" (41cm × 51cm)
Transparent watercolor on cold-pressed paper
Collection of the artist

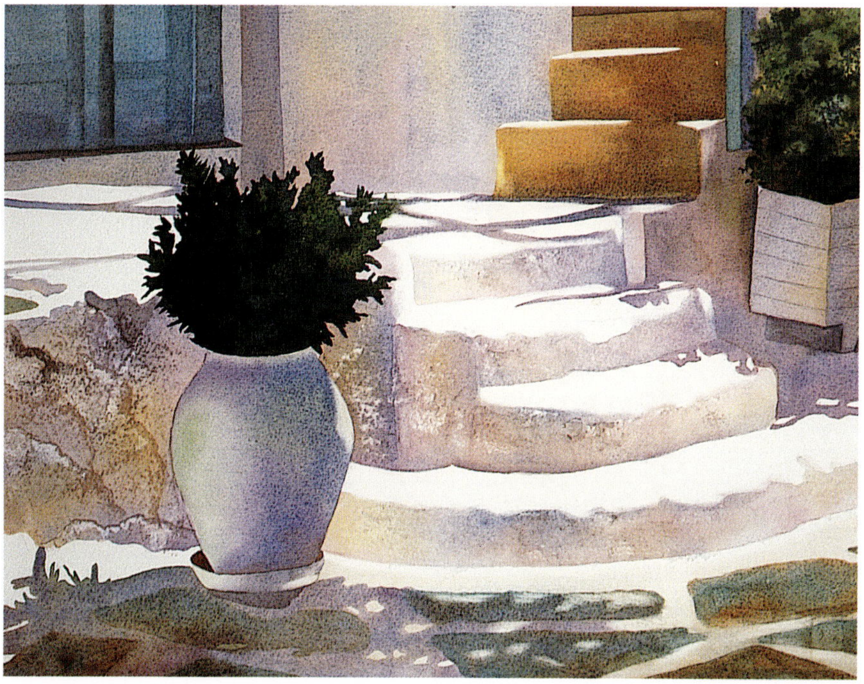

Painting From a Black-and-White Photocopy

MATERIALS

BRUSHES
Nos. 4, 10 and 12 round • ½-inch (12mm) flat

COLORS
Aureolin Yellow • Brown Madder • Cobalt Blue • Cobalt Teal Blue • Mineral Violet • New Gamboge • Olive Green • Permanent Rose • Permanent Sap Green • Quinacridone Red Orange • Scarlet Lake • Undersea Green

SURFACE
300-lb. (640gsm) Arches cold-pressed paper

TRY WORKING IN A SERIES

I've done many different versions of these olives: I've cropped into the photos, added other objects and painted them really big. It's fun to get into "the zone," where all the creative juices are flowing, and let one painting inspire the next. Also, when I'm working on multiple paintings at once, I don't have to spend as much time waiting for paint to dry.

Here you'll do a simple composition following the value patterns in the black-and-white photocopy. As you apply the paint, remember to look back at the photocopy to check the value pattern. Use thicker paint (watercolors with more pigment than water) for areas with darker values. The light and dark areas of the olives create their form.

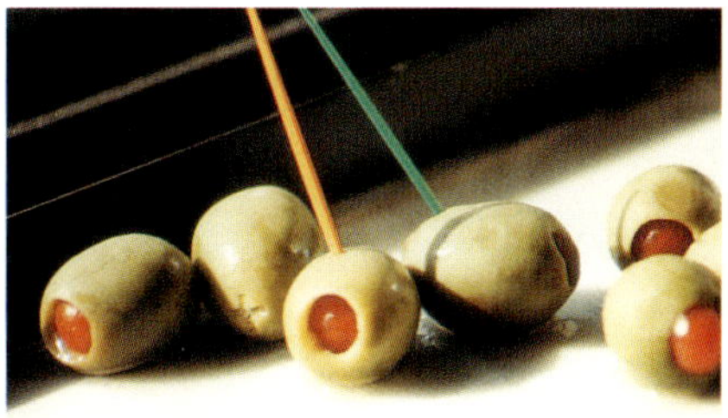

Color Reference Photo

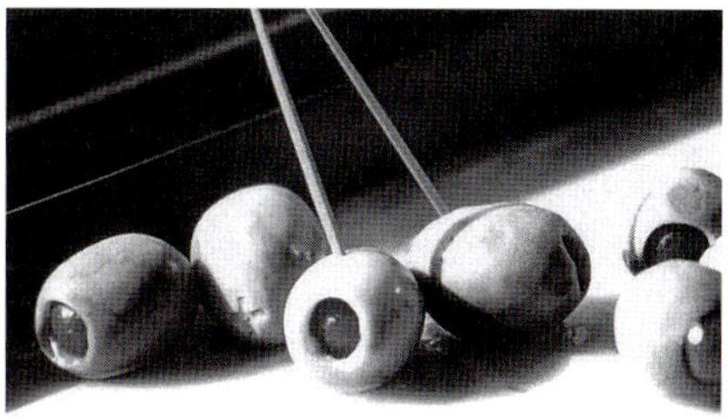

Black-and-White Photocopy

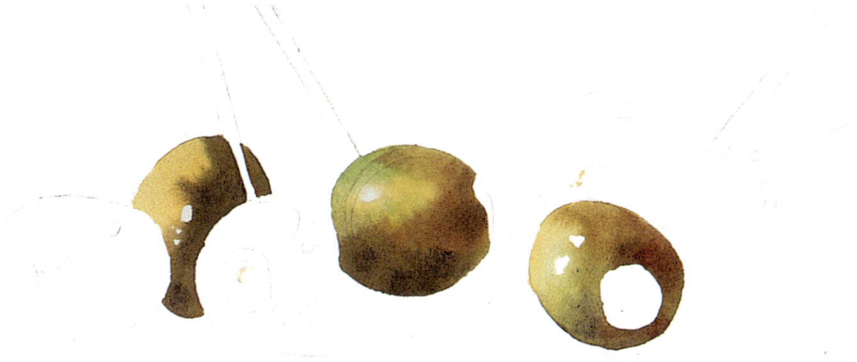

1 START THE OLIVES
Draw or trace the image onto your watercolor paper. Following the patterns of light and dark in the black-and-white photocopy, wet the light areas of the olives with a no. 10 round. To preserve the highlight, let those areas of the paper remain dry. Starting at the area farthest away from the water, mingle Aureolin Yellow, Permanent Sap Green, Cobalt Teal Blue and Olive Green and paint toward the water. Let the paint flow into these areas.

Switch to the ½-inch (12mm) flat. While the olive is damp with pigment, work thicker paint into the areas that need darkening, using the black-and-white photocopy as your guide. Mingle Olive Green, make two strokes, and clean your brush. Apply two or three more strokes with Brown Madder. Repeat using Undersea Green and Permanent Sap Green in other areas.

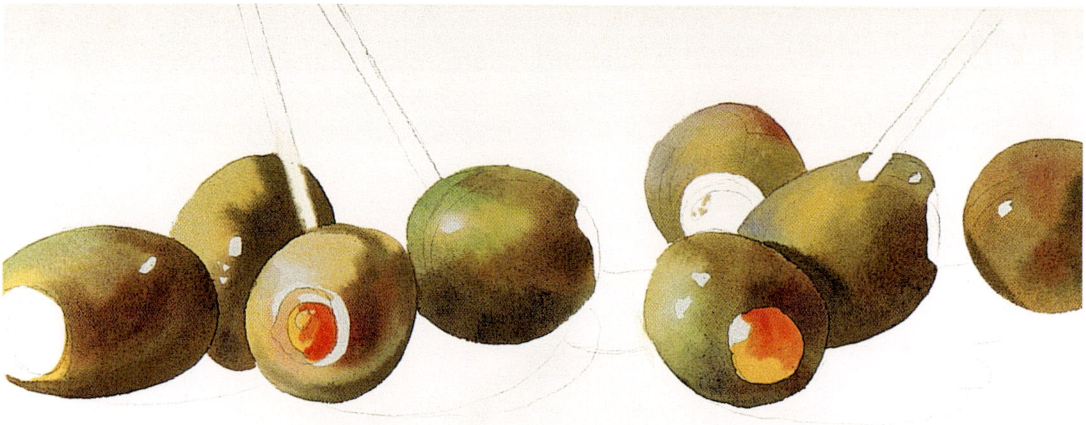

2 DEVELOP THE REMAINING OLIVES AND BEGIN THE PIMENTOS

Follow the process in step 1 to paint the rest of the olives. Remember to use the black-and-white photocopy as your guide. Suggest reflections of the red pimentos by dropping Brown Madder into some of the olives with the ½-inch (12mm) flat.

Use a no. 10 round to paint the whole pimento with New Gamboge. A light wash won't work here, so use lots of pigment. Paint around the highlights, leaving dry white paper. While the New Gamboge is still damp, drop in Scarlet Lake and Permanent Rose. The yellow will push through and glow. Paint the rest of the pimentos with this technique.

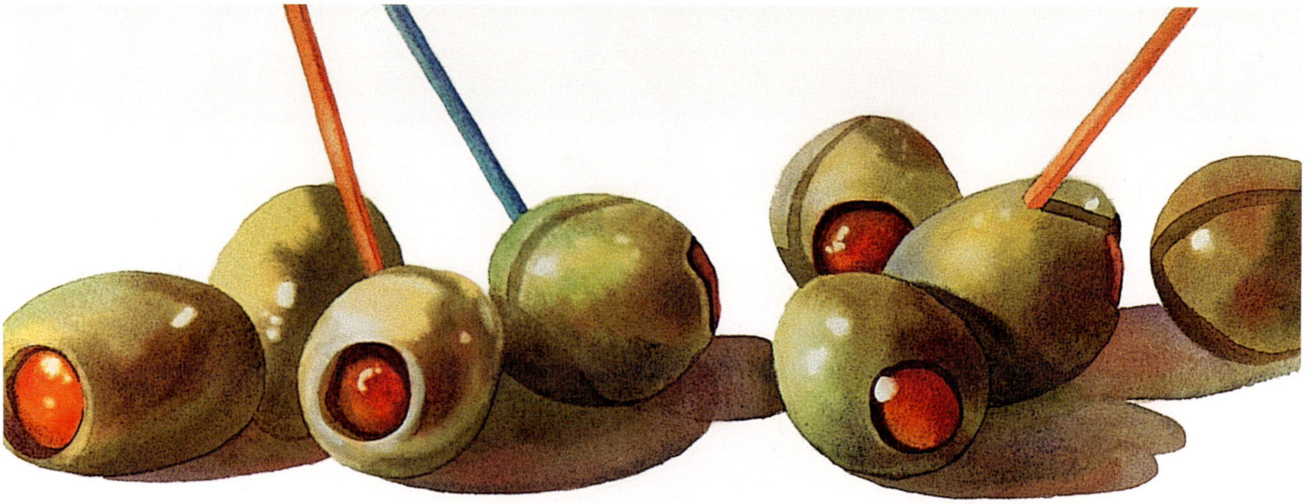

3 ADD THE SHADOWS

While the pimentos are wet, load the no. 4 round with thick Mineral Violet and paint the shadows between the pimentos and the olives. Do not outline the entire pimento, but let the edges get soft and blurry.

With a no. 12 round, mingle Brown Madder, Mineral Violet and Permanent Sap Green. Vary the colors and let them mingle together on the dry surface. When the paper is wet, drop in a little Cobalt Blue along some of the edges. Join and connect all of the shadows, repeating the above colors. Paint the toothpicks using New Gamboge and Quinacridone Red Orange for the glowing orange and Cobalt Teal Blue for the turquoise.

ALL IN A ROW
10" × 18" (25cm × 46cm)
Transparent watercolor on cold-pressed paper
Collection of the artist

Mingling Whites on a Wet Surface

MATERIALS

BRUSHES
Nos. 4, 12, 16, 26 and 36 round • no. 6 scrubber

COLORS
Aureolin Yellow • Brown Madder • Burnt Sienna • Cobalt Teal Blue • Cobalt Violet • Greenish Yellow • Mineral Violet • New Gamboge • Permanent Rose • Quinacridone Magenta • Quinacridone Red Orange • Scarlet Lake • Ultramarine Blue • Verditer Blue • Yellow Ochre

SURFACE
300-lb. (640gsm) Arches cold-pressed paper

OTHER
Absorbing pad • paper towels

We all know that watercolor will dry at least one value lighter, but if you wet the surface first it will dry even lighter. This is a technique that I use throughout this book for saving whites and lights. Knowing how to mingle color onto a wet surface to create shape and volume is also important. Painting a white vase on a white surface while reflecting colors from surrounding objects can be a fun challenge.

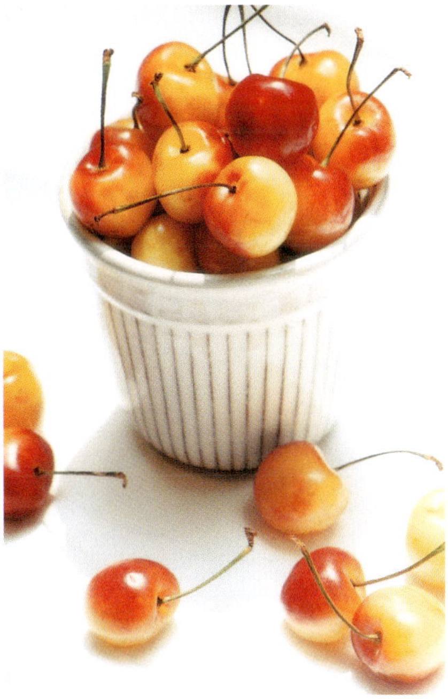

Reference Photo

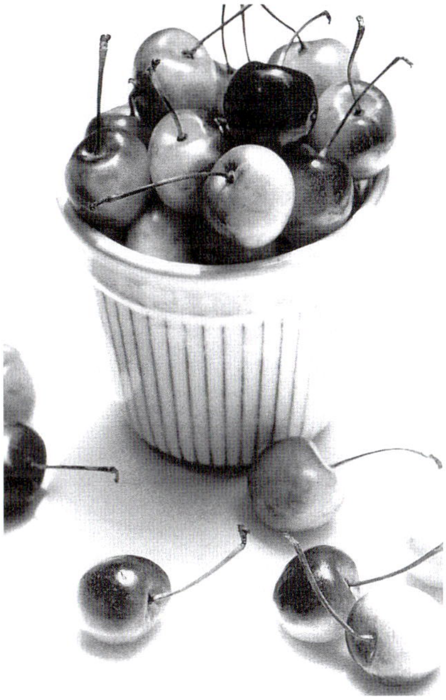

Black-and-White Photocopy

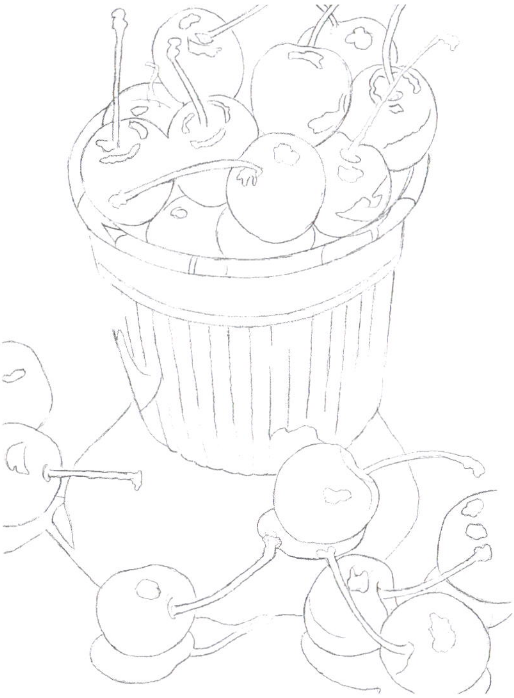

1 SKETCH THE COMPOSITION
Draw or trace the image onto your watercolor paper. Make sure you outline the shadow areas on the surface and on the bowl. Also outline the highlights on the cherries.

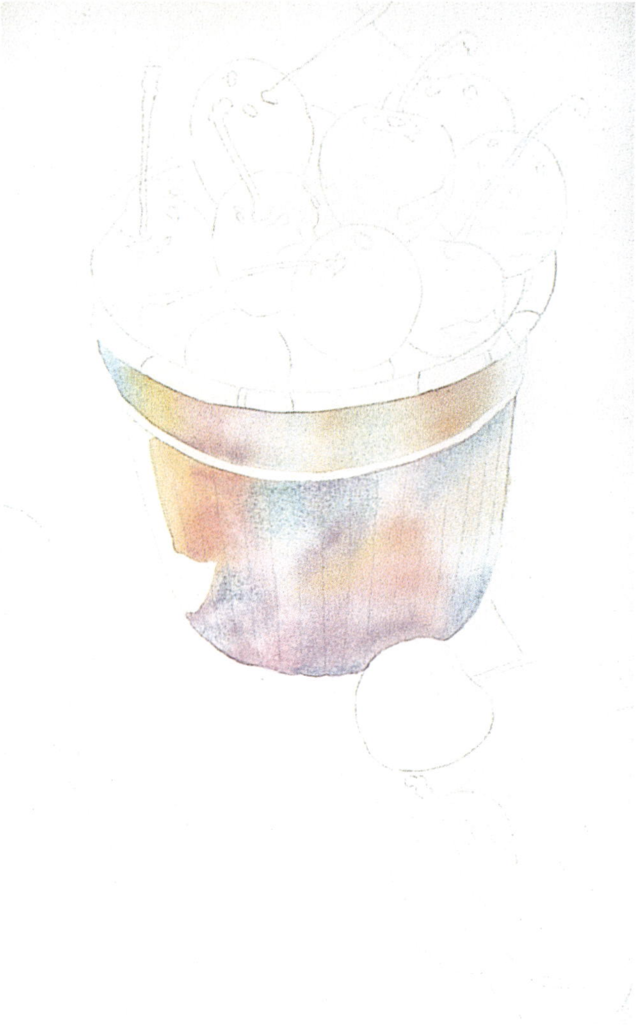

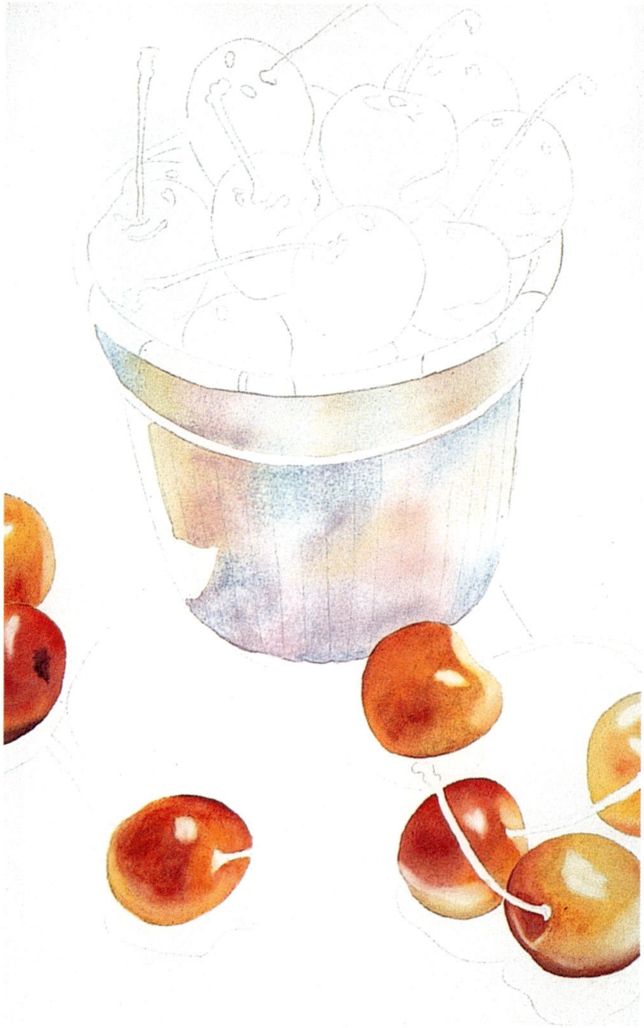

2 CREATE THE BOWL

With a no. 36 round, wet the surface of the bowl with clean water. Allow any white areas that you see in the black-and-white photocopy to dry slightly. Mingle Cobalt Teal Blue, Permanent Rose, Quinacridone Red Orange, Verditer Blue and Cobalt Violet across the wet surface with a no. 26 round. Drop more Quinacridone Red Orange to reflect the cherries—especially behind the cherry almost touching the bowl on the upper right. As you do this, constantly touch your brush to the absorbing pad. Drop Yellow Ochre onto the other colors for warmth.

3 ADD THE FOREGROUND CHERRIES

Wet some of the lightest parts of the cherries. You can paint around highlights on the cherries. The highlights will be hard-edged; wetting the highlights will give you soft edges. Allow them to dry. With a no. 12 round, paint from dry to wet mingling Aureolin Yellow, Yellow Ochre, New Gamboge, Permanent Rose, Quinacridone Red Orange and Scarlet Lake. The cherries in shadow should be darker, so use more pigment and darken them with Brown Madder and Mineral Violet.

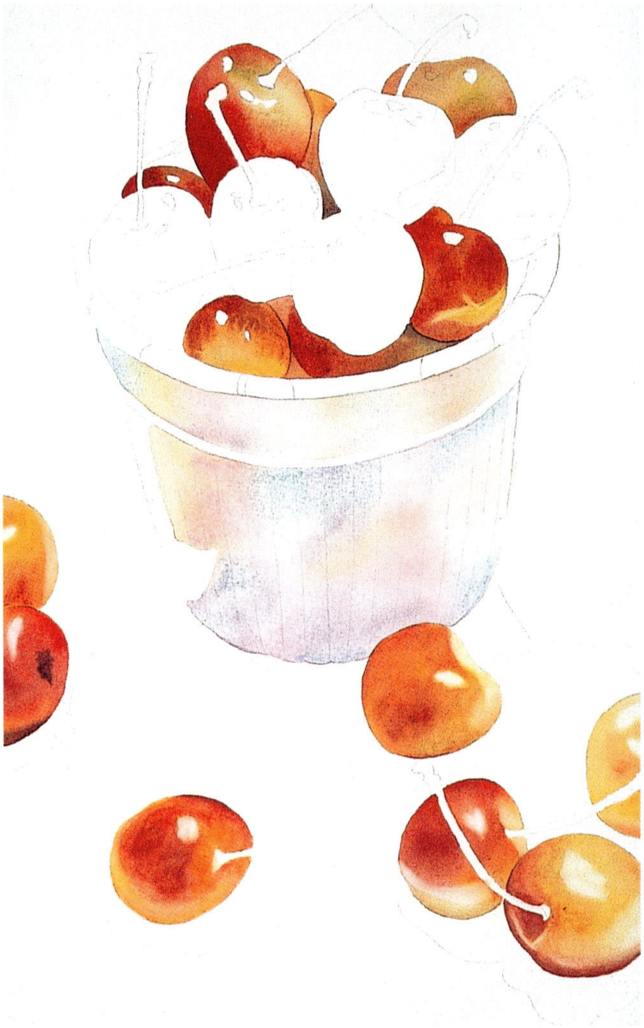

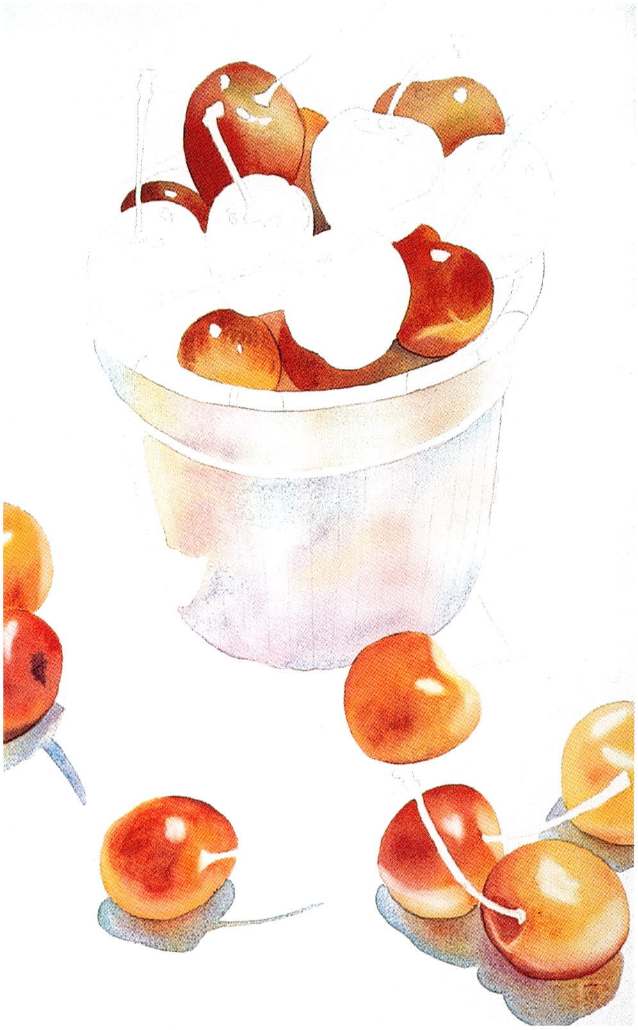

4 ADD THE DARK CHERRIES IN THE BOWL

By painting the darker cherries in the back of the bowl first, it will be easier for you to keep the front cherries a lighter value. For the darker cherries mingle Scarlet Lake, Permanent Rose, Brown Madder, Quinacridone Magenta and Mineral Violet with a no. 12 round.

5 ADD SHADOWS TO THE CHERRIES

Use a round brush that is appropriate to the size of the area you wish to cover—if the shadow is of a stem, use a no. 4 round; if the area is larger, use a no. 12 round. Mingle Cobalt Teal Blue, Cobalt Violet, Brown Madder and Yellow Ochre in the shadow areas of the stems. Under the cherries, use the same colors and in the same order. While the shadows are wet, drop in Quinacridone Red Orange and then some Yellow Ochre under the cherries. This reflects the color of the subject into the shadow.

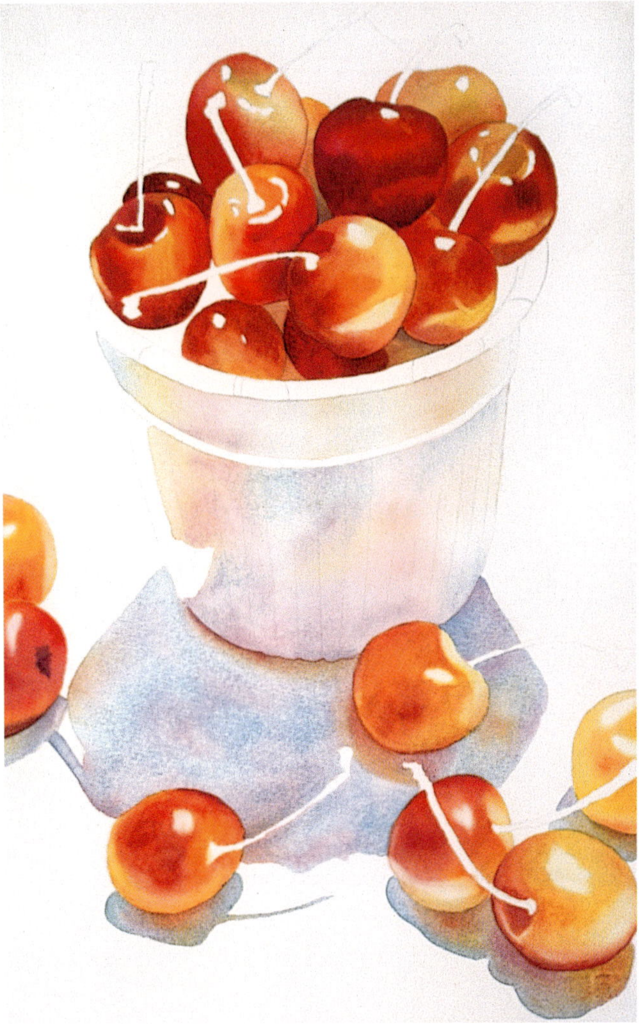

6 FINISH THE CHERRIES AND ADD THE BOWL'S SHADOW

Using lighter values, more water and less pigment and a round brush appropriate to the size of the area, wet and mingle the lighter cherries in the front of the bowl. Use Scarlet Lake, Quinacridone Red Orange, New Gamboge, Aureolin Yellow and Mineral Violet with a no. 12 round.

With a no. 16 round, mingle and connect the large shadow under the bowl to the stems and the cherries. Use the cherries' shadow colors of Cobalt Teal Blue, Cobalt Violet, Quinacridone Red Orange and Yellow Ochre. Drop in reds and yellows only where there would be a reflection of a cherry.

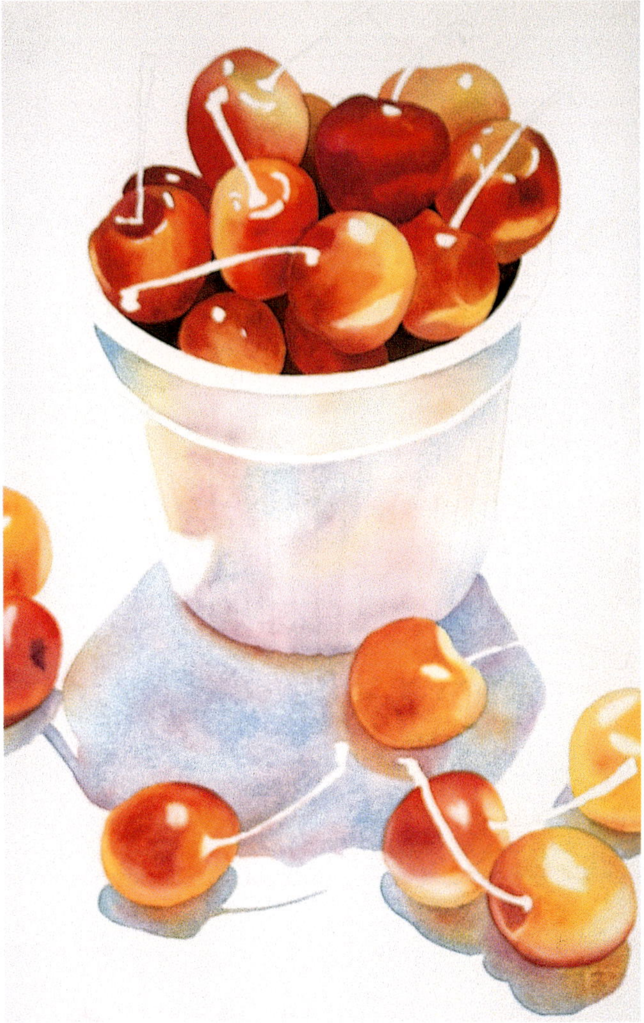

7 CONNECT THE CHERRIES TO THE BOWL

The cherries seem to be floating in the bowl, so you need to anchor the cherries to the bowl. Let the surface dry, then with a no. 12 round, mingle the dark areas under the cherries in the bowl with Mineral Violet and Brown Madder. Pull the wet paint over the dry cherries. Use a no. 12 round and gently add a little water to loosen the hard dry edge of the cherries.

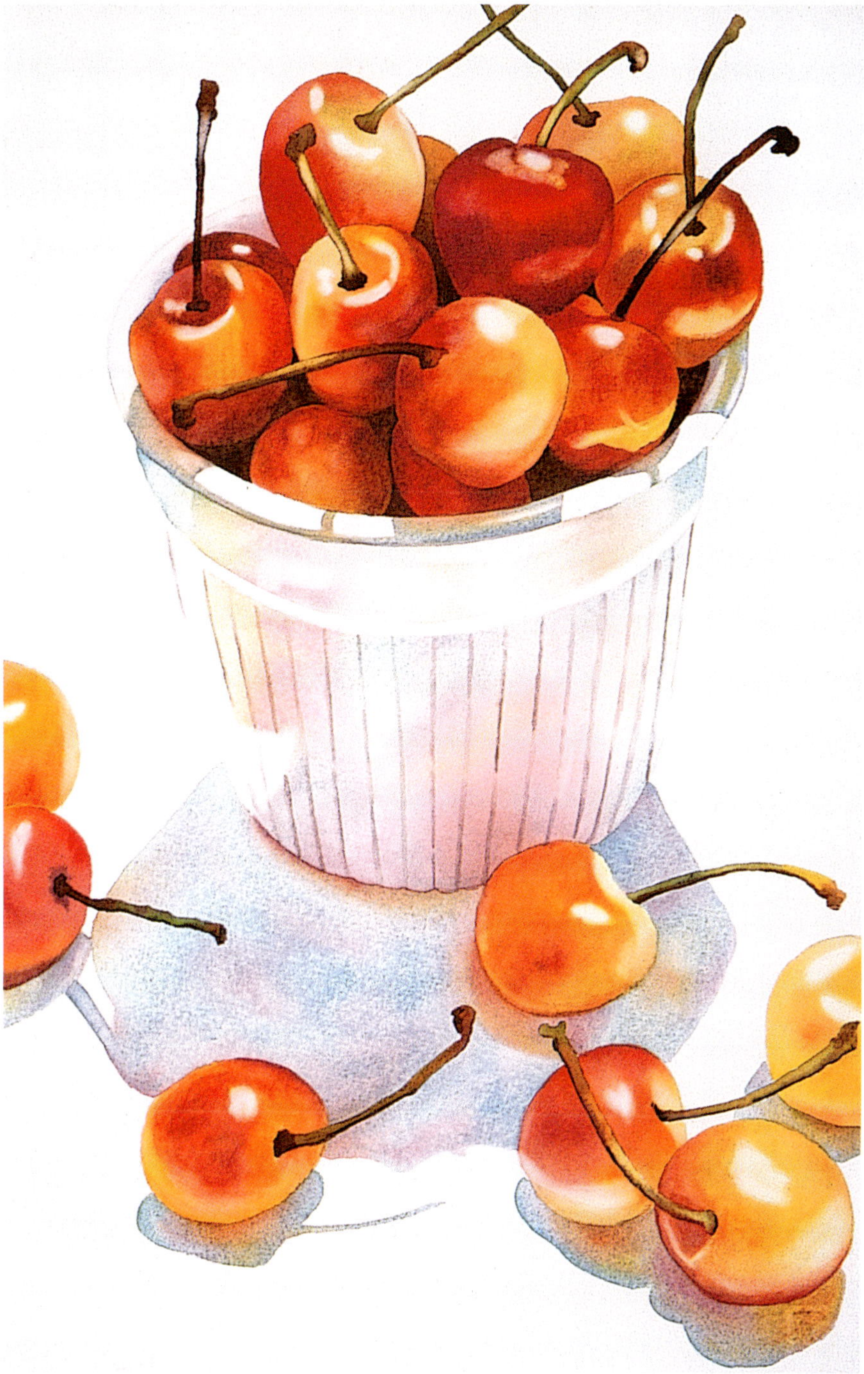

8 PAINT THE STEMS AND FINISH THE PAINTING

Use Greenish Yellow for the highlights on the stems. Mingle Brown Madder, Burnt Sienna, and Ultramarine Blue in the darkest areas.

Use your no. 6 scrubber to lift and soften any highlights on the cherries and your bowl. Apply water to the areas you wish to soften and keep the scrubber very wet. Lift and blot with a paper towel. Repeat if necessary, always keeping the area wet for the best results.

The dark stripes on the bowl are tricky. If you paint them wet on dry, they will appear very definite. So, first draw the lines with water using a no. 4 round. Then, quickly drop Brown Madder and Ultramarine Blue into the water. This will create the appearance of the subtle lines .

CHERRIES JUBILEE
22" × 15" (56cm × 38cm)
Transparent watercolor on cold-pressed paper
Collection of the artist

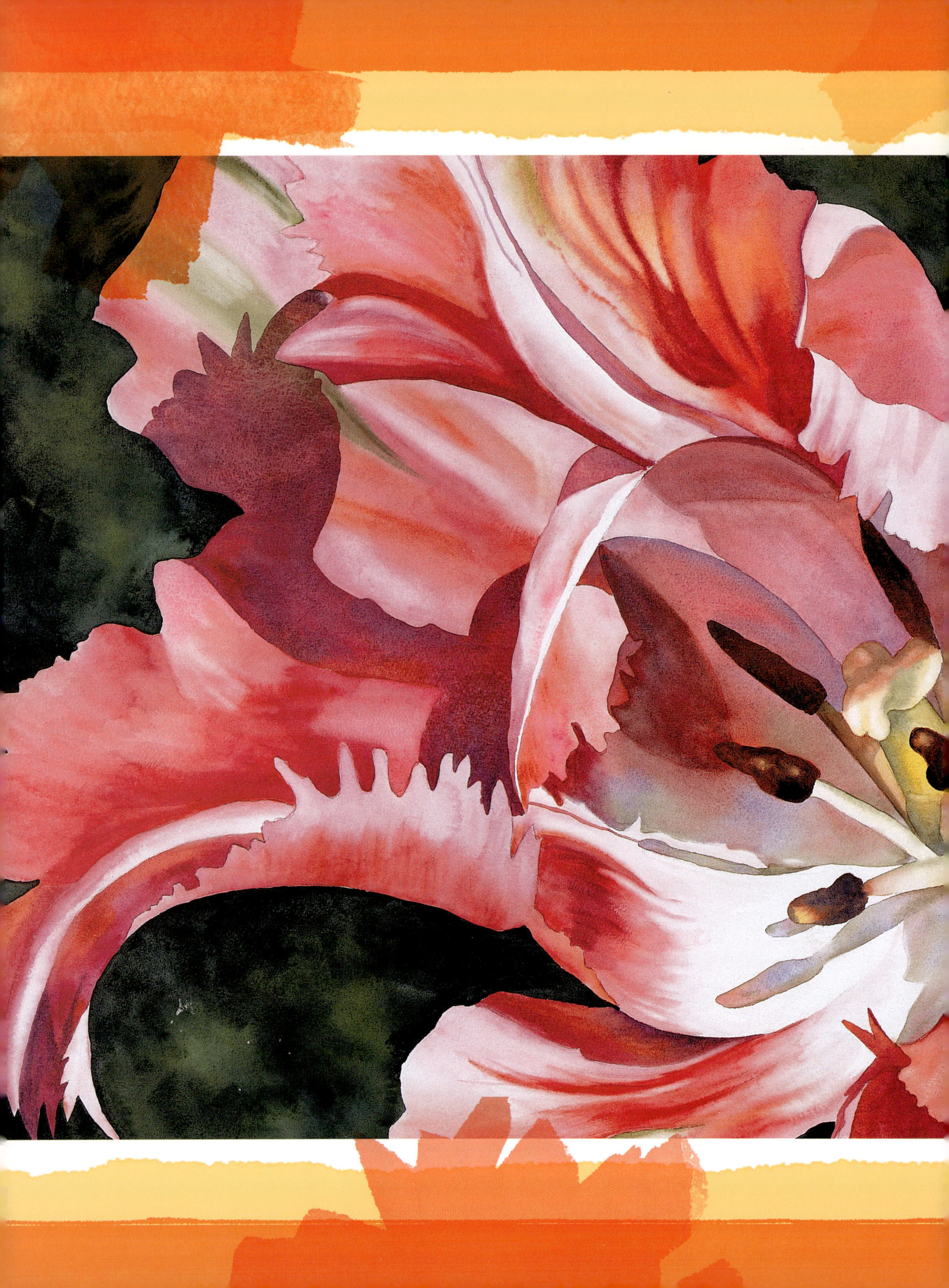

5

Other Useful Techniques

Over the years I've taken many workshops and classes from artists I admire. I'm always looking to learn what magic technique or brush enabled them to create the beauty of their paintings.

In this chapter I share with you several techniques that I use to make my colors glow.

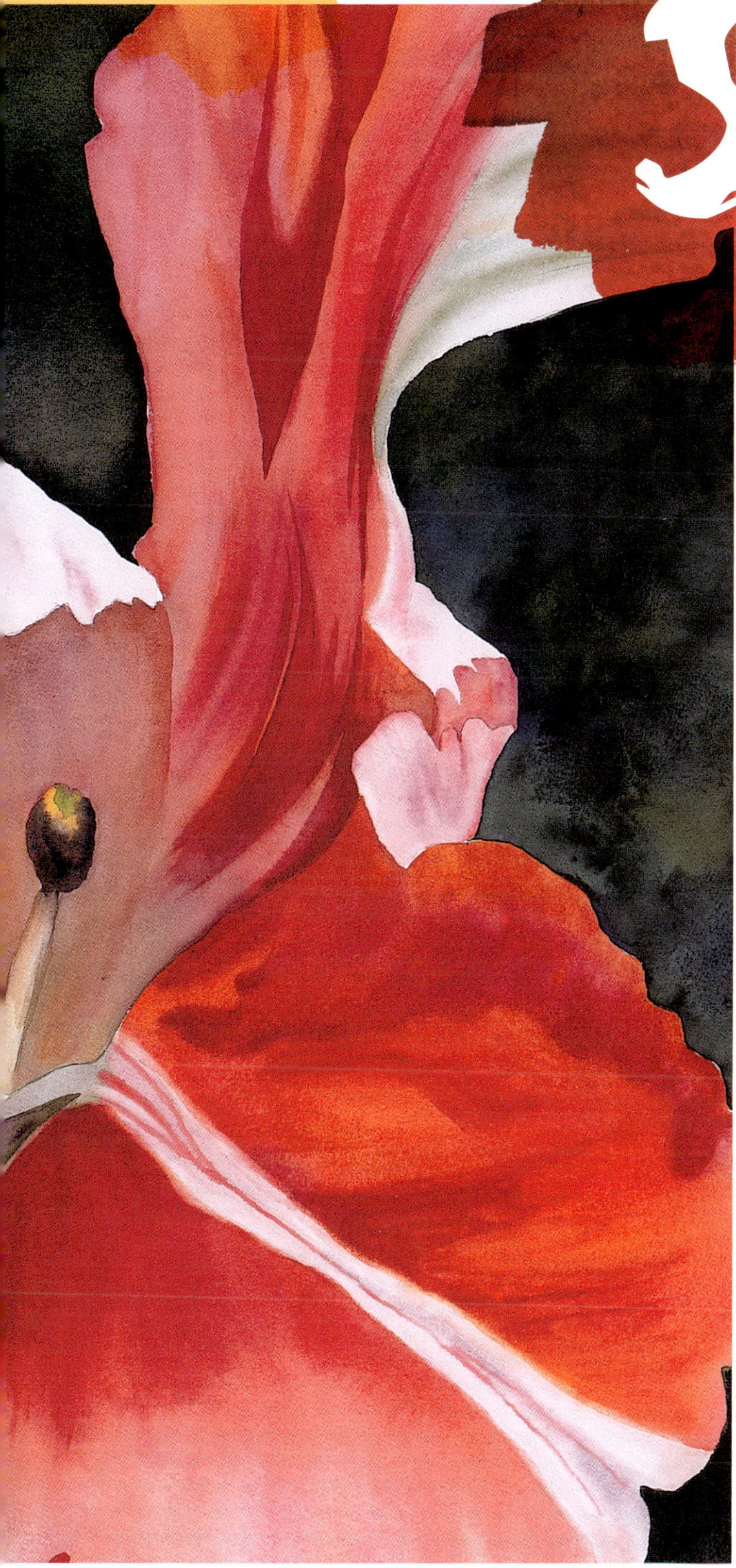

REUNION
22" × 30" (56cm × 76cm)
Transparent watercolor on cold-pressed paper
Collection of the artist

Water: Not Too Little, Not Too Much

You need water to spread watercolor paints, but you must learn to control the water or it will control you. Pay attention to the sheen of the wet pigment on the paper as a guide in judging how wet your surface should be. If there is a lot of water on the paper (producing a high sheen), the paint will dissipate too much. On paper that is barely moist (with little sheen), pigment will hardly spread at all. The most effective amount of water is somewhere in between.

I recommend that you work on 300-lb. (640gsm) cold-pressed paper because it will stay wet and workable longer. As the paper absorbs the water, you can continue to build up color intensity by using thicker paint.

HOW TO CONTROL THE WATER WITH YOUR ABSORBING PAD

After your paper is covered with paint and water and you begin to intensify the values with thicker paint, your brush will pick up excess water from the paper. Keep tapping the point of any brush you are using on the absorbing pad that I showed you how to make on page 16. This will keep extra water out of your brush and help you maintain control. You will go from the paper to the pad and then back to the paper again many times during the course of a painting.

No Control
Paper with too much water and high sheen offers no control over paint flow.

Little Control
The paper has absorbed some of the water, but there is still high sheen and you will have very little control.

Perfect Control and Flow
Very little sheen means your ability to control the flow of paint will be greater.

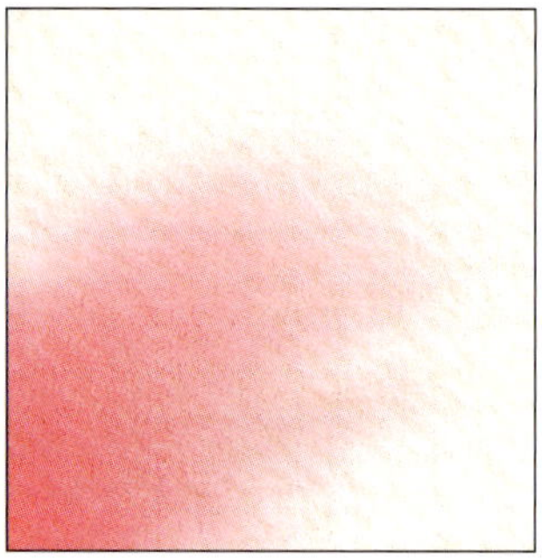

Too Dry
If the paper is too dry, there is no flow and you will have uneven, uncontrollable edges.

Mingling on Wet Paper vs. Mingling on Dry Paper
Mingling on wet paper involves wetting the paper first with clean water; this makes your watercolors appear lighter when dry. Mingling on dry paper involves simply putting the pigments on the dry paper; colors will dry darker.

Mingled colors on wet paper

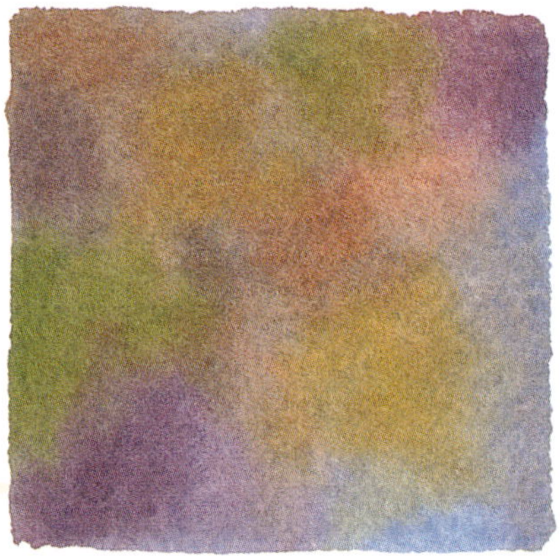

Mingled colors on dry paper

Masking Fluid or Water?

Masking fluid can be a potential disaster. It can ruin a painting when applied to paper in a sloppy manner. When you remove the mask, the hard-edged mechanical appearance of those saved white areas can overpower the painting and ruin the appearance of spontaneity.

I do use masking fluid—at times it's invaluable—but I prefer to use water as a masking agent. It saves your lights, yet also gives you soft edges.

To do this, wet the area to be saved or preserved with clean water and wait a few seconds before painting. Apply pigments to the other areas, starting as far away from the wet area as possible, mingling and joining the various colors. Paint toward the wet area, let the pigment hit the edges of the wet area, and then stop. The pigment will creep into that area and you will have a little flow, but not a lot. If the paint quickly flows into the wet area, then it is too wet and the water has not had enough time to absorb into the paper.

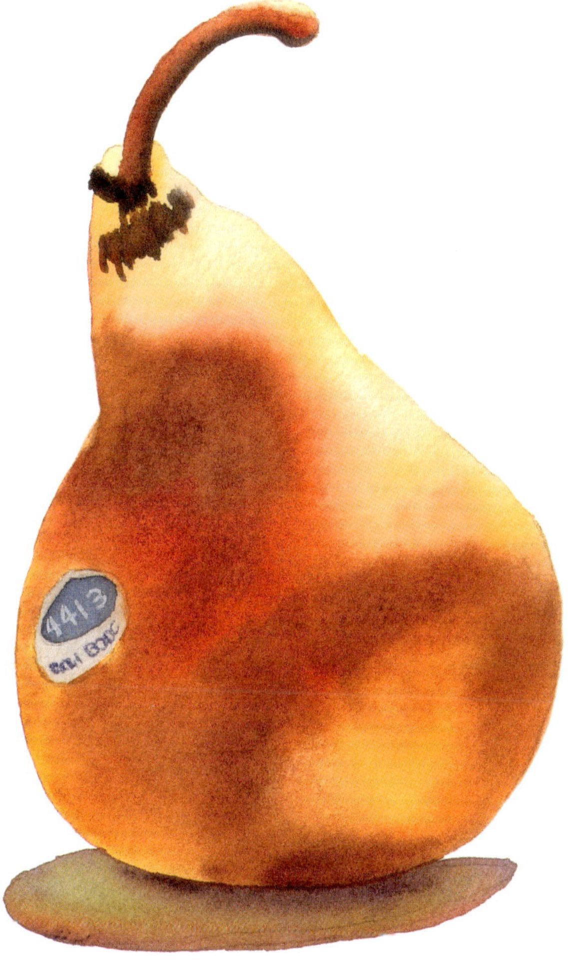

"Masking" With Water...
This painting of a pear was done using the technique of wetting the highlights and light shapes with water instead of using masking fluid. Note the natural-looking light shapes.

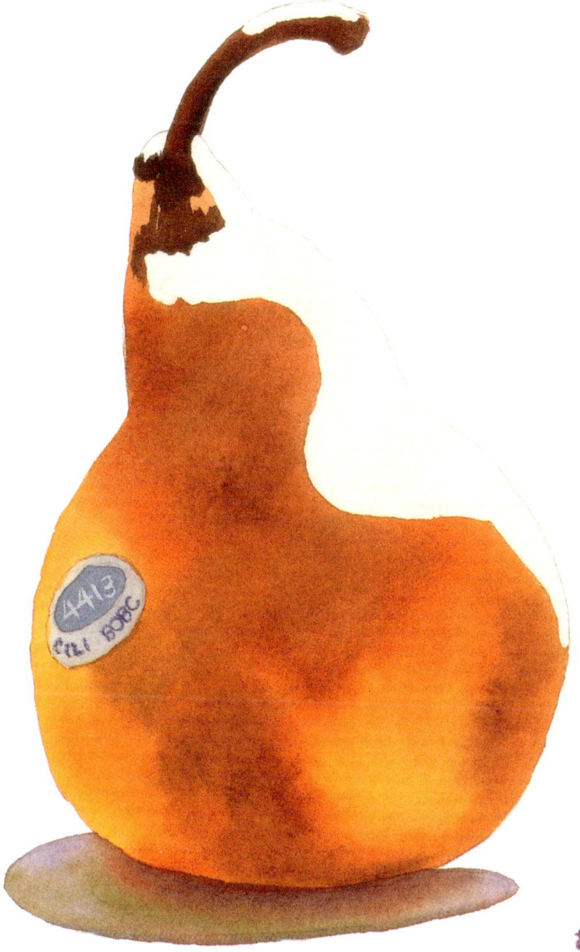

...and With Masking Fluid
This is the same pear painted using masking fluid to preserve the whites and lights. Notice the scary hard-edged shape that's left to work with.

Save the Lights With Water, Not Masking

You can use water to save the lights and middle values in your paintings instead of using masking fluid. Using water gives very soft edges so you won't have to deal with the hard edges left by masking fluid. This is one of my favorite techniques and it's not hard if you practice. It's also very simple to paint a subject and complete it with no additional glazing using this technique.

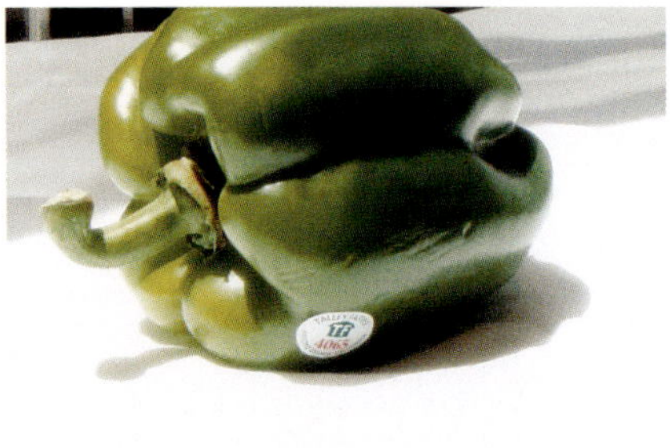

Color Reference Photo
Look carefully at your color photo and the black-and-white photocopy to see the light values in the green pepper.

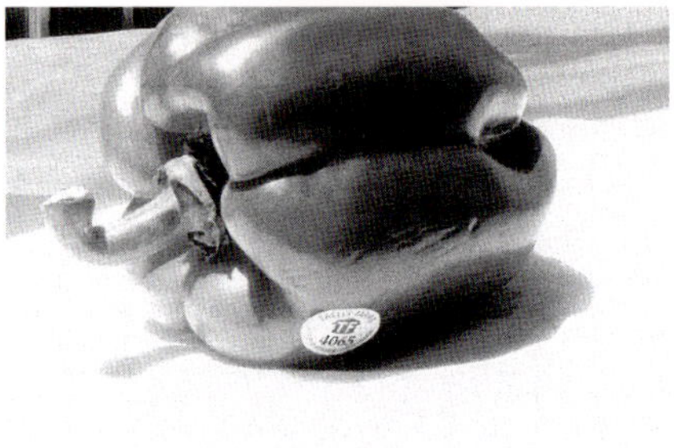

Black-and-White Photocopy

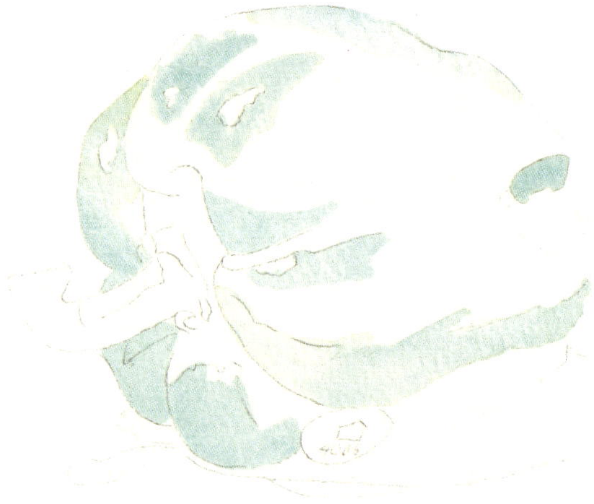

1 WET THE HIGHLIGHTS
With a no. 12 round, carefully wet the light shapes with clear water. (Note: I have tinted those areas on the paper with a little blue so that you can see them more easily.)

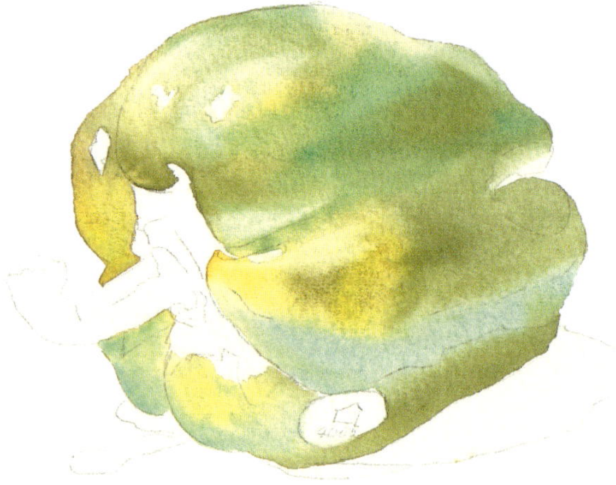

2 PAINT FROM DRY TO WET
When the water settles into the paper, use the no. 12 round to mingle and alternate colors on the dry paper, working toward the wet area. Paint up to the edge of the dampened areas. The colors I used are Cobalt Teal Blue, Undersea Green, Permanent Sap Green, Olive Green and Aureolin Yellow.

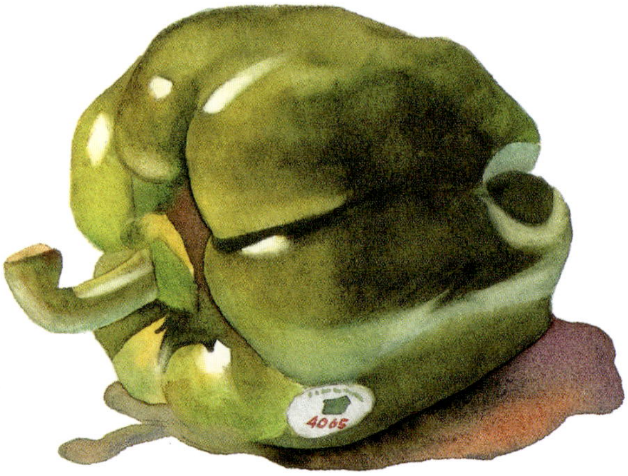

3 CHARGE IN MORE VALUES
When the pepper is completely wet with pigment, pick up a ¾-inch (19mm) flat. Be sure that the wells holding your pigment are wet, then pick paint directly out of them. Using this thicker paint, darken the values in the shapes. Mingle and vary the color, making sure that you clean your brush between color applications and remove the extra water on the tip of the brush with your absorbing pad. Use the following colors to increase your values: Undersea Green, Olive Green, Permanent Sap Green and a little Brown Madder.

When the gloss leaves the paper, use the same ¾-inch (19mm) flat to lift out some color for more highlights and shapes.

Saving Highlights With Masking Fluid and Water

It is easy to identify soft edges and hard edges, but difficult to know how to achieve the effect. Soft edges occur where wet meets wet and hard edges occur where wet meets dry. You can use both masking fluid and wet paper to achieve these effects. To learn this technique, be patient. The wetness of the paper will affect the paint flow. Let the water permeate the paper, and then work the wet area with thicker and thicker paint.

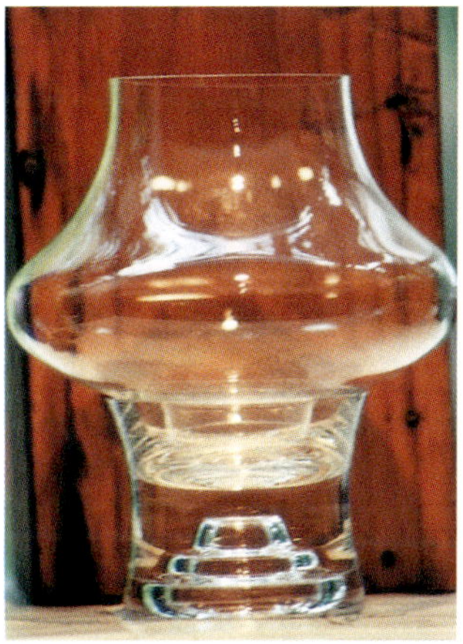

Color Reference Photo
This clear glass candle holder shows hard and soft edges and lights and darks.

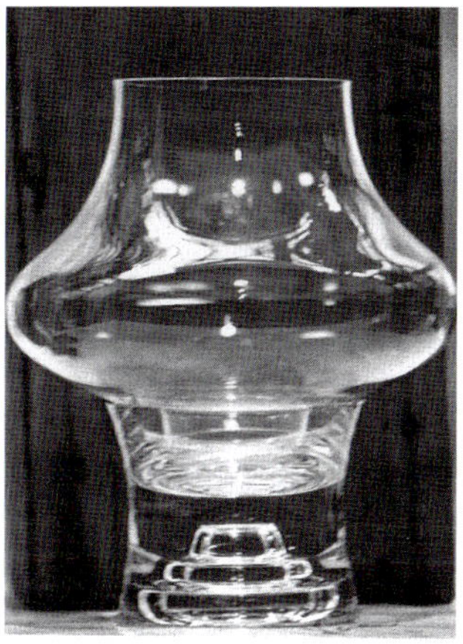

Black-and-White Photocopy

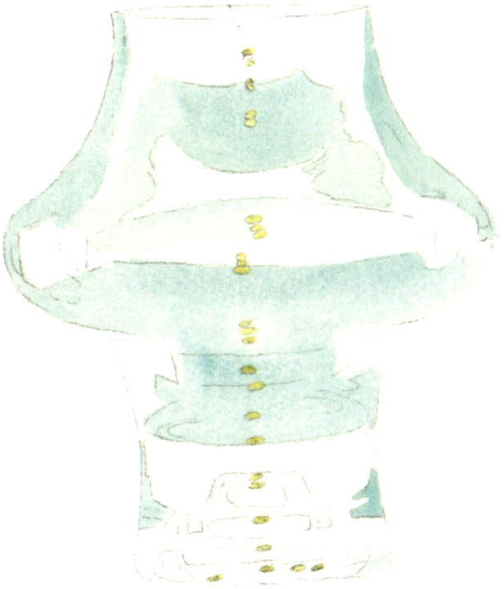

1 WET THE PAPER
Use a no. 6 round to cover the small sparkles of light with masking fluid. These are the lines of small light reflections down the center front area of the glass. Let this dry. Take a no. 12 round and wet the lightest areas of the glass with clean water. (I've tinted those light areas with blue to make them easier to see.)

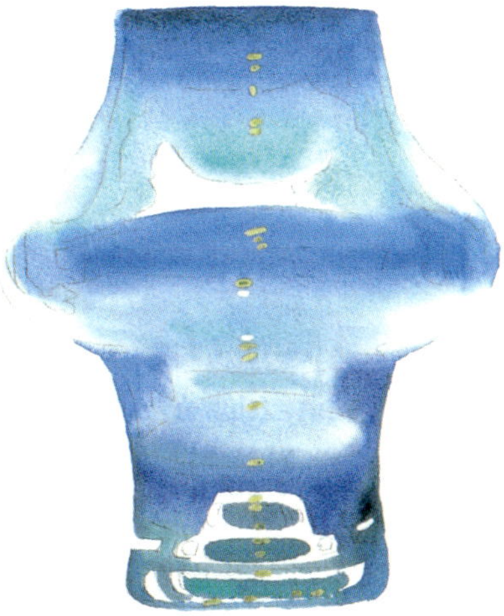

2 MINGLE COLORS
With a no. 12 round, mingle whatever colors you prefer for the glass. (I used Cobalt Blue, Verditer Blue, Cobalt Teal Blue, Ultramarine Blue and Permanent Blue.) Leave a few areas completely dry and paint around the dry areas and over the masking fluid. You can see these white areas in the center of the lower portion of the candle holder.

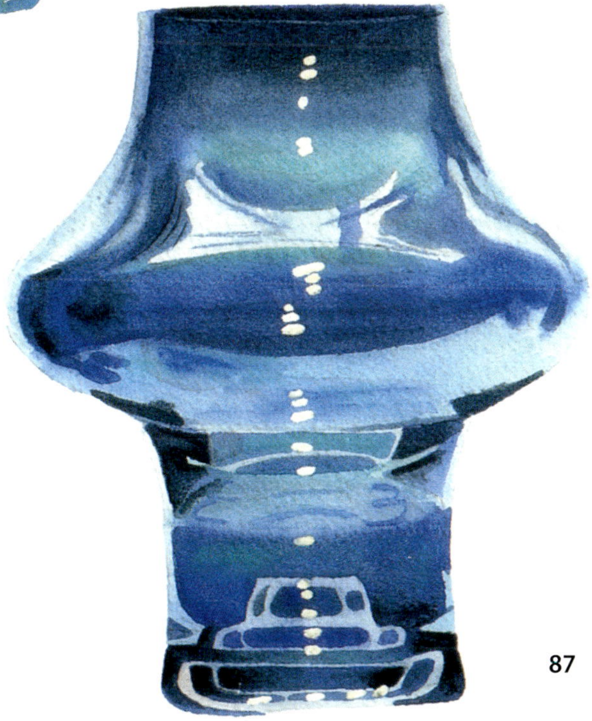

3 DROP IN THE DARKS
With most of the paper still wet (except where I painted wet to dry at the bottom) take a ¾-inch (19mm) flat brush and drop in more pigment for the darks. I used Ultramarine Blue, Permanent Blue and Indigo. Soften some edges and paint over the lights you don't like. When everything is dry, remove the mask.

Saving Whites With Gesso

MATERIALS

BRUSHES
Nos. 4, 6, 12, 16 round • ¾-inch (19mm) and 1-inch (25mm) flats

COLORS
Brown Madder • Burnt Sienna • Cobalt Blue • Cobalt Teal Blue • Cobalt Violet • Indigo • Mineral Violet • New Gamboge • Opera • Permanent Rose • Permanent Sap Green • Quinacridone Red Orange • Scarlet Lake • Ultramarine Blue • Verditer Blue • Yellow Ochre

SURFACE
300-lb. (640gsm) Arches cold-pressed paper

OTHER
Absorbing pad • gesso • paper towels • pencil • scissors • toothbrush • tracing paper

Gesso is a water-based acrylic used primarily to prime canvases. For years, I just saved the white of my paper, but then I started to use gesso mixed with my transparent watercolors to paint hair and water and to fix damaged areas of the paper. Here, I mixed gesso with light shades of Brown Madder and New Gamboge to create the lighter tendrils in the girl's ponytails. The instructions below will show you how to use gesso to create lights in the waves. I have great success using gesso to create lights, and you will too.

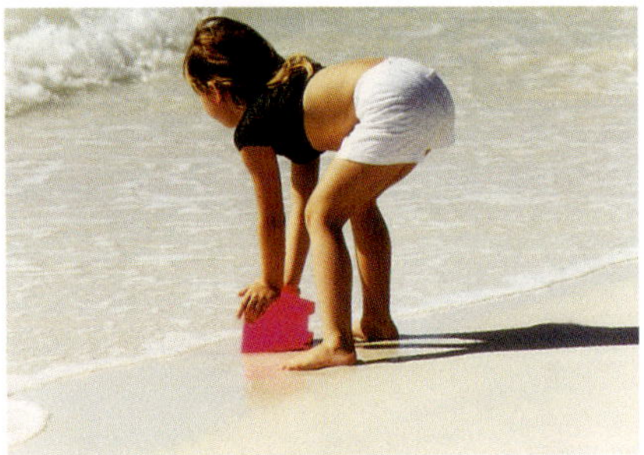

Reference Photo
Photo by Delores Pastorius

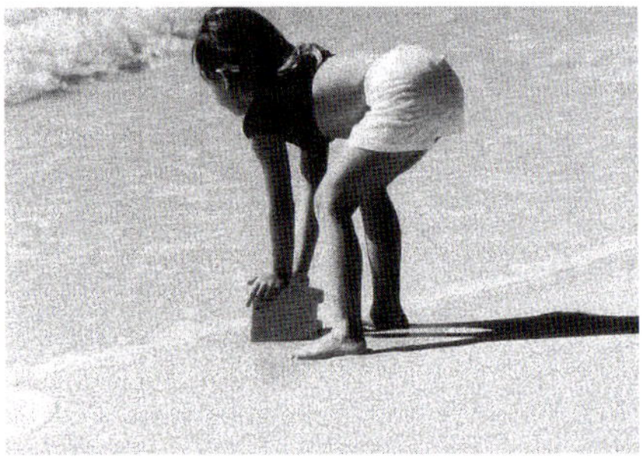

Black-and-White Photocopy
This photocopy shows you the lightest areas of the legs, the midtones and the shadows—both form and cast—that make the legs and arms have dimension. Without these value changes, the arms and legs would appear flat, not round.

1 SKETCH THE COMPOSITION
Sketch the subject onto your watercolor paper.

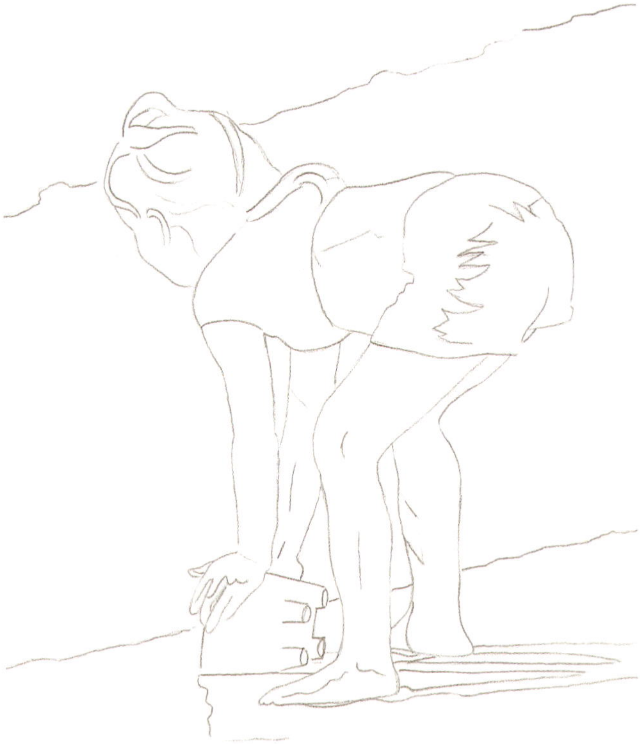

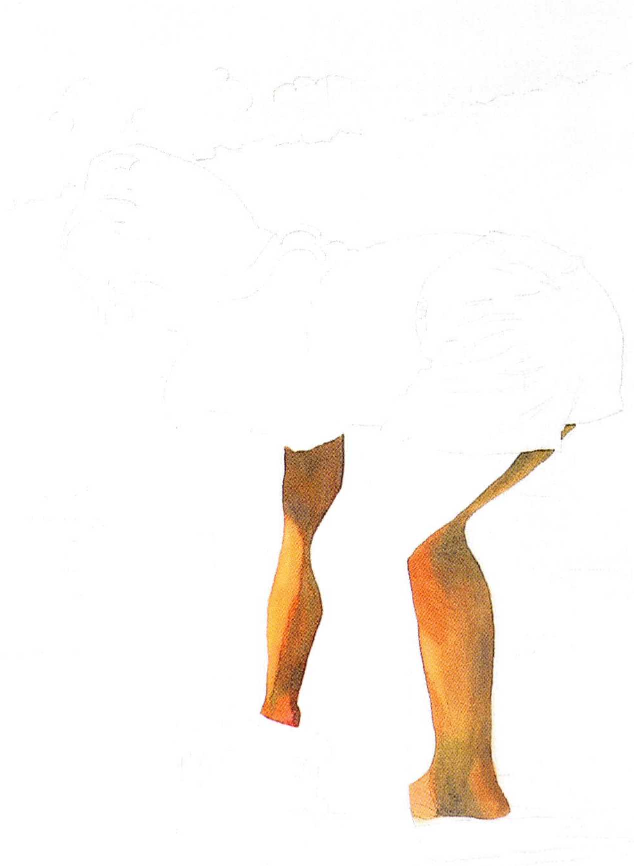

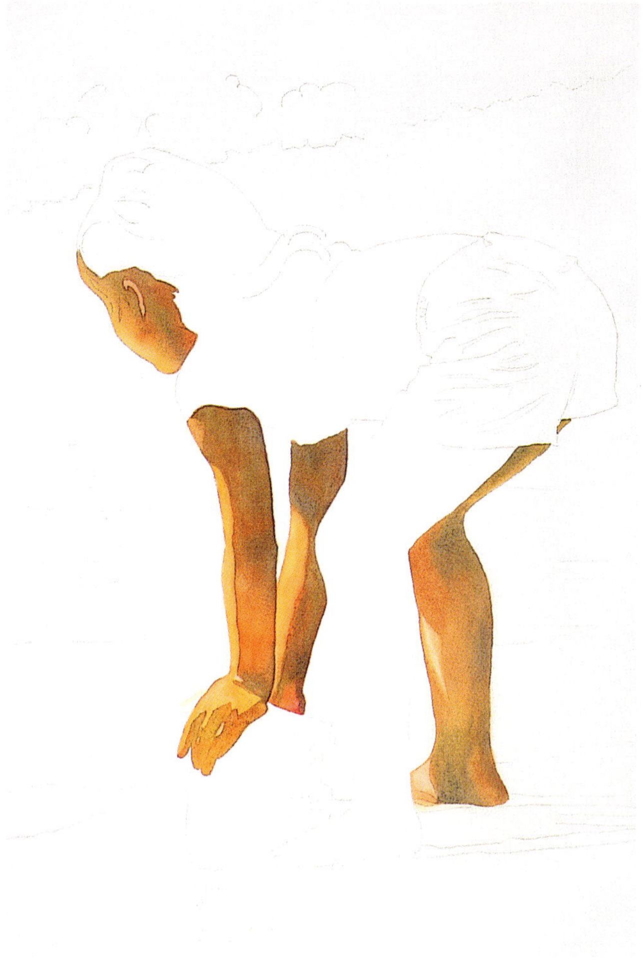

2 ESTABLISH THE BACKGROUND SKIN TONES
Begin by painting the leg and arm that are in the background. Use a no. 12 round to cover the entire back leg with New Gamboge. Mingle some Permanent Rose into that. Add some Brown Madder and mingle a tiny bit of Permanent Sap Green and Cobalt Blue into the shadow areas, such as the crook of the leg. Repeat this process for the arm in the background.

3 CATCH THE LIGHT-STRUCK AREAS
With a no. 12 round, wet the top of the hand, the side of the face and the tiny, light-struck edge of the arm with water. Working from the farthest dry edge, cover the face and then the arm with New Gamboge. Mingle in a little Permanent Rose. Add Brown Madder, Permanent Sap Green and Cobalt Blue where you see the darker skin tones or shadow areas in your black-and-white photocopy.

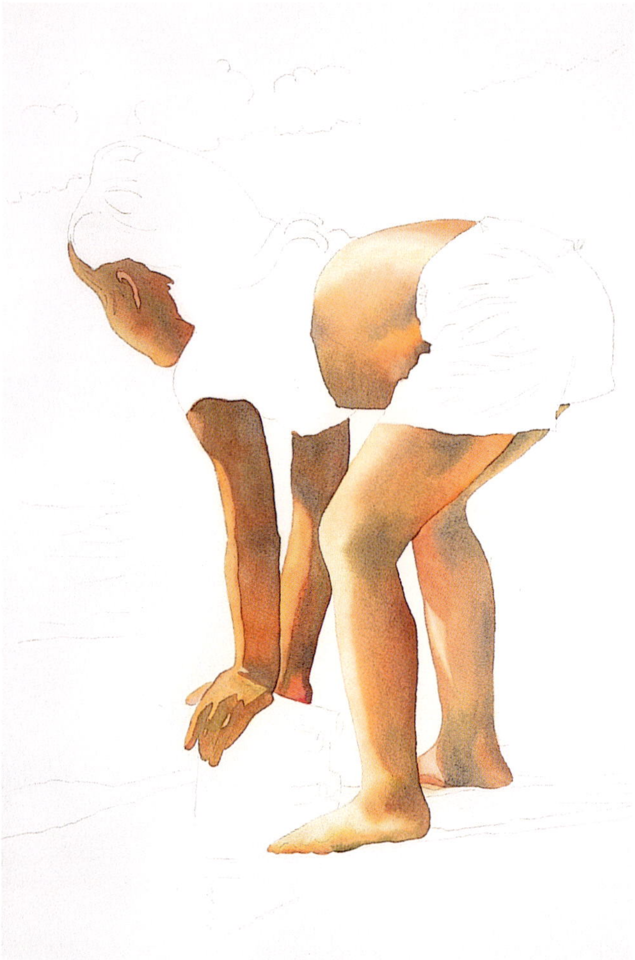

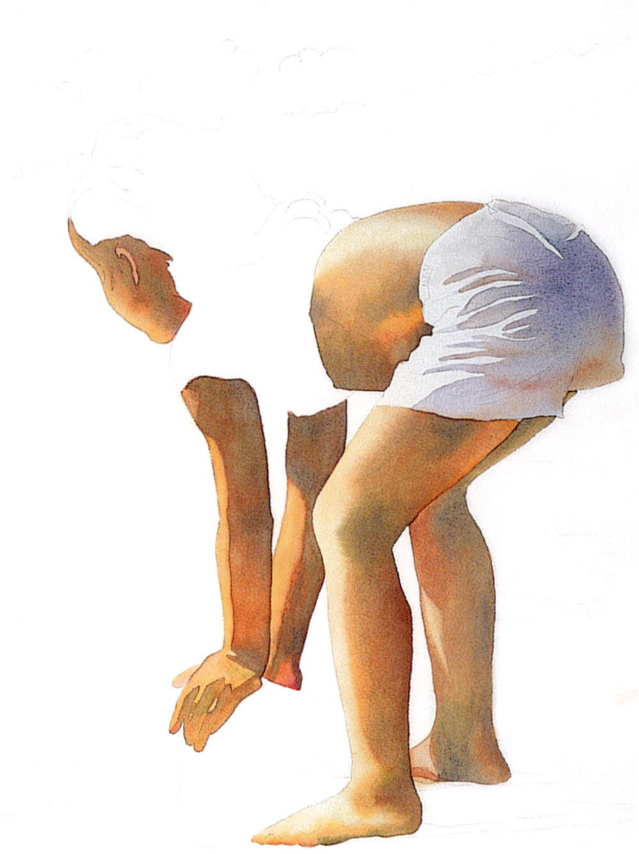

4 ADD THE FRONT LEG AND TORSO

Wet the highlight areas of her torso and front leg with lots of water with a no. 16 round brush. Wait a few minutes, then mingle New Gamboge, Permanent Rose, Brown Madder, Permanent Sap Green and Cobalt Blue to create the shape and form of the leg with a no. 16 round. When your paints hit the wetness, they will move a little and create soft shadows. While the area is still wet, drop in more pigment to darken. Switch to a damp ¾-inch (19mm) flat and gently add more pigment in the areas that need it. Use your absorbing pad to control any extra water that is on the brush by tapping the absorbing pad with the brush between strokes. Repeat the same process for the torso.

5 ADD THE SHORTS

Using the black-and-white photocopy as a guide, paint the shadow shapes on the white shorts with a no. 12 round, mingling Verditer Blue, Permanent Rose, Mineral Violet and Quinacridone Red Orange. (You may need to turn the painting and the photocopy upside down to see the shadow shapes better.) While the paper is wet, switch to a ¾-inch (19mm) flat and add more value to the middle area of the shorts with some Mineral Violet.

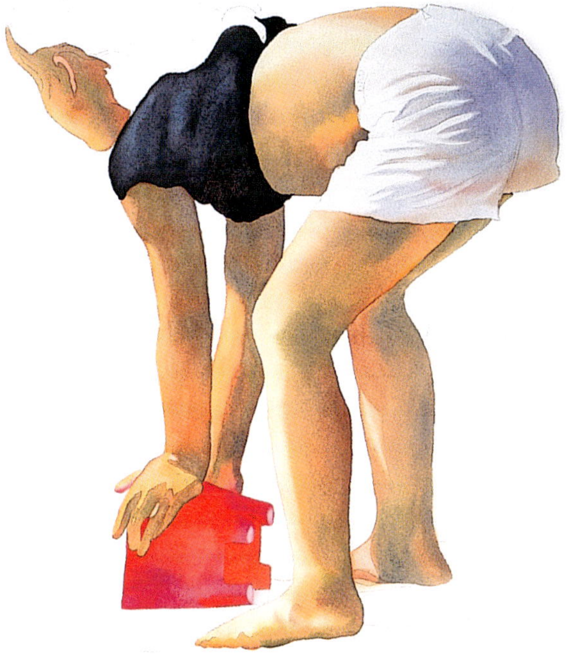

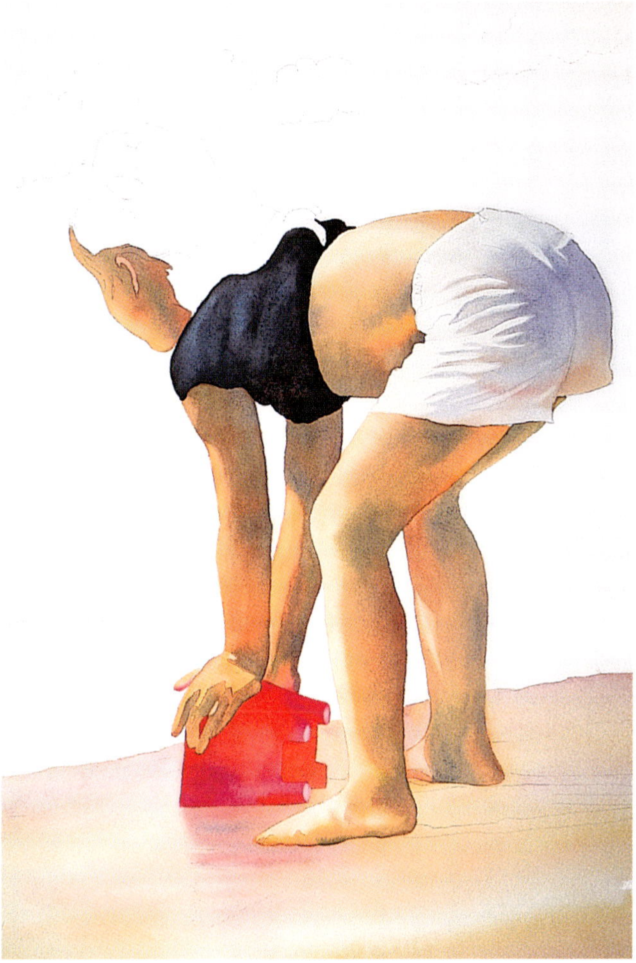

6 ADD THE TOP AND SAND PAIL
Take a no. 6 round and charge Scarlet Lake and Indigo into the halter top. Let the colors mingle together. While this is wet, use a ¾-inch (19mm) flat to lift the lights out of the darks. You can see the shapes of the lights more easily by turning your black-and-white photocopy upside down. Mingle Quinacridone Red Orange, Opera and Permanent Rose to paint the sand pail. Life the lights out with a no. 6 round while it's still wet.

7 CREATE THE SAND
Using a no. 16 round, apply a strip of water to the surface of the paper where the light areas of sand will be. Mingle Burnt Sienna, Yellow Ochre and Permanent Rose on the dry paper. Paint toward the wet area of the sand, let the pigment hit the wet area and stop. Painting around the wetness creates value changes that keep the area interesting. Use water to create these value changes. Slash the water on the paper in a few places (you would do the same thing if painting a meadow or lawn). Paint and mingle the Burnt Sienna and Yellow Ochre from the dry paper to the wet. Stop when you hit the wet. Start again at the dry. The water will create lighter areas than those where the paint was applied to dry paper. Let the painting dry.

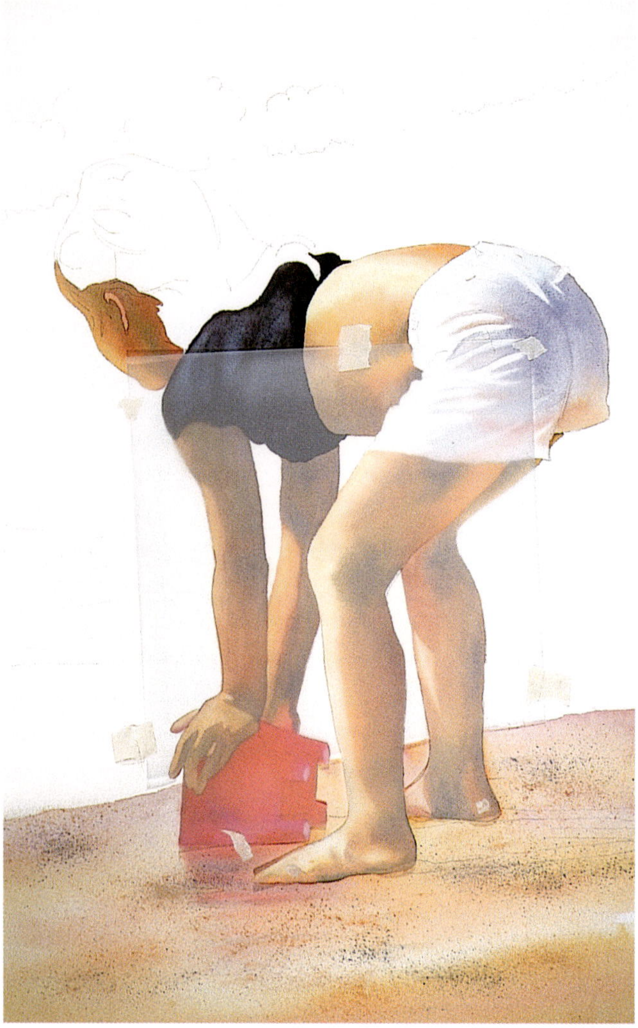

8 ADD TEXTURE TO THE SAND

To avoid adding texture to the skin or the water, cut a piece of tracing paper small enough to cover just the legs and arms and place it over your painting. Wet a toothbrush with water and tap out excess water on the side of your water container. Dip your middle finger in the Burnt Sienna well on your palette, then tap the paint onto the toothbrush. Hold the toothbrush at an angle in the hand you don't use for painting and use a finger to pull back the bristles, spattering paint droplets onto the surface of the sand. This will create a very fine-textured spatter. If you have blotches, you have too much water in the toothbrush. Repeat the process using Permanent Rose and then Ultramarine Blue, cleaning your brush between each application. Use a damp ¾-inch (19mm) flat to soften any areas of spatter you don't like. If some of the spatters get on the area where the water will be, immediately take a brush dampened with clean water and soften the spatter. Blot with a paper towel.

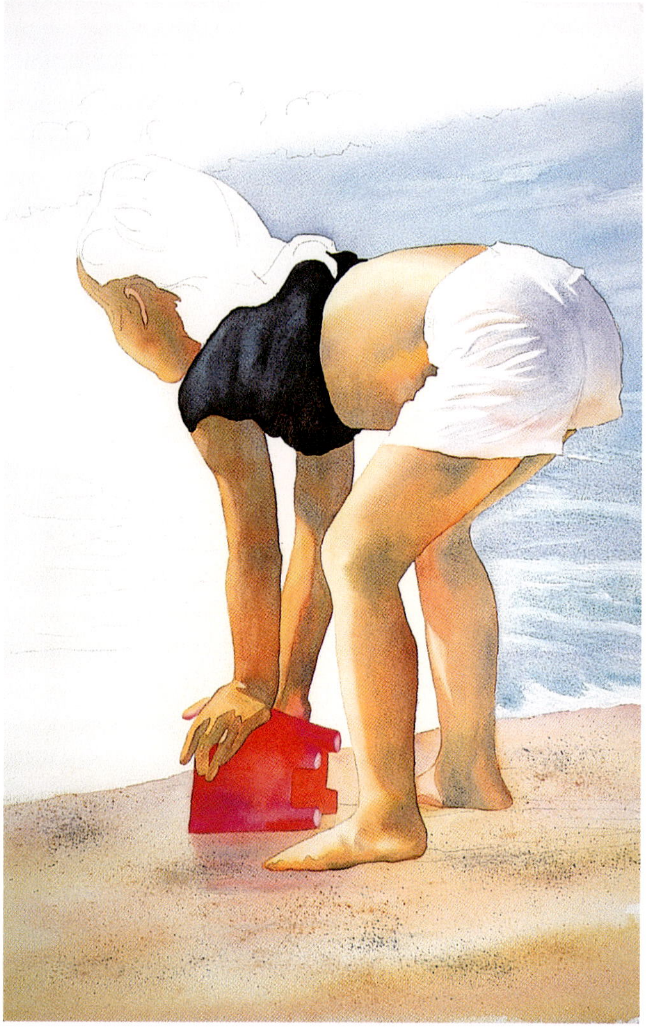

9 PAINT THE WATER

Mingle Cobalt Teal Blue, Verditer Blue and Cobalt Blue on the surface of the water to the right of the figure with a no. 16 round brush. While the blues are still wet, take a ¾-inch (19mm) flat and stroke in a little gesso to suggest some waves.

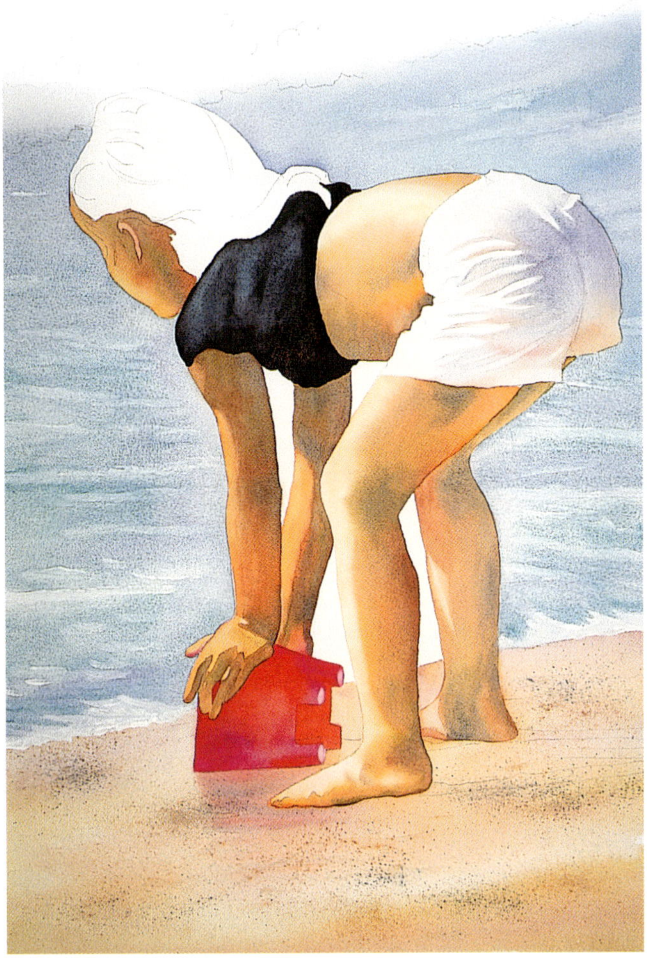

10 COMPLETE THE WATER

Continue to mingle Cobalt Teal Blue, Verditer Blue, Cobalt Blue and some Cobalt Violet onto the water area, stopping at the lower edge of the wave. Use a ¾-inch (19mm) flat to drop passages of gesso into the damp paint, using the black-and-white photocopy as your guide. The light streaks in the water differ in size and have angles that create movement in the water.

Take some Brown Madder, Burnt Sienna and Mineral Violet to mingle the little girl's shadow on the sand and under her feet. While the shadow is damp, drop a little Cobalt Blue along some of the edges of the shadow. Don't outline the shadow; just apply the blue here and there. Drop a little Opera into the shadow created by the pail on the sand.

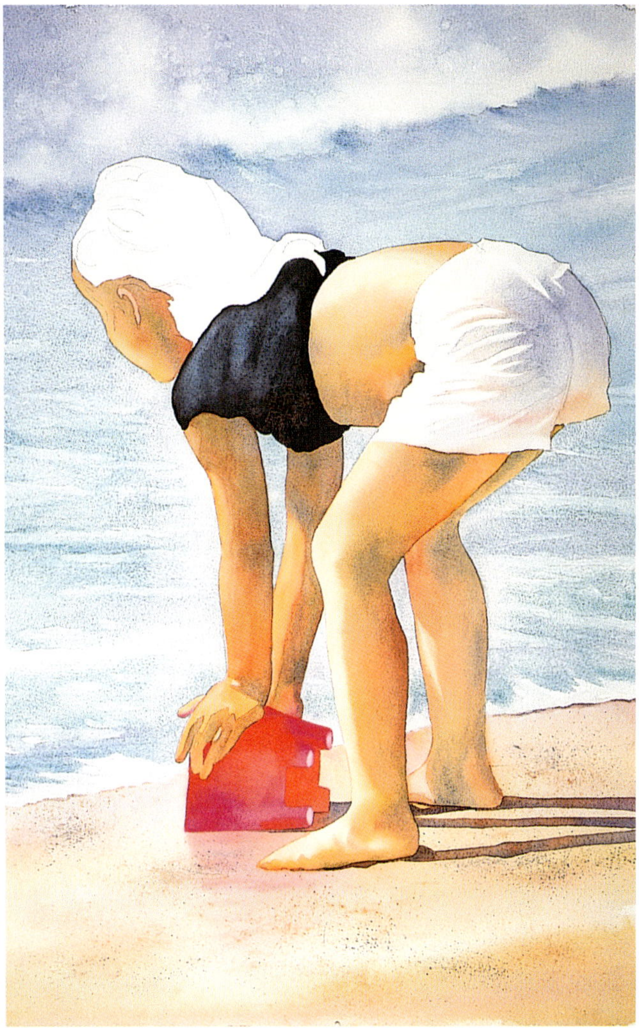

11 ADD THE BACKGROUND WAVE

With the blue of the water still damp, use a no. 12 round to apply gesso in a circular motion to imitate the foam on the top of the wave. Clean your brush and add some Verditer Blue or Cobalt Blue to the gesso. Add this to the pure gesso on the paper to give added value to the waves.

12 PAINT THE HAIR AND FINISH THE PAINTING

Charge Burnt Sienna, Brown Madder and Ultramarine Blue (using lots of pigment on the brush) onto the hair. While the paint is wet, use a no. 4 round to mix some New Gamboge with some gesso and touch it into the wet darks to suggest hair tendrils caught by the wind.

I thought that the value of the back right leg was a little light, so I mixed a puddle of Brown Madder using a loaded no. 16 round and gently put a glaze over the back leg to darken the shadows. This can be done over and over, but you must let the paint dry thoroughly between applications of transparent paint. When using 300-lb. (640gsm) paper, the painting should dry for at least a day.

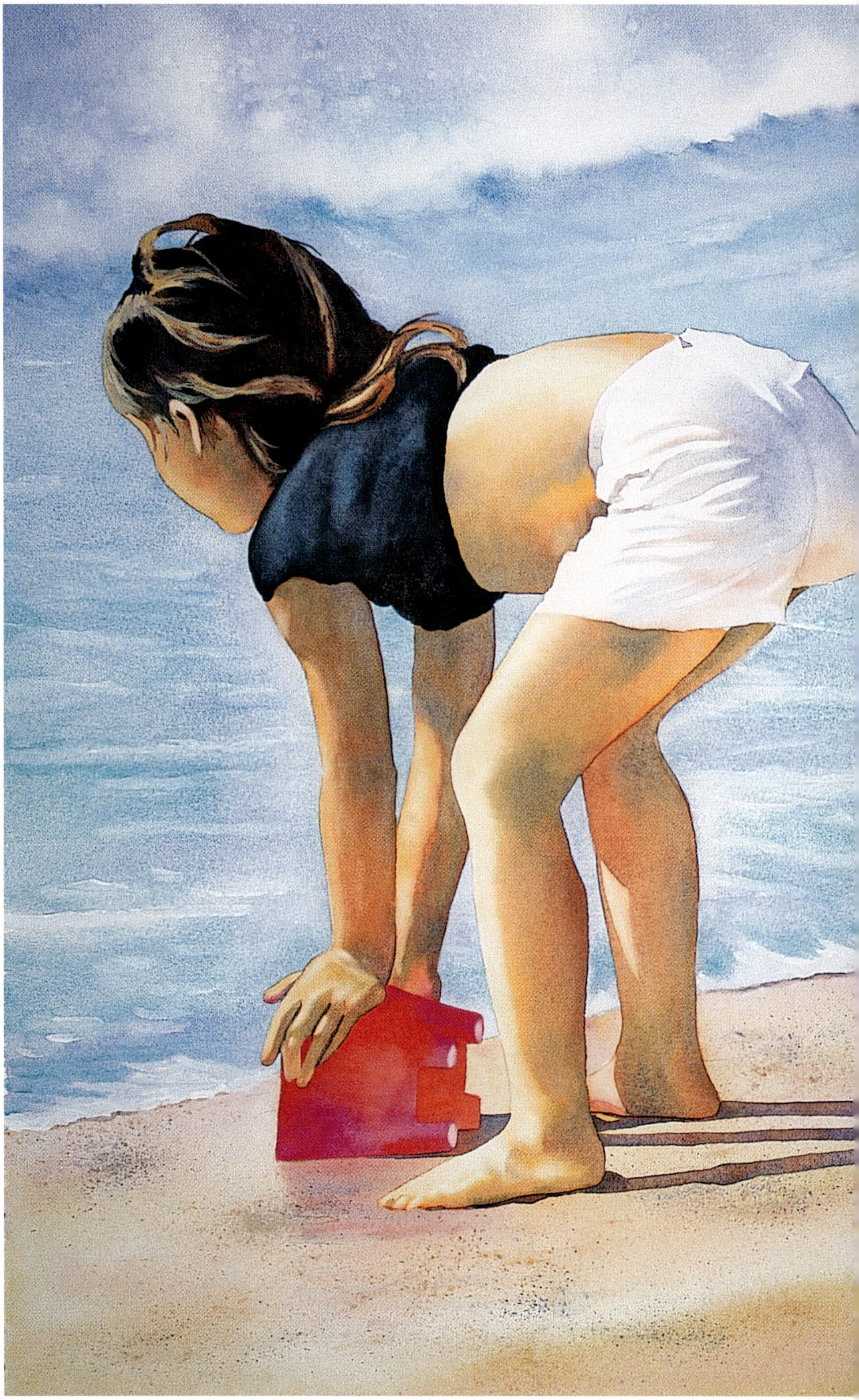

WHITNEY ON WHITNEY BEACH
22" × 15" (56cm × 38cm)
Transparent watercolor on cold-pressed paper
Collection of Mr. and Mrs. Ben Johnson

Creating Texture on Different Surfaces

To create texture, I like to use a single-edge razor blade because it's safe and easy to hold. Lay your pigment down and wait a few minutes for the shine to go off the paper. You will know when you've scraped too soon, because the paint will run back into itself. Be patient and wait. It's a good idea to practice this before you take on a big project with the razor blade.

Grip the razor blade with your fingers (I use the whole edge of the blade as well as the tip) and apply pressure to the front edge with your thumb, with the back edge of the blade off the paper. Scrape into the paint, pulling it back to the white paper or your initial wash. Then, using all of your fingers, flatten the blade and scrape some more. I alternate the pressure on the blade from the flat edge with the blade completely on the paper to just the tip of the blade on the paper.

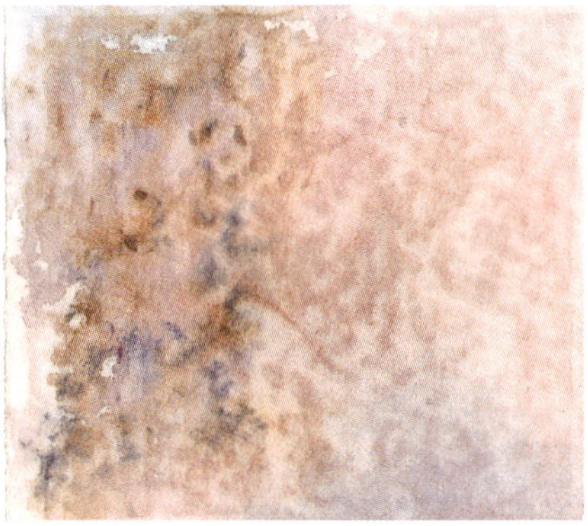

Razor on Damp Surface
On a painted surface, I used a razor blade to roughen up the damp paper. On one side, I took a flat loaded with Burnt Sienna and Cobalt Blue and lightly dragged this over the top of the paper. There wasn't enough pigment on the brush, so the texture does not show through.

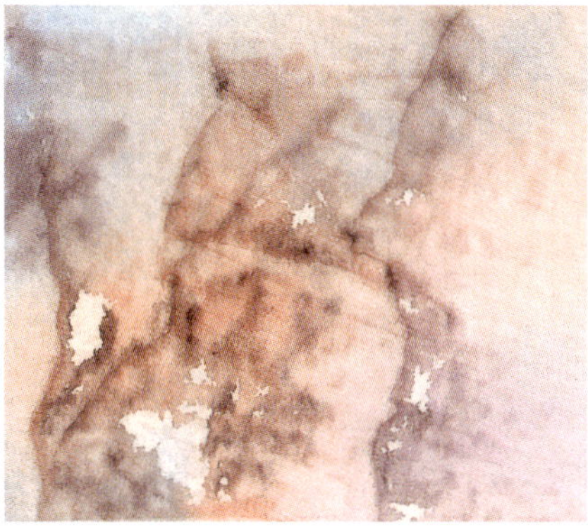

Bruised Surface
This paper was very wet when I used the razor blades, which bruised the paper. The paint went into the bruises and created dark lines. The blade also pushed the paint around. This effect can be useful in many places, especially when painting stucco or bark on a tree.

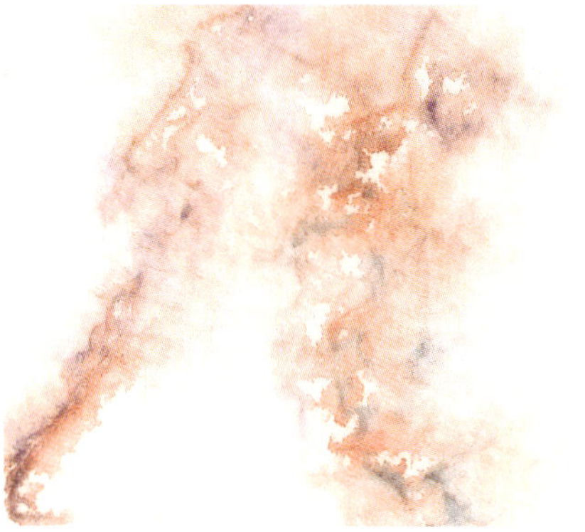

Razor on Wet Surface
Here I wet the paper with water and let it sit to soften, then used a razor blade to create texture. Next, I used a no. 4 round loaded with pigment and, while the paper was still very wet, touched the brush's tip to the raised areas of the paper. I let the colors (Brown Madder and Cobalt Blue) seep into the paper. It dried very light because of all the water, so use more paint than you might think.

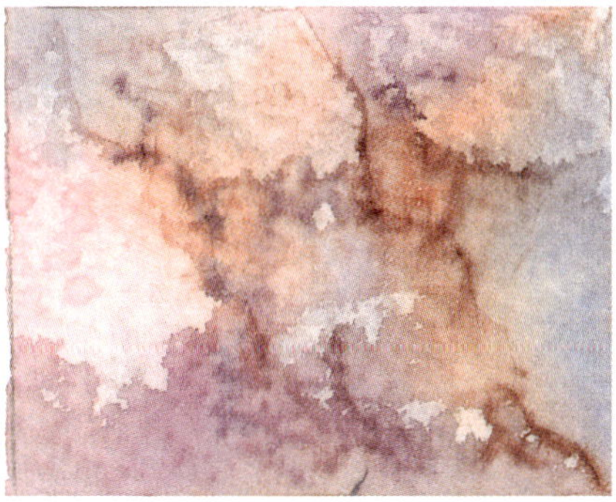

Razor on Tinted Surface
Mingle colors on the paper and wait until the shine begins to disappear. Add texture with the razor blade while the paper is still damp. Switch to a small round, load it with pigment and touch the roughened areas with the tip of the brush. Add several colors if you want.

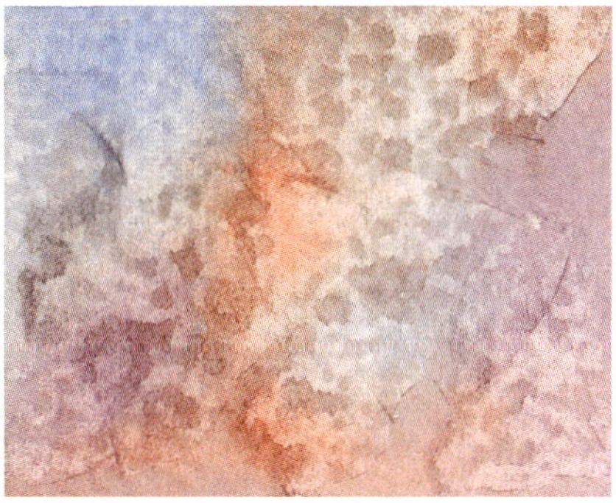

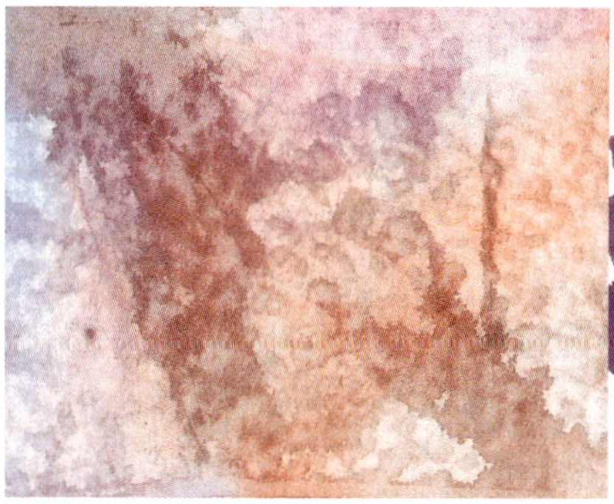

Removing a Layer
This is a technique that you should practice before attempting on a painting. Feel comfortable with it first! You are pulling the paint off with the razor blade to show the white paper underneath. The razor blade also damages the paper in some areas, creating interesting effects. The slight dark smudges result from paint that has been absorbed into a bruise on the paper's surface.

Mingle Intense Colors for a Dark Background

Dark backgrounds enhance the feeling of light on a subject, but are difficult to master. Watercolor fades as it dries, and if you add water when trying to darken an area, you'll just lighten it even more.

The keys to achieving a dark background are:

- *Paint with your paper flat, not tilted.*
- *Use as little water as possible, just enough for flow.*
- *Use a flat brush; it will carry less water than a round. I prefer the Loew-Cornell ¾-inch (19mm) or 1-inch (25mm) angled flat, series 7400, because it offers good control.*
- *Dampen the paint in the wells rather than mixing a puddle on your palette.*
- *Use intense colors, and change colors every four or five strokes.*
- *Rinse the brush before each application of color.*
- *Continually remove the excess water from the brush by touching it to your absorbing pad.*
- *Work from one area into another; don't paint all over the paper at once.*
- *To keep the dark consistent, work with very thick paint. That is why keeping your pigments dampened in your palette wells is so important.*

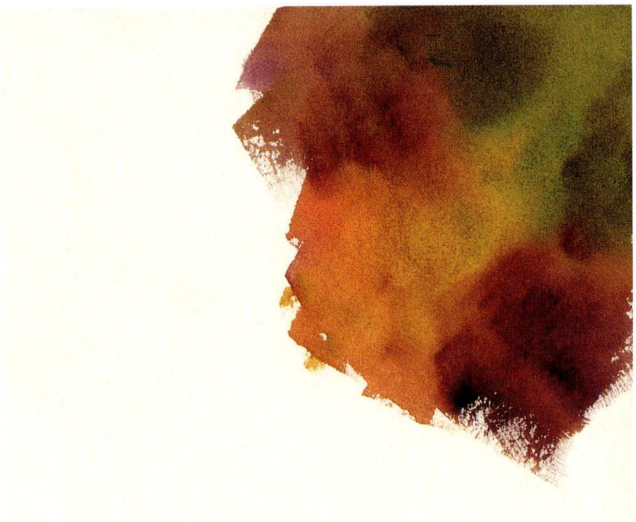

1 BEGIN THE BACKGROUND
Keeping your paper flat and the pigments dampened, start on dry paper with a 1-inch (25mm) angled flat. Pick up paint from your palette's dampened wells (remember, no puddles; you need thick paint for this). Begin with several strokes of Permanent Sap Green and Olive Green, then clean your brush. Add Quinacridone Gold to the greens. Repeat the process using Permanent Violet Reddish. Do this several times, repeating and varying the colors. Work from the corner down. I like to use a crosshatching stroke, while increasing the color intensity with lots of thick paint and as little water as possible.

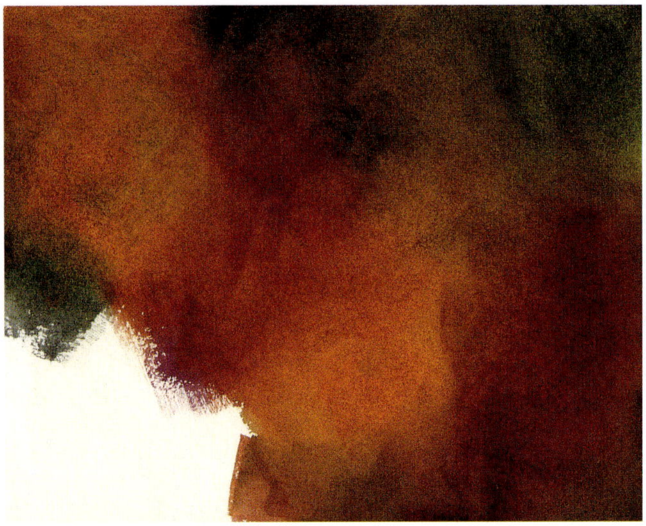

2 ADD MORE PAINT
Cover the area with thick paint, varying the colors. This will look very colorful at this stage but will quiet down when more color is added. Repeat using the previous colors. Decide for yourself which colors to use. I like to repeat the colors of the subject in the background. For instance, if the flower is red or pink, I use Brown Madder or Quinacridone Red Orange. I always use Permanent Sap Green for a floral to suggest green leaves in the background. Essential colors are Mineral Violet and Indigo.

3 FINISH THE BACKGROUND
In the damp area, use the 1-inch (25mm) angled flat to go over some areas with Indigo. Remember, you are not painting a wall. Use the same crosshatching stroke and let the first layer of colors show through in some places. Be sure to control the amount of water on your brush, remembering that the brush is also picking up water from the wet surface, so keep touching it to the absorbing pad to remove the excess water.

HINT FOR MASKING BACKGROUNDS

We're all nervous about damaging the edges of the subject when covering the background, especially around light areas. Do yourself a favor and wait a day to be sure that your subject is dry before applying masking fluid. Using a no. 6 round, carefully apply masking fluid right over the dry edges of the subject, working from the outside edge into the dry subject ¼-inch (6mm) to ½-inch (12mm). Be careful not to take the masking fluid onto the unpainted white background. Once the mask is dry, you can paint freely. When the painting is thoroughly dry again, remove the mask.

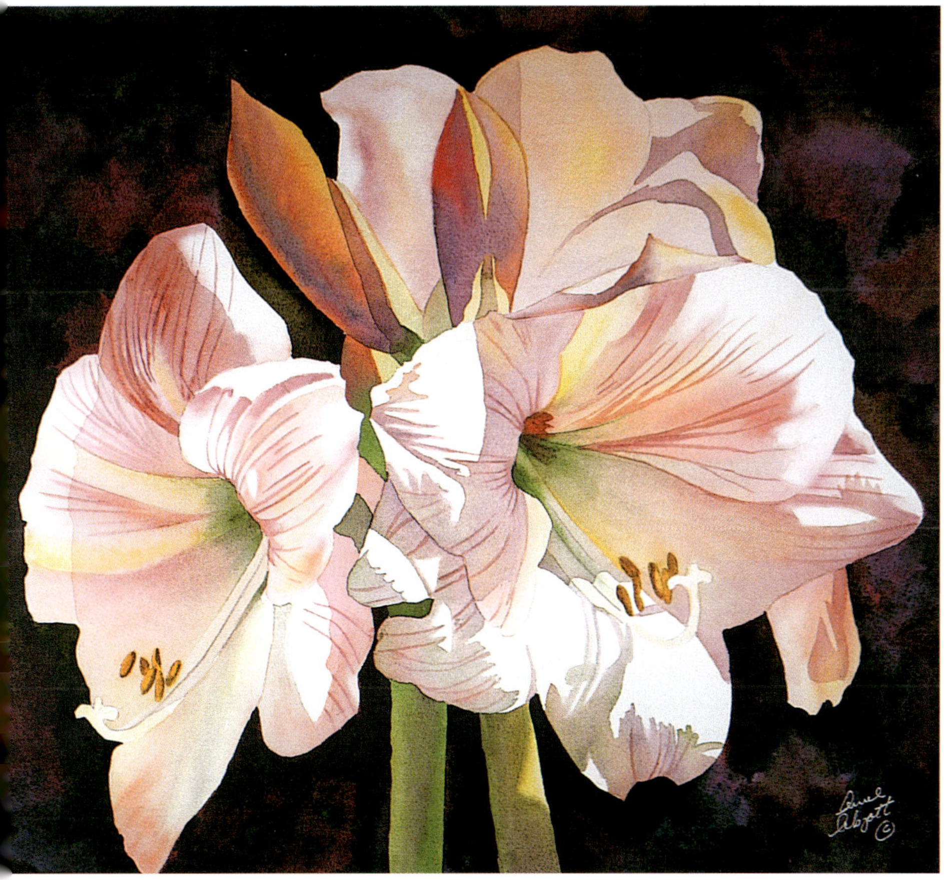

Completed Painting
This amaryllis painting was done by masking the edges of the subject before adding the dark background, which enhances the light flower. I repeated the colors of the flower in the background to suggest life and movement behind the subject.

BRILLIANT BLOOMER
15" × 22" (38cm × 56cm)
Transparent watercolor on cold-pressed paper
Collection of the artist

Putting in a Dark Background

MATERIALS

BRUSHES
Nos. 4, 10, 12 and 16 round • 1-inch (25mm) angular flat • no. 8 scrubber

COLORS
Aureolin Yellow • Brown Madder • Greenish Yellow • Indigo • Mineral Violet • New Gamboge • Olive Green • Opera • Permanent Magenta • Permanent Rose • Permanent Sap Green • Quinacridone Red Orange • Scarlet Lake • Ultramarine Blue • Undersea Green

SURFACE
300-lb. (640gsm) Arches cold-pressed paper

OTHER
Absorbing pad

Now that you've had a chance to practice mingling a dark background, try creating one around a bright subject. You'll also try mingling on wet and dry paper, which will save you from having to do any glazing.

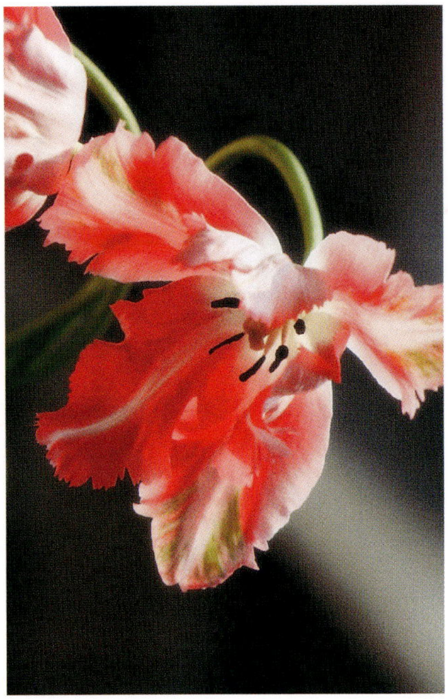

Reference Photo

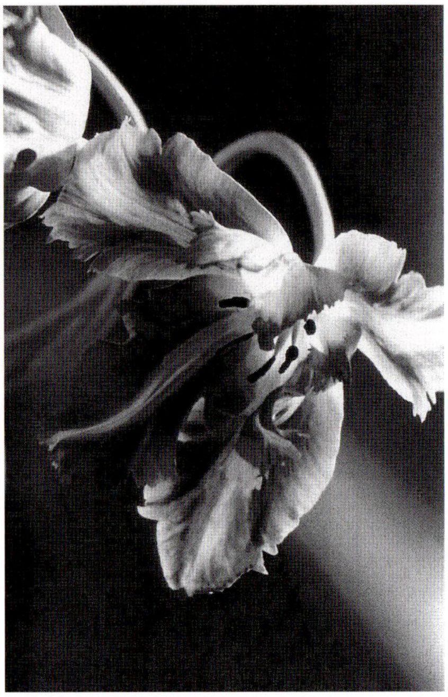

Black-and-White Photocopy

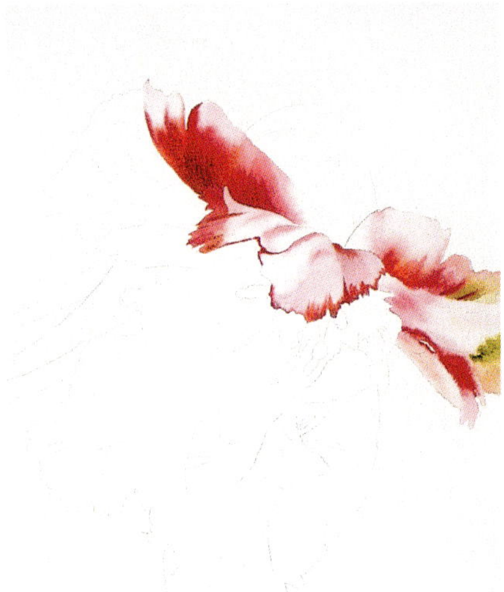

1 ESTABLISH THE LIGHTEST VALUES
Draw or trace your composition onto the watercolor paper. Wet the lightest areas of the right upper petal with the no. 12 round and gently drop Permanent Rose, Greenish Yellow, Quinacridone Red Orange and Opera onto the dry paper, letting them move into the wet areas. Paint the petals on either side using the same process. Let this dry. Wet the upper edge of the left petal. Starting under the dry middle petal, use thicker paint and mingle Quinacridone Red Orange, Permanent Rose and Permanent Magenta, painting toward the wet upper edge. When the paint hits the wet edge, stop and let it flow.

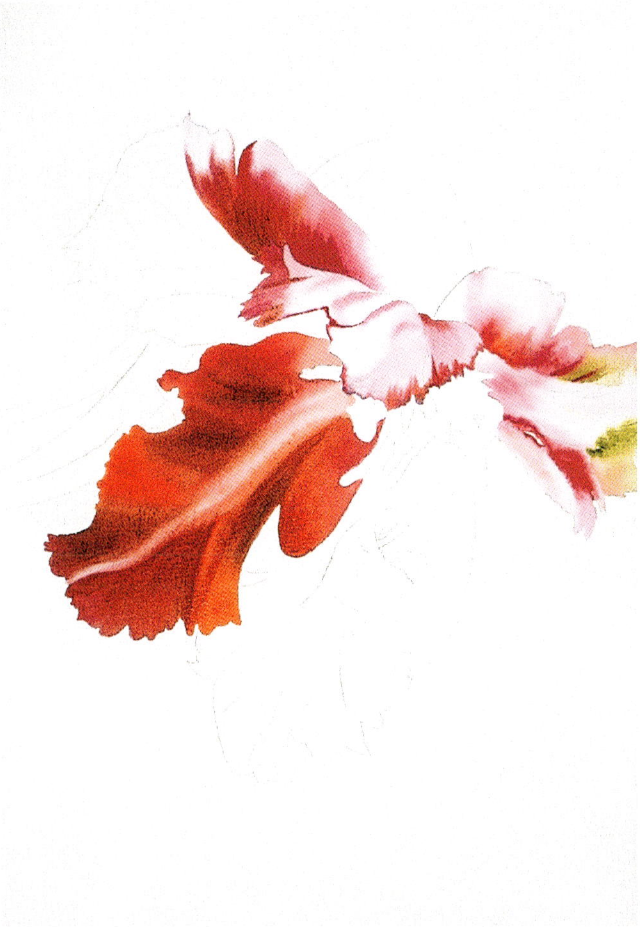

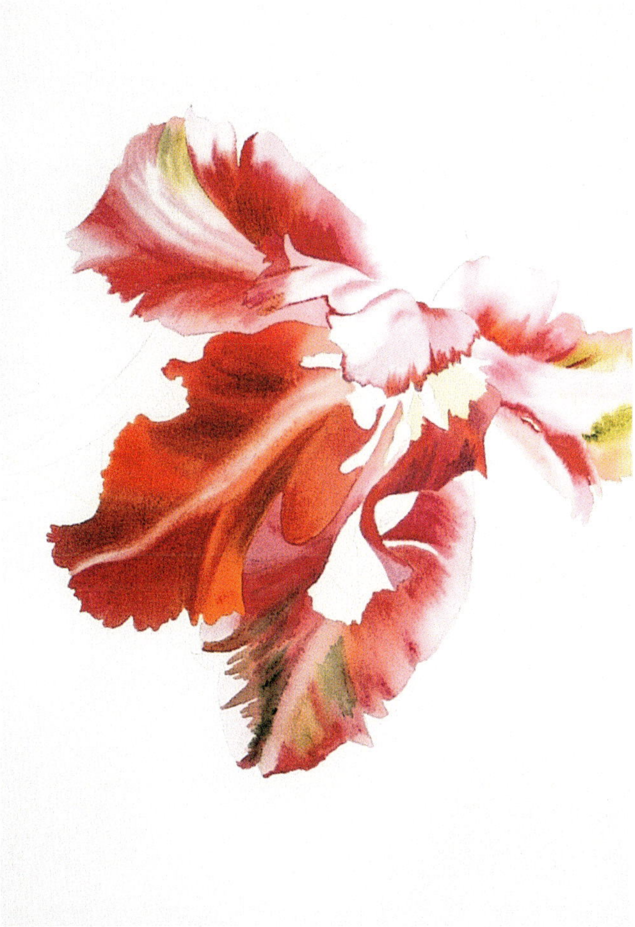

2 PAINT THE DARKER PETALS

Using a no. 16 round, apply an underpainting of New Gamboge to the areas of the foreground petal where the petal is warmer and light-struck. While the underpainting is wet, mingle Scarlet Lake, Quinacridone Red Orange, New Gamboge and Permanent Rose with a no. 16 round on the wet and dry areas of the surface. While the petal is still a little damp, use a 1-inch (25mm) angular flat to lift a white stripe out of the center of the petal. Lift until you have the desired effect. You may also let the petal dry and simply dampen the area with water and use a no. 8 scrubber to lift until you have the white stripe on the petal.

3 DARKEN THE VALUES

Here you will use your black-and-white photocopy as a guide as you increase the intensity of some petals with thick paint. In the lower, darker petals, wet some of the light areas with clear water. Using a no. 16 round, mingle Quinacridone Red Orange, Opera, Scarlet Lake, Permanent Rose and Permanent Magenta in the lower-right petal. Drop in some Greenish Yellow and some Permanent Sap Green along the edges and into some of the petals. Lift a light stripe out of the paint using a 1-inch (25mm) angular flat if the paint is damp or a no. 8 scrubber if the paint is dry.

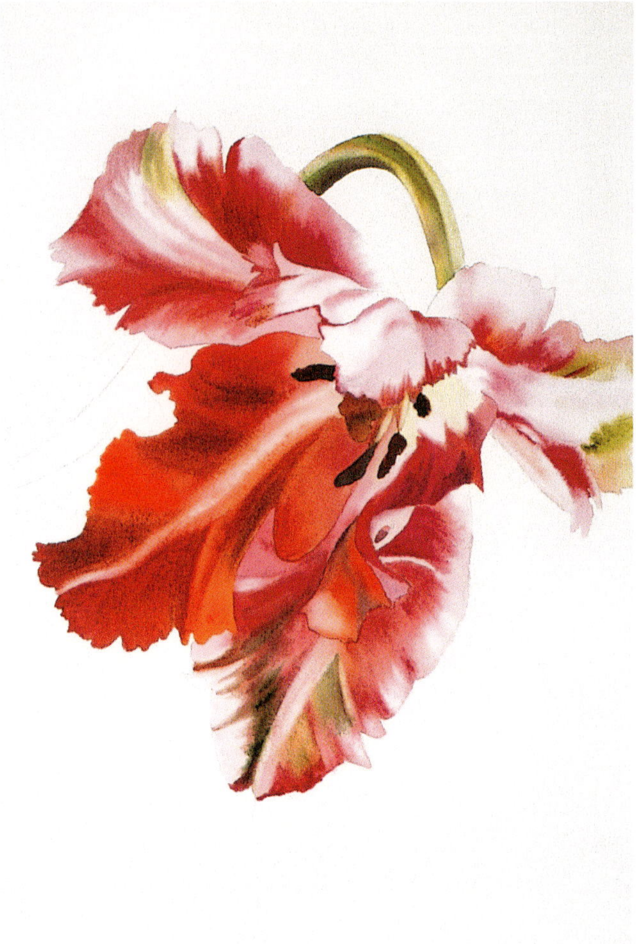

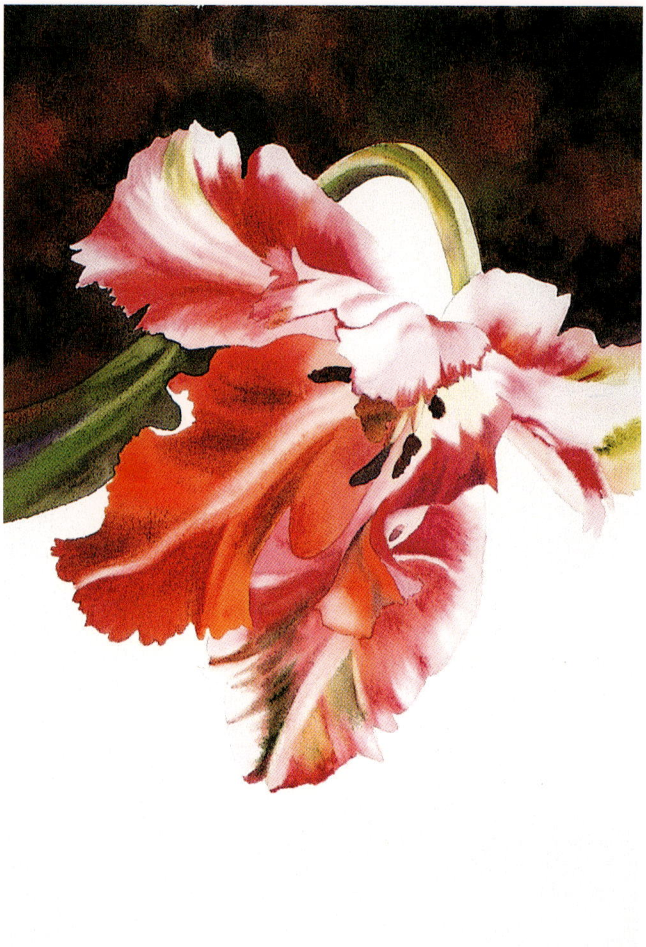

4 ADD THE STEM AND STAMENS

Wet the lightest areas of the stem using a no. 10 or 12 round. Mingle Aureolin Yellow, Greenish Yellow, Olive Green and Permanent Sap Green, working from dry areas toward the wet. When the whole stem is covered with pigment and while it is still damp, take a no. 4 round and drop in some Mineral Violet and Brown Madder, darkening the values in those areas.

With a no. 4 round, underpaint the stamens with Brown Madder and drop Ultramarine Blue into the wet paint to darken some areas. Let some of the Brown Madder show through.

5 MINGLE THE DARK BACKGROUND

On dry paper, use a 1-inch (25mm) angular flat to mingle the dark background using Brown Madder, Mineral Violet, Quinacridone Red Orange and Permanent Sap Green. Alternate the colors, joining them side by side. Do not paint one color over another; instead join them, allowing them to mingle on the paper as they flow into each other. Control the amount of water on your paper by using the absorbing pad; you want only enough for flow. If you don't use enough paint here, it will dry too light, so use lots of pigment on your brush. While the other colors are still damp, add Indigo to further darken the color. Avoid covering all of the underpainting—let some of the colors show through to give the background life. While the background is damp, paint the left side of the stem with a no. 16 round, mingling Olive Green, Permanent Sap Green and Undersea Green. Doing this while the background is damp will create soft edges.

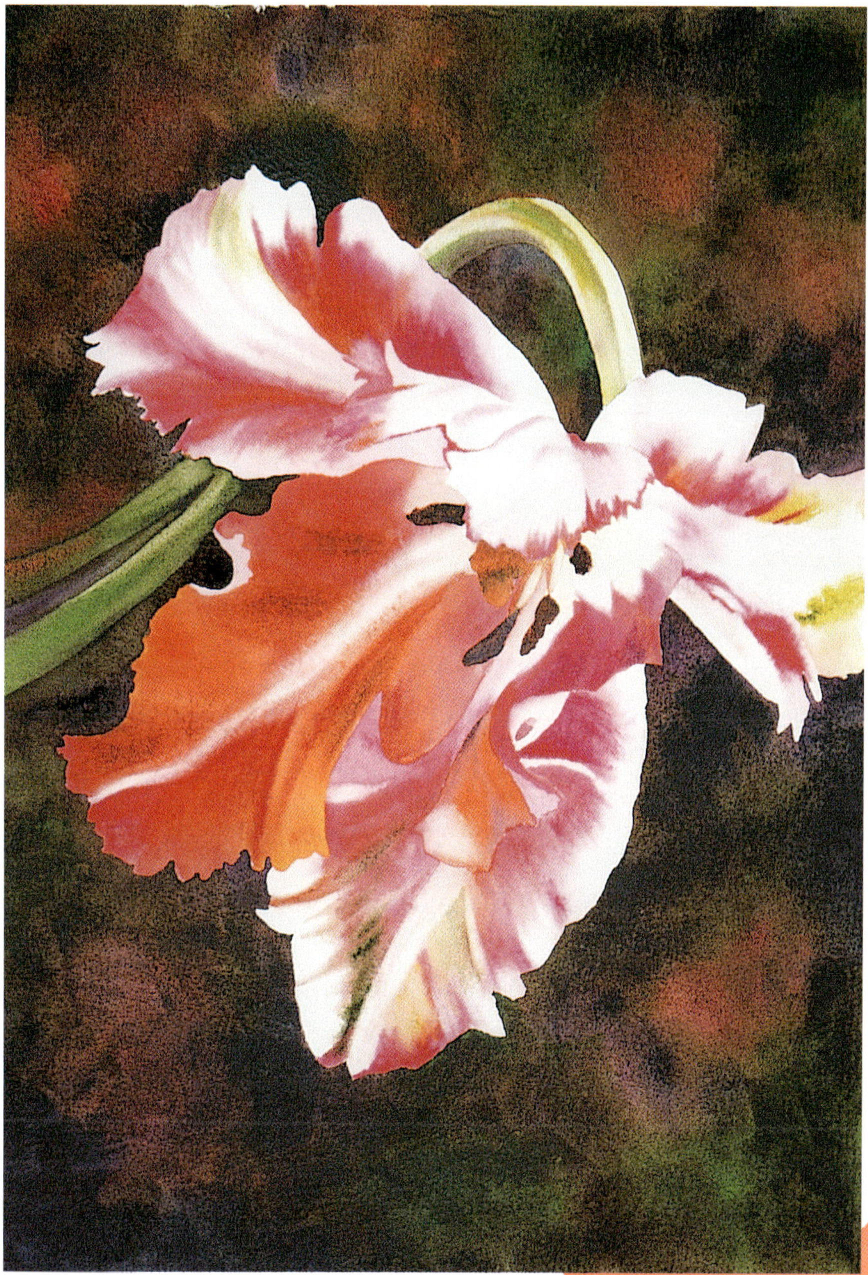

6 FINISH THE PAINTING
Here is where your black-and-white photocopy is so important; use it as a guide. When the dark background is fully dry, take a no. 8 scrubber to lift and adjust the lights and areas of the flower that need adjusting. Use the same brush to clean up any edges.

THE CAROL HEWITT
22" × 22" (56cm × 56cm)
Transparent watercolor on cold-pressed paper
Collection of Mr. and Mrs. J. Furman

Push Back With Yellow

Yellow paint always seems to push its way through other colors and make itself known. Try painting any color on a scrap of paper, then drop yellow into it. Watch the yellow push the other colors away.

Yellow's pushing quality can be used in an underpainting to lend a warm glow to your entire subject, or just in areas you want to glow. You can use any yellow you want, but I prefer New Gamboge, Gamboge Nova or Aureolin Yellow. Stay away from underpainting with opaques such as Naples Yellow and most Yellow Ochres or you will create mud.

People often tell me that my paintings seem to glow, and for that I give full credit to this technique.

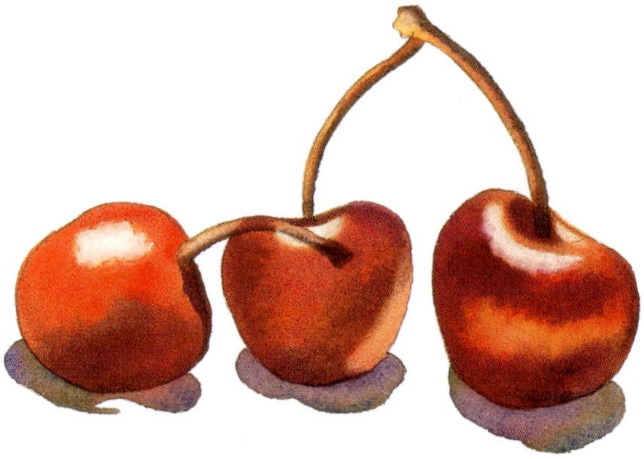

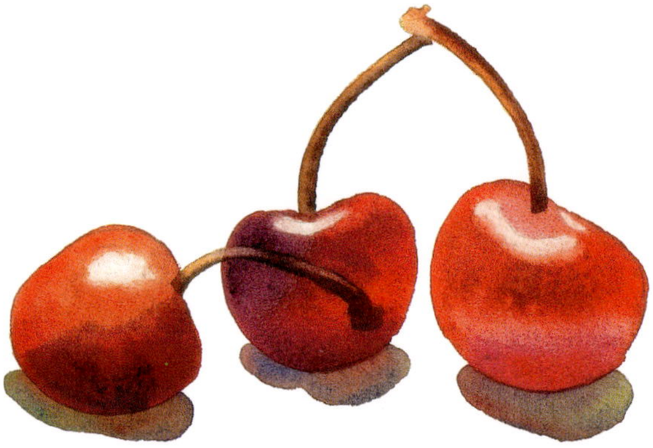

Compare and Contrast
The cherries with the golden glow were underpainted using New Gamboge.

A Yellow Underpainting Adds Warmth
In this cherry painting it's clear where the yellow has given the cherries added warmth.

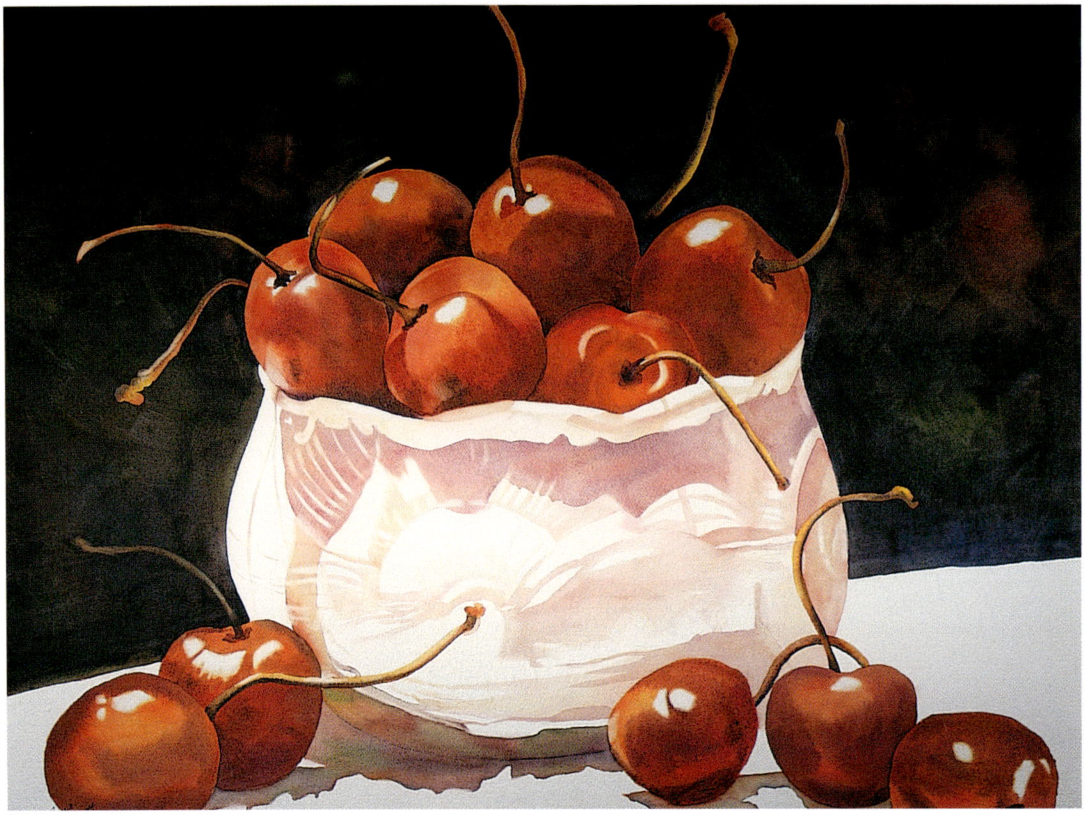

LIFE IS JUST A BOWL OF . . .
22" × 30" (56cm × 76cm)
Transparent watercolor on cold-pressed paper
Collection of the artist

Creating Intense Darks Without Glazing

MATERIALS

BRUSHES
Nos. 4, 12, and 26 round • ¾-inch (19mm)

COLORS
Aureolin Yellow • Brown Madder • Cobalt Blue • Cobalt Teal Blue • Cobalt Violet • Cobalt Violet Light • Compose Green 1 • Greenish Yellow • Mineral Violet • New Gamboge • Permanent Blue • Permanent Violet • Quinacridone Red Orange • Scarlet Lake • Ultramarine Blue • Verditer Blue • Yellow Ochre

SURFACE
300-lb. (640gsm) Arches cold-pressed paper

OTHER
Masking fluid • old no. 4 round (for applying masking fluid) • soapy water

Glazing *is the technique of placing a layer of paint over a layer of dry paint. In this demonstration, you'll learn how to get in and out of a painting without going back to glaze. Start a bottle and a cherry and finish it at one time—no glazing.*

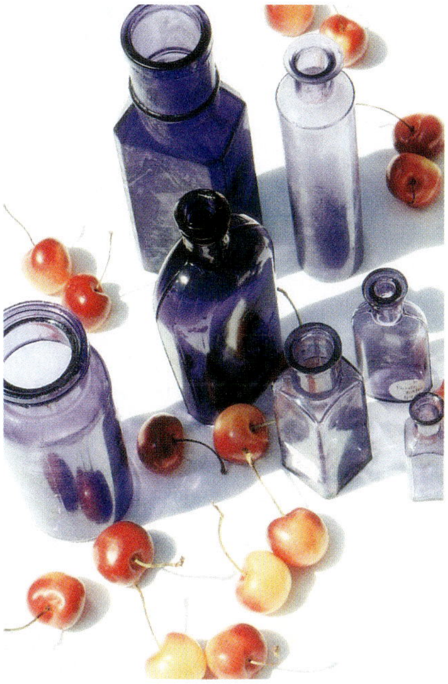

Reference Photo
I found these colored bottles in an antique store. I decided to group the bottles with Rainier cherries and paint them. I played with different arrangements and shadow shapes, then stood on a ladder to take the photo.

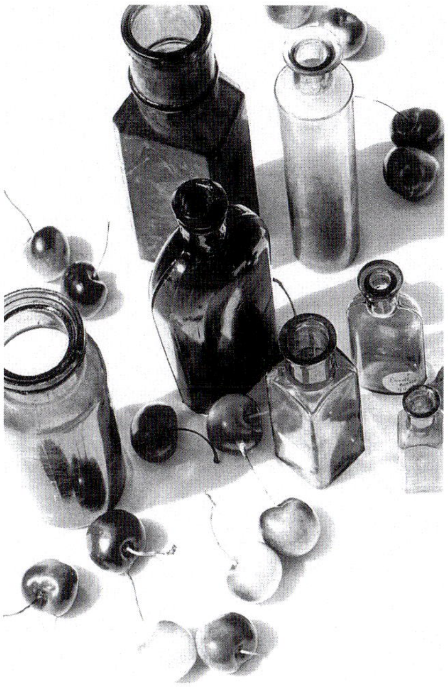

Black-and-White Photocopy

1 ESTABLISH THE VALUES IN THE LIGHTEST AND DARKEST BOTTLES
Draw or trace the composition onto the watercolor paper. Mask the brightest highlights in the bottles and cherries. Then wet the bottom of lightest bottle. Let the water settle into the paper, then with a no. 12 round, mingle Cobalt Teal Blue, Cobalt Violet and Mineral Violet in the lightest bottle. Where the cherries are reflected in the glass, drop in Quinacridone Red Orange. Mingle the light green reflection on the right side of the bottle with Compose Green 1. Add more pigment where you see the darker values.

For the darker bottle, mingle Cobalt Violet and Permanent Violet with a little Permanent Blue without applying water to the paper first. Wetting the paper will make it difficult to achieve transparent darks.

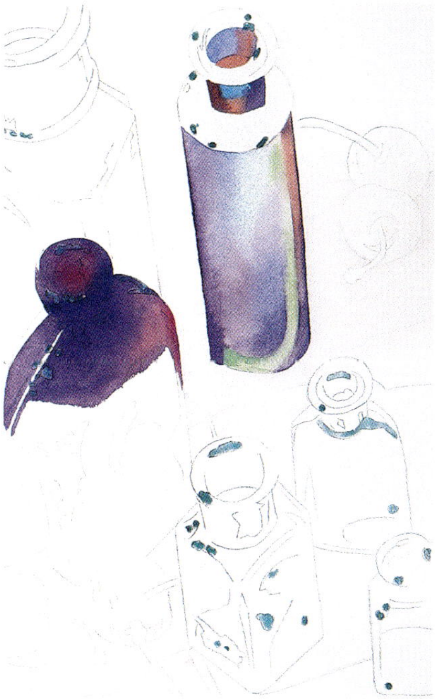

2 CREATE THE REFLECTIONS

With a no. 12 round, wet the rest of the darkest bottle. Let the water settle into the paper, then mingle Cobalt Blue, Permanent Blue, Mineral Violet and Permanent Violet. Drop in red reflections with Scarlet Lake and use the Compose Green 1 for the green reflection on the left side of the bottle. While damp, take a ¾-inch (19mm) flat and lift some highlights out of this bottle.

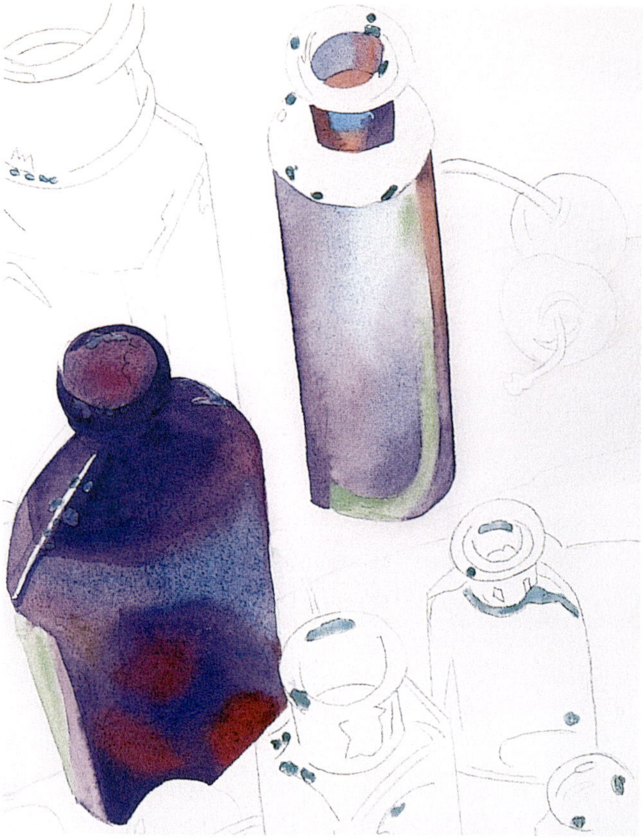

3 PAINT THE FOREGROUND CHERRIES

Wet some areas of the cherries with a no. 12 round, leaving the highlights dry. Paint from dry areas to wet, mingling Yellow Ochre, New Gamboge, Aureolin Yellow, Quinacridone Red Orange, Scarlet Lake and Brown Madder with the no. 12 round. Let the colors mingle and join around the dry highlights. Mingle the stems using Greenish Yellow, Brown Madder, Mineral Violet and Ultramarine Blue. Mingle the shadows on dry paper using Cobalt Teal Blue, Verditer Blue and Cobalt Violet. While these colors are damp, drop in Yellow Ochre and Quinacridone Red Orange. The cherries in the shadow areas have no lights and will need to be darker, so use more Brown Madder and Mineral Violet .

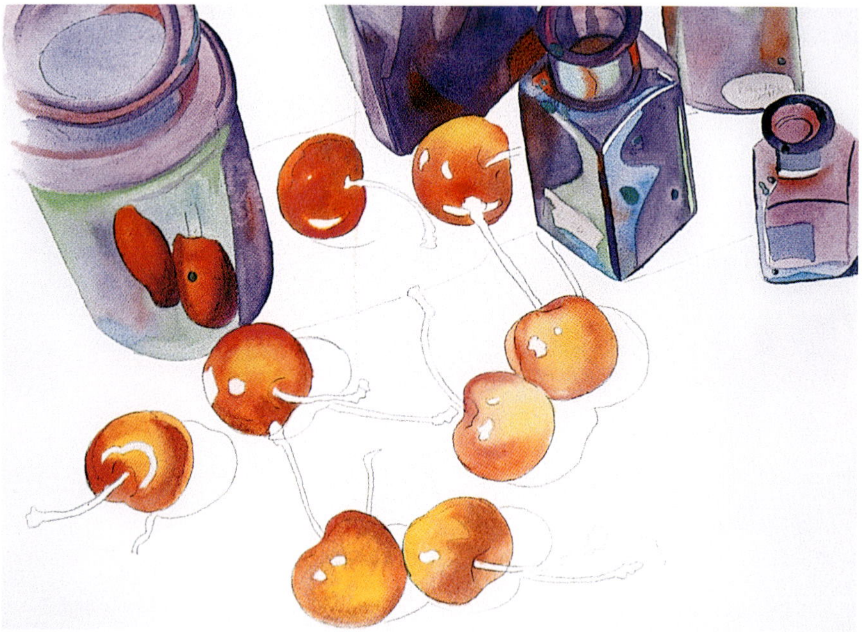

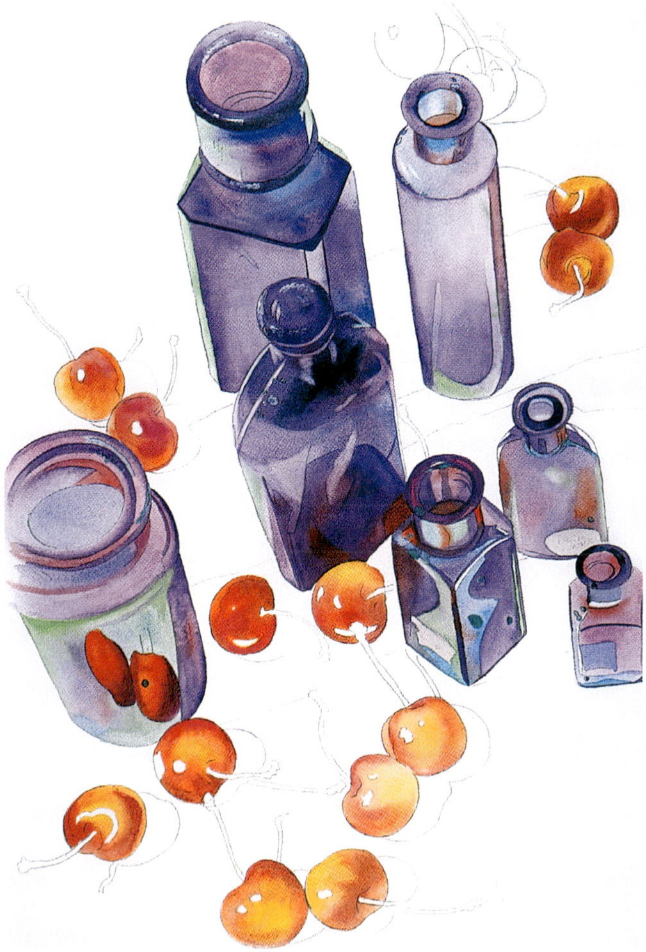

4 FINISH THE BOTTLES AND THE CHERRIES

Paint the red cherry reflections in the bottle in the left front, making the cherry's shape appear distorted by the glass. Charge in some darks in the bottles with a no. 4 round loaded with thick Permanent Violet to complete the rim of the bottle. Continue mingling the blues, violets and greens to complete the rest of the bottles. Be sure to mingle in some yellows and reds to suggest the reflected color of the cherries. Complete the background cherries by mingling the yellows and reds, following the process described in step 3.

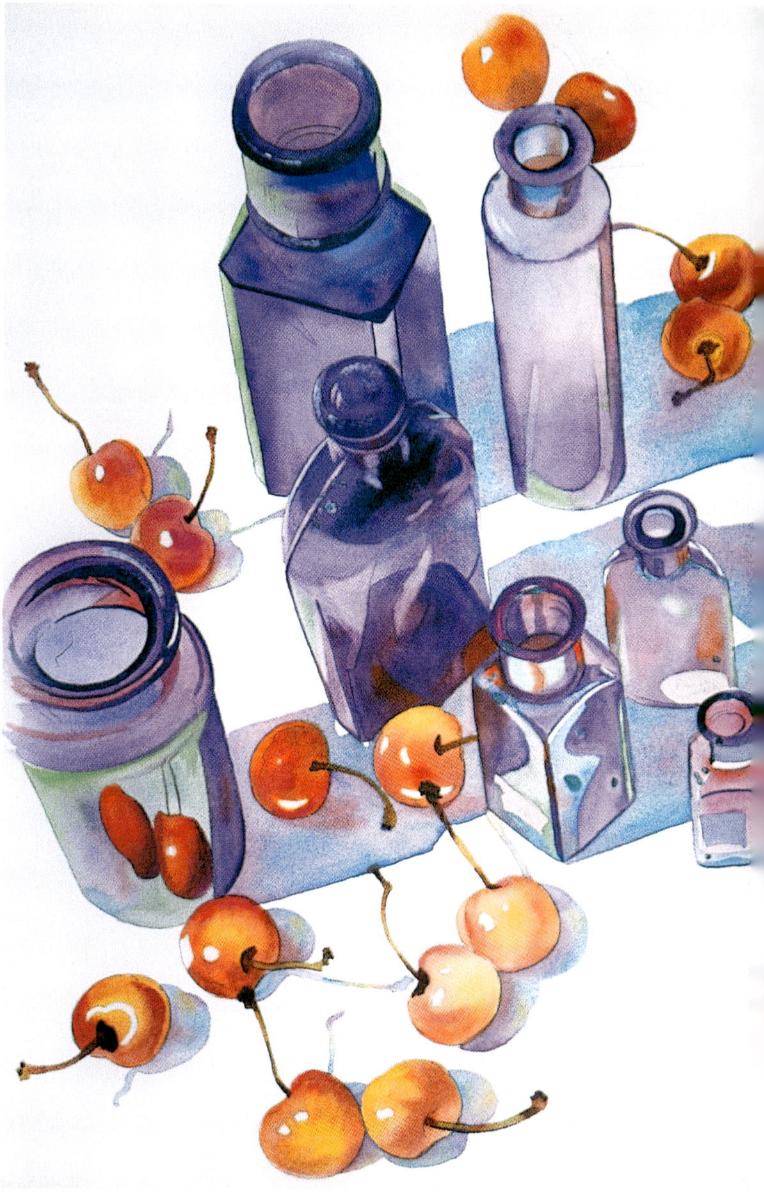

5 PULL THE PAINTING TOGETHER WITH SHADOWS

Connect the different shapes of the bottles and the cherries with their shadows. Using a no. 26 round, mingle the shadows using Cobalt Teal Blue, Cobalt Violet Light and Cobalt Violet. While the shadow area is still wet, switch to a ¾-inch (19mm) flat and drop Quinacridone Red Orange and Yellow Ochre into the shadows under the cherries. Then drop in some Cobalt Blue along the edges of some of the shadows.

MOOSE CROSSINGS
28" × 22" (71cm × 56cm)
Watercolor on cold-pressed paper
Collection of the artist

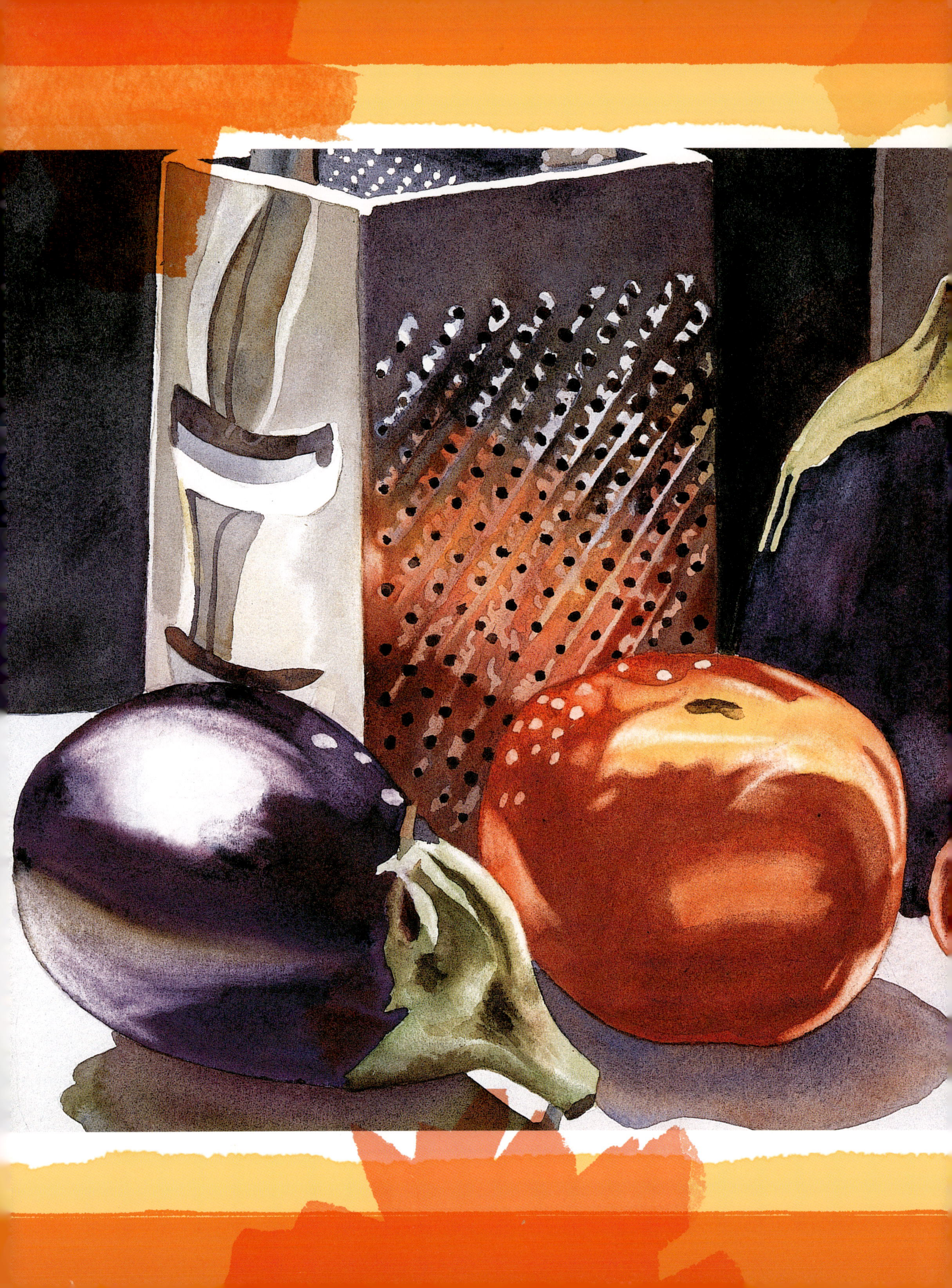

6

Shadows

This chapter explores the importance of shadows in painting. You'll learn the difference between good and bad shadows, the color of shadows, and how mingled colors can add excitement and life to all shadows.

Shadows are longest in the early morning and late afternoon. Subjects float off the page without a shadow to ground them in the painting. Think of shadows as ghosts of the objects that reflect the object's color and shape.

Shadows define sources of light, create dimension and establish mood in paintings. Dramatic shadows bring a painting to life.

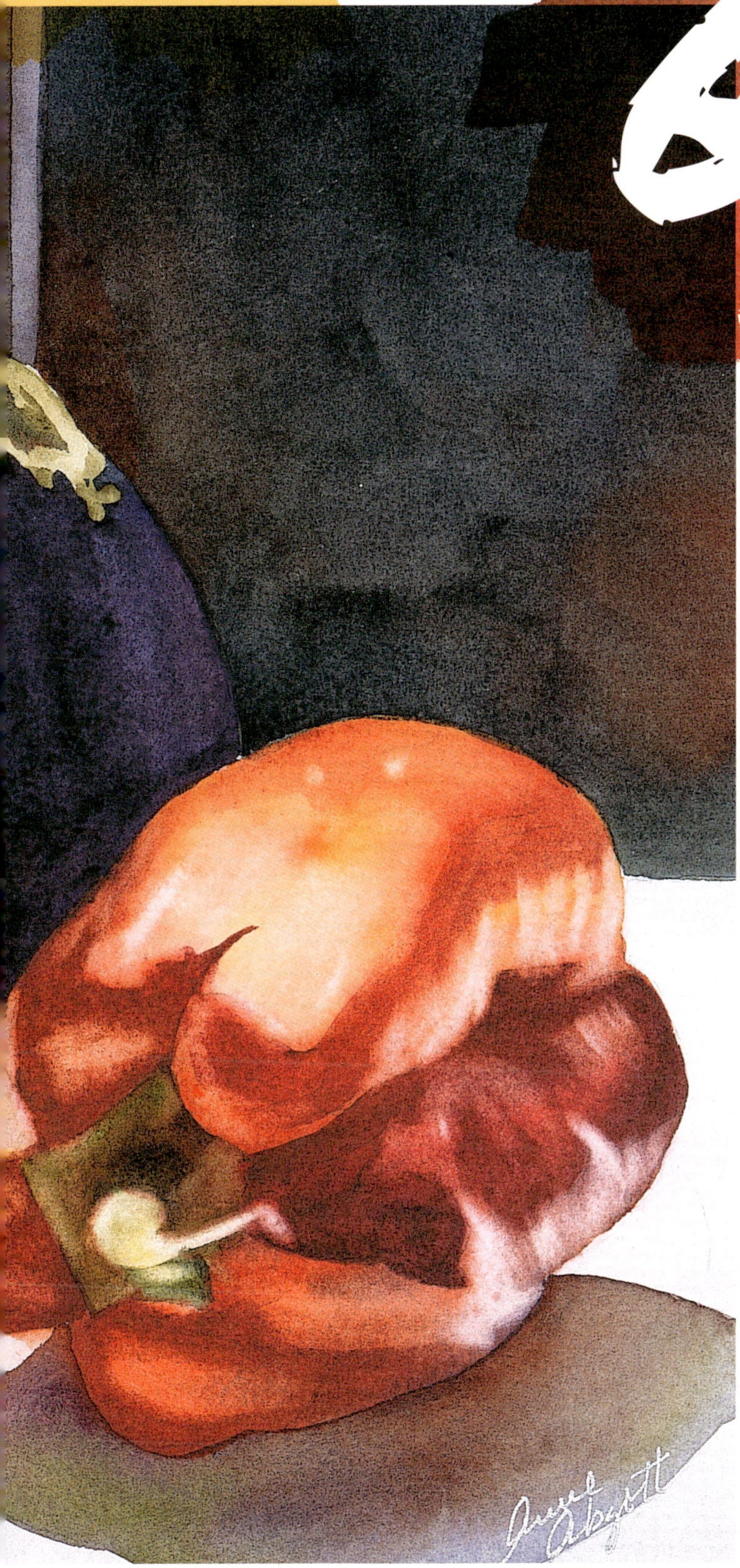

WHERE'S THE PASTA? WHERE'S THE CHEESE?
15" × 20" (38cm × 51cm)
Transparent watercolor on cold-pressed paper
Collection of the artist

Light and Shadow in Reference Photos

Light and shadow are a big part of what inspires me to paint. It's easier for me to design a painting from photographs than from life because I don't have to race the sun. The photo freezes the moment for me.

Take reference photos early in the morning or late in the afternoon when the light is at a low angle, creating more interesting cast shadows.

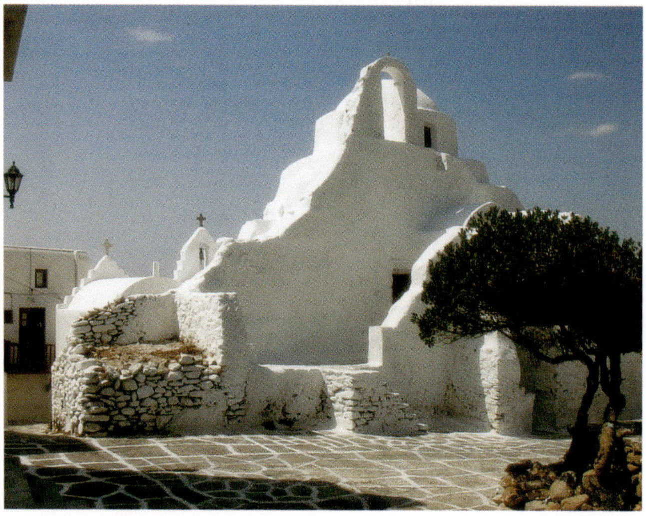

Good Light and Shadow
This photo provides all the elements you need for a successful painting: large, light-struck areas to leave as white paper surrounded by many other values. The sky is a midvalue that will make the white stand out. Notice how the shadows on the building have varying values. Also notice how the shadows connect; this connection holds the painting together.

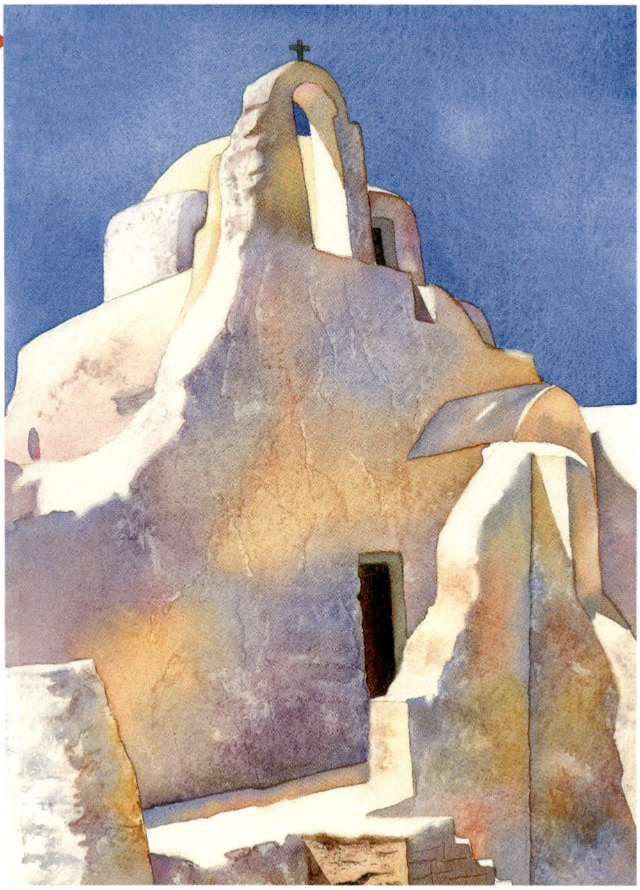

Use Artistic License to Create Dramatic Shadows
This painting is successful because I was able to enhance the lights on the building with the sky and the shadows. The shadows here vary in depth of color and clearly make the painting.

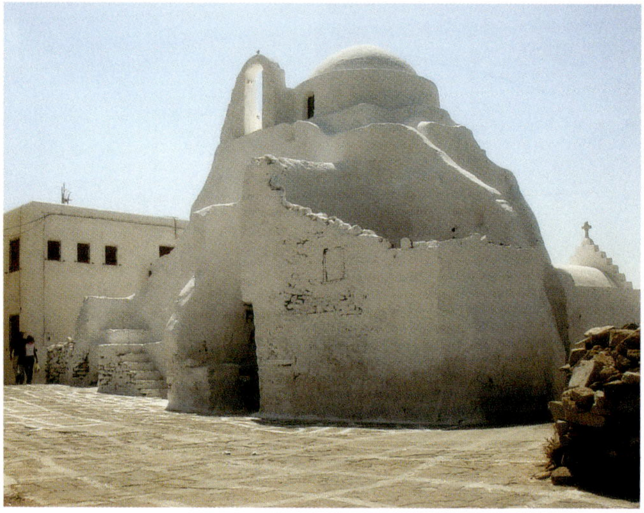

Too Much Shadow
Here we have too much shadow and not enough light-struck areas. I always evaluate a photo by looking for the lights. By squinting my eyes, I can clearly see there is not enough contrast between light, medium and dark values here to make a good painting.

Identifying the Types of Shadows

Portraying light and shadow effectively will make your subjects leap off the page, creating a dynamic painting. Understanding the basic characteristics of light and shadow will help you create beautiful shadow shapes.

- *Form shadow*: This is the area of an object where light does not hit the object directly. The darkest part of the form shadow is called the *core shadow*.
- *Cast shadow*: This is the shadow cast from one object onto another object.
- *Highlight*: This is where the light hits the object most directly, making it the lightest area of the object.

I like to think of shadows as hard-edged and soft-edged. *Hard-edged* shadows have a very distinct change from the light areas to the dark. Cast shadows are usually hard-edged. *Soft-edged* shadows have a gradual, blended transition from the light areas to the dark. Form shadows are usually soft-edged.

Paintings should include both hard and soft edges, with one being more dominant than the other. Hard edges attract attention, but too many can make a composition look overworked, so it is best to have a variety of edges.

By dragging a wet brush along one edge of the wet paint you can soften any edge. Hard edges are made by painting wet against dry. You can also create soft edges by working damp-into-damp, not wet-into-wet. If the painting is too wet, you will lose control of the edges. Using your absorbing pad (page 16) will give the paint enough water to travel on.

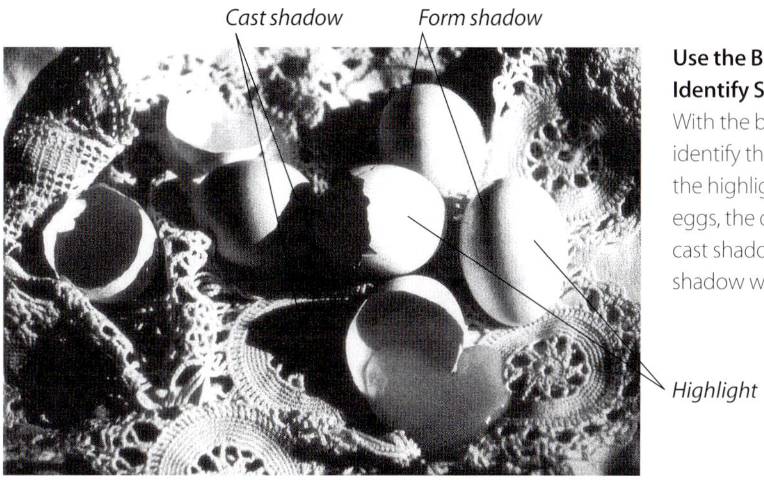

Use the Black-and-White Photocopy to Identify Shadows
With the black-and-white photocopy you can identify the form shadows, cast shadows and the highlights. Notice that of the center two eggs, the one on the left has a hard-edged cast shadow; the egg on its right has a cast shadow with a softer edge.

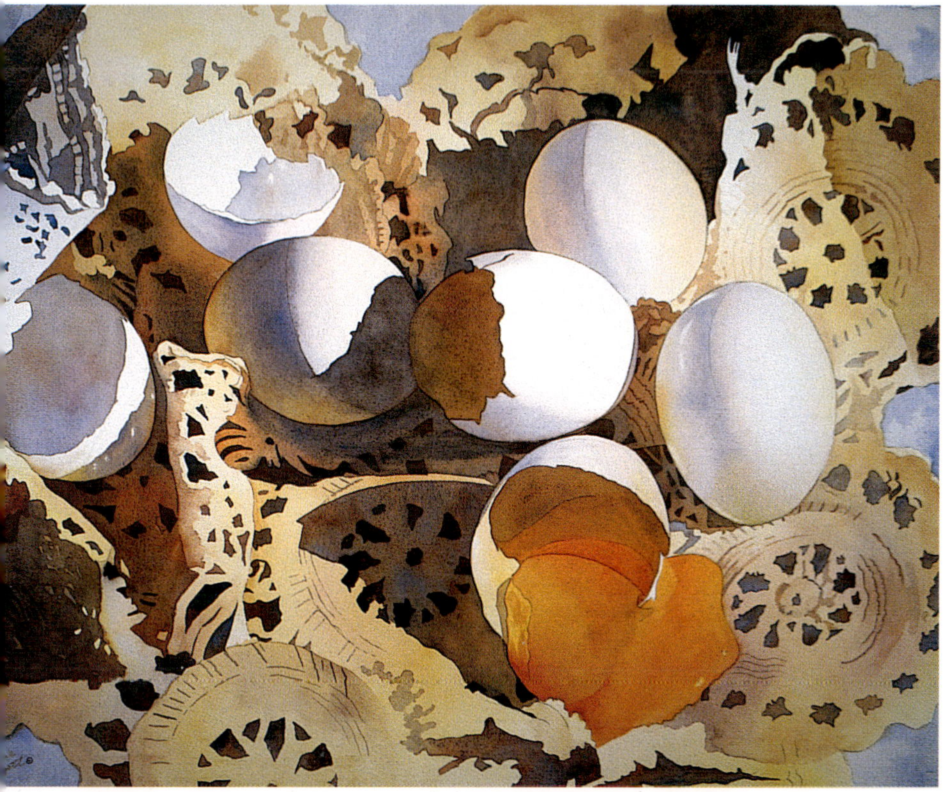

Connect the Shadow for Interesting Shapes
The dark connecting shadows surrounding the white eggs and the light-struck lace areas demonstrate the importance of shadows in a composition.

I'VE GOT EGG ON MY LACE
22" × 30" (56cm × 76cm)
Transparent watercolor on cold-pressed paper
Collection of the artist

The Color of Shadows

Seeing colors in shadows can be difficult. Shadows are not uniform in color because they reflect the color of objects and surfaces around them. Shadows also become lighter and cooler as they get farther from the object casting them. Many artists see shadows as only gray, but they are not gray. Colorful shadows are necessary for a good painting. They anchor objects, create wonderful shapes and unify a painting. As you try to paint the colors of the shadows, consider the following:

- The actual color of an object is the local color. Local color is unaffected by light or shadow.
- Light is reflected from the ground into the form shadow. This is called *reflected light;* it separates the object from the shadow.
- The color reflected from the object into the cast shadow is called the *reflected color.* It shows the relationship between the object and its shadow.

As you paint, create gradual color changes. Be brave and put colors in whether you see them or not. Many times the reference photo will show you colors in the shadows you may have missed.

Remember, shadows are darkest and most dense at the base of the subject where the light is completely blocked. The shadow edge, where some of the light penetrates into the shadow, is softer and more transparent.

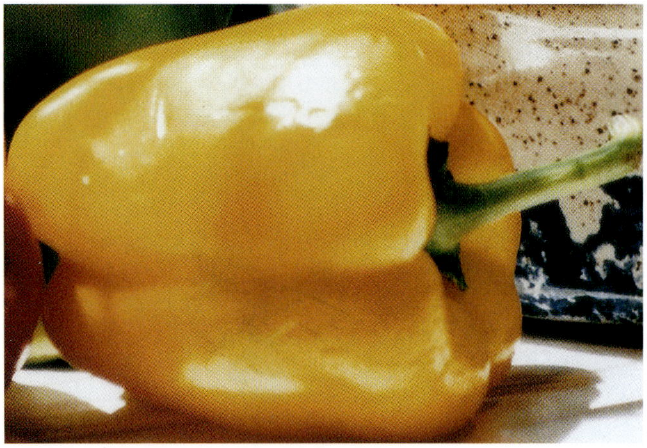

Reference Photos Show a Shadow's Colors
This pepper clearly has a lot of yellow in its shadow. If you look closer, you can also see some greens, blues and purples.

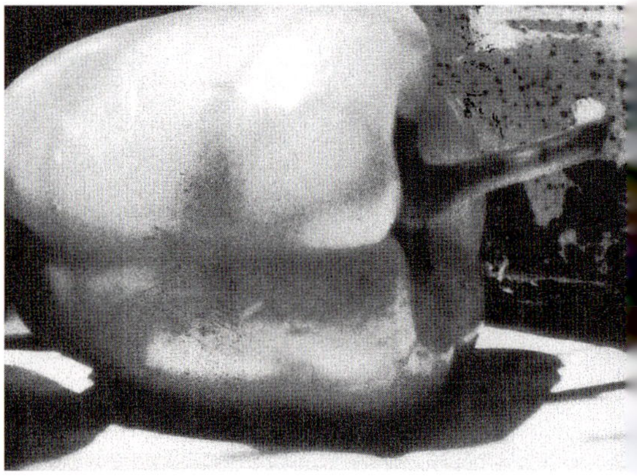

Photocopies Show Patterns of Light and Shadow
Use the lights and shadows you see in the photocopy to help you create the right value pattern in your painting.

TIPS FOR REFERENCE PHOTOS

When combining photos, make sure the light source is located in the same place. Photograph light clothing rather than dark. Dark has flat shadows.

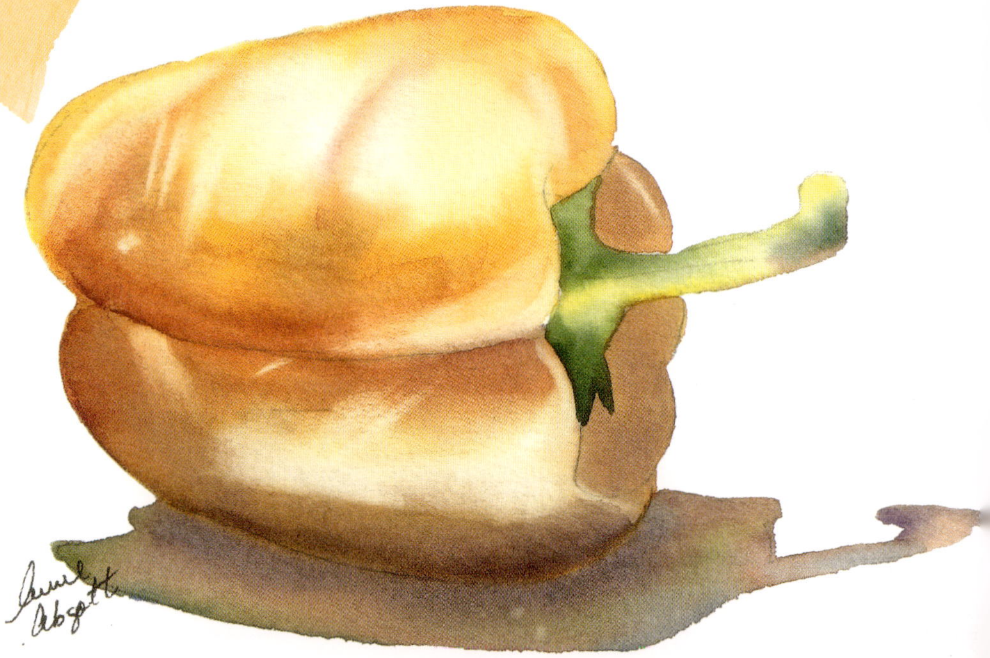

Use Your References to Create Lively, Colorful Shadows
Following the shadow pattern on your black-and-white photocopy, create form shadows, cast shadows and highlights on your subject. Remember, shadows reflect the colors of the object, though not always uniformly.

Mingled Shadows

Shadows are wonderfully colorful. They anchor subjects and indicate the direction of the light. They add dimension and drama. Most importantly, shadows are not gray; they are a transparent veil through which you see the reflected color of the object on another surface. I like to mingle colors in my shadows to give them life and interest. Flat passages of gray do little to convey to the viewer that the shadow reflects the color of the object.

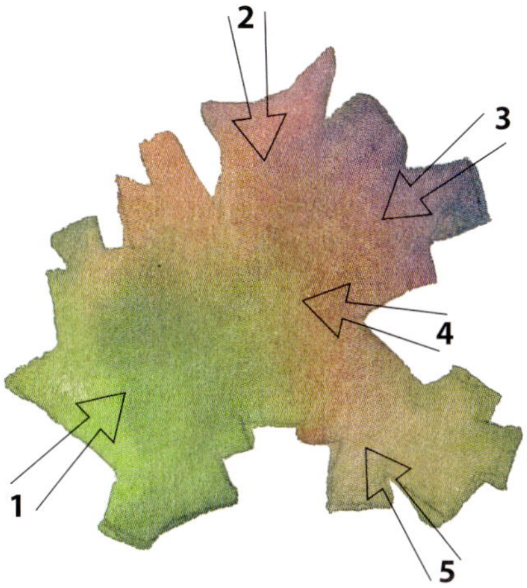

Foliage Shadows
These are colors I often mingle for the shadows in foliage or grass.

1. Permanent Sap Green
2. Brown Madder
3. Cobalt Blue
4. Mineral Violet
5. Olive Green

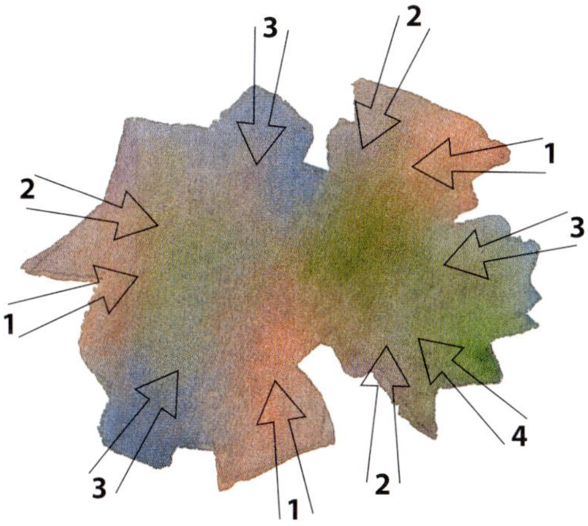

Background Foliage
These are great colors to use if you want to create the appearance of background foliage.

1. Quinacridone Red Orange
2. Mineral Violet
3. Cobalt Blue
4. Permanent Sap Green

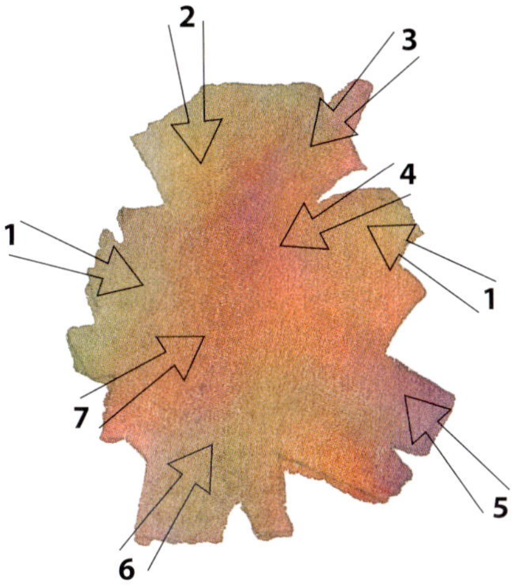

Shadows of Reds and Greens
Mingle these colors for the shadows of red fruits, vegetables or a red flower with a green stem.

1. Olive Green
2. Yellow Ochre
3. Cobalt Violet
4. Quinacridone Red Orange
5. Quinacridone Magenta
6. Permanent Sap Green
7. Permanent Rose

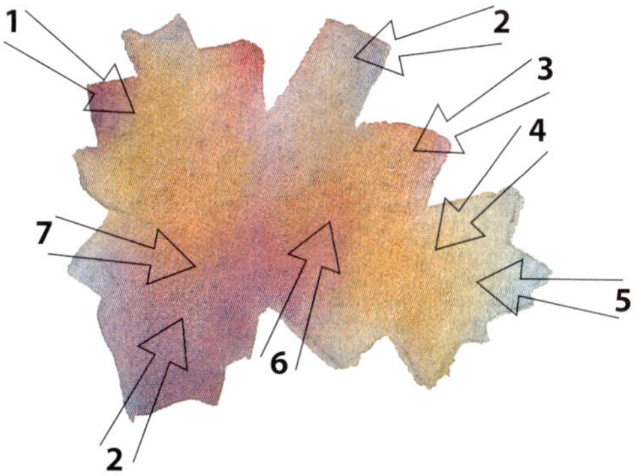

Shadows for Red and Yellow Objects
Use these for shadows under a red or yellow pear.

1. Brown Madder
2. Cobalt Blue
3. Permanent Rose
4. Yellow Ochre
5. Verditer Blue
6. Quinacridone Red Orange
7. Mineral Violet

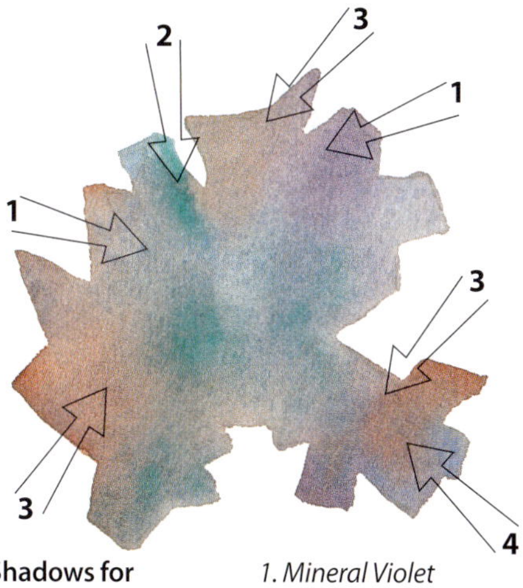

Shadows for Buildings
Try these colors for the dark side of a stucco wall or as the shadow of a rusty piece of machinery.

1. Mineral Violet
2. Cobalt Teal Blue
3. Brown Madder
4. Cobalt Blue

Create Different Effects With the Same Colors
Here I used the same colors but varied their placement. Notice how this changes the way the colors look.

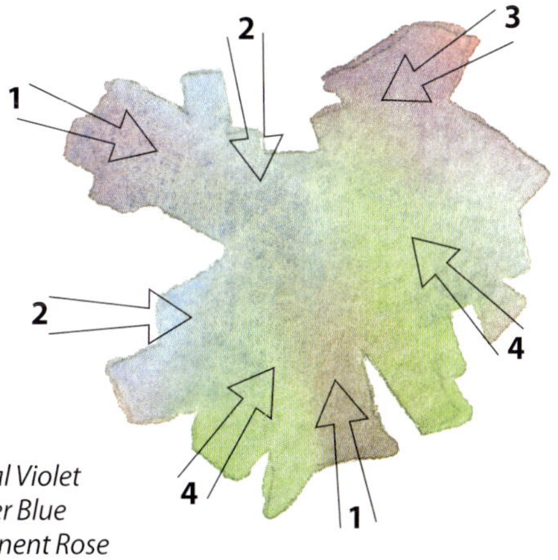

1. Mineral Violet
2. Verditer Blue
3. Permanent Rose
4. Permanent Sap Green

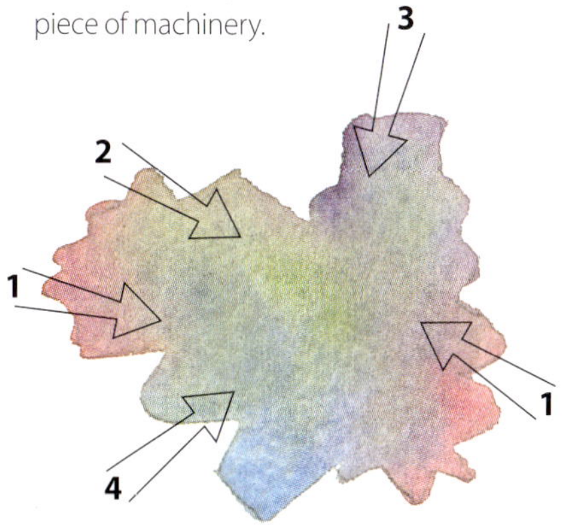

1. Permanent Rose
2. Permanent Sap Green
3. Mineral Violet
4. Verditer Blue

Glazing Shadows

MATERIALS

BRUSHES
Nos. 6, 12, 16 and 26 round • no. 8 scrubber

COLORS
Brown Madder • Mineral Violet • New Gamboge • Olive Green • Permanent Rose • Permanent Sap Green • Quinacridone Red Orange • Scarlet Lake • Ultramarine Blue

SURFACE
300-lb. (640gsm) Arches cold-pressed watercolor paper, natural color

OTHER
Paper towels • spray bottle filled with water

I seldom glaze, but the technique is essential when I paint shadows on flowers. When you glaze watercolors, each layer of paint must be completely dry before you add the next layer. Use a hair dryer or wait for the paint to dry naturally. You can glaze as many times as you want. Remember, each layer of glazed paint will darken the area.

When you use transparent paints to glaze (especially Verditer Blue), you can correct the values in a background, pull two separate subjects together or turn a hard edge into a soft edge.

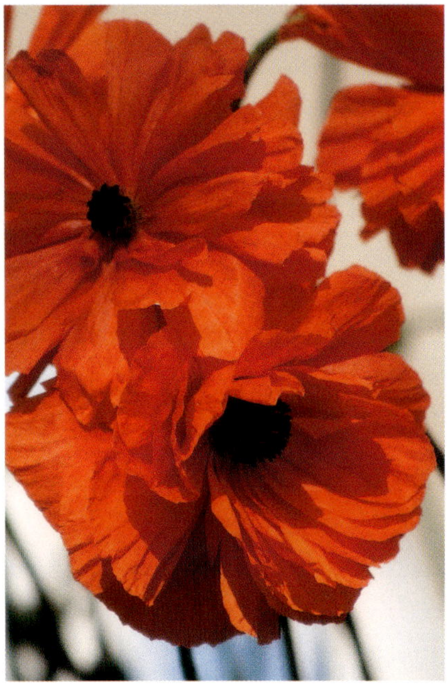

Reference Photo

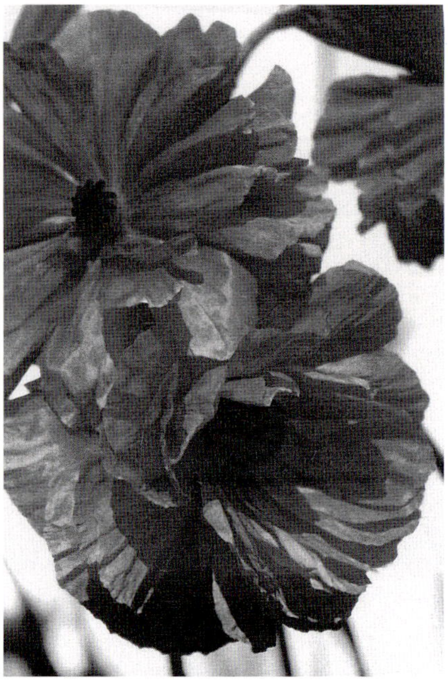

Black-and-White Photocopy

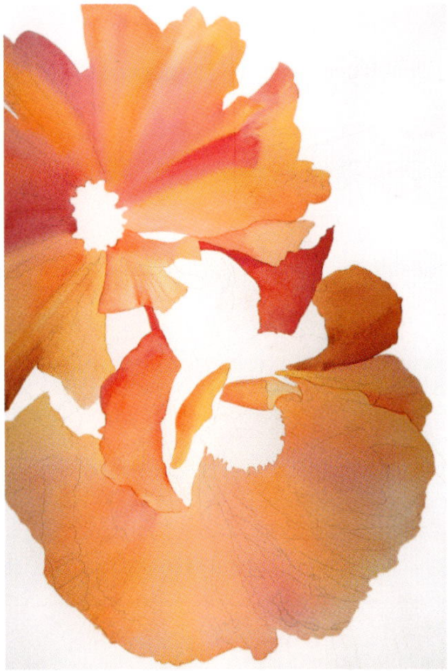

1 MINGLE THE COLORS
Sketch or trace the drawing onto the watercolor paper. With a no. 26 round, paint all of the flower's petals, mingling New Gamboge, Permanent Rose, Scarlet Lake and Quinacridone Red Orange across the flowers' shapes. Change and vary colors as you mingle, leaving a few light petals as shown in the black-and-white photocopy. Drop in thicker paint to darken some areas while the paint is still damp.

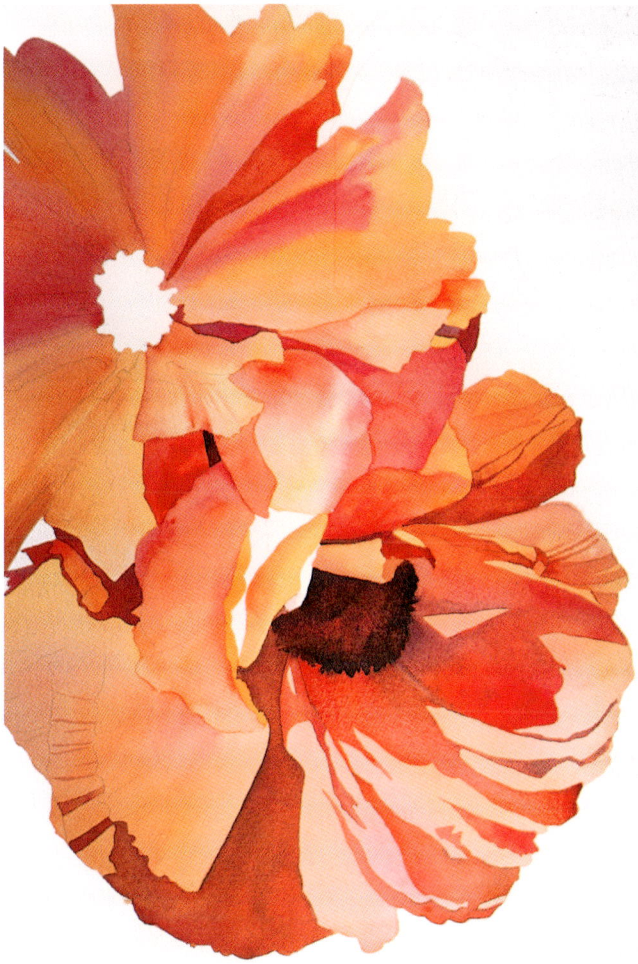

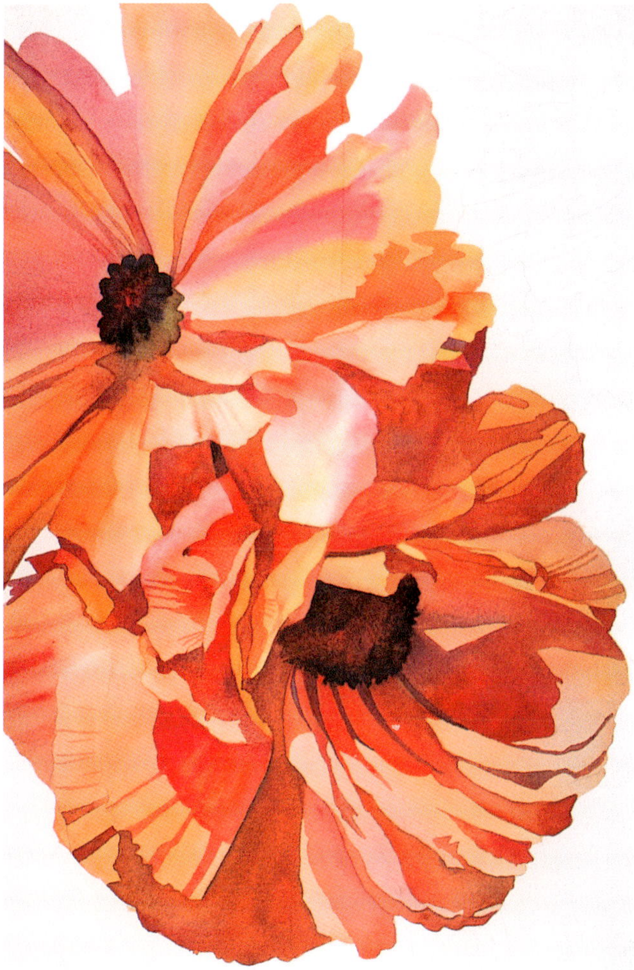

2 ADD THE DARK CENTER AND SOME LIGHTER PETALS

To paint the center, underpaint the whole area with Permanent Rose using a no. 12 round. Also use the no. 12 round to cover this with Brown Madder and Ultramarine Blue. Let some of the Brown Madder show through, creating a lively shape instead of a black hole.

Glaze shadows into the lower flower with a no. 16 round, mingling Quinacridone Red Orange and Brown Madder side by side. While the area is still damp, drop Mineral Violet into the corners to darken.

Darken the bottom petals of the upper flower with Scarlet Lake, Brown Madder and Mineral Violet using a no. 12 round. When dry, wet the light petals on the top of the lower flower and float New Gamboge and Quinacridone Red Orange into the water.

Connect the shadows on the lower edge of the upper flower with Quinacridone Red Orange, Brown Madder and Mineral Violet. Charge in the Mineral Violet to darken while the paint is wet.

3 ADD TEXTURE AND THE OTHER DARK CENTER

With a no. 6 round, create a crepelike texture on the petals by dropping in Quinacridone Red Orange and Permanent Rose. Do this on dry paper for hard lines or create soft lines by wetting the lines with clear water first. Finish the dark center of the upper flower with Brown Madder and Ultramarine Blue by repeating the process in step 2.

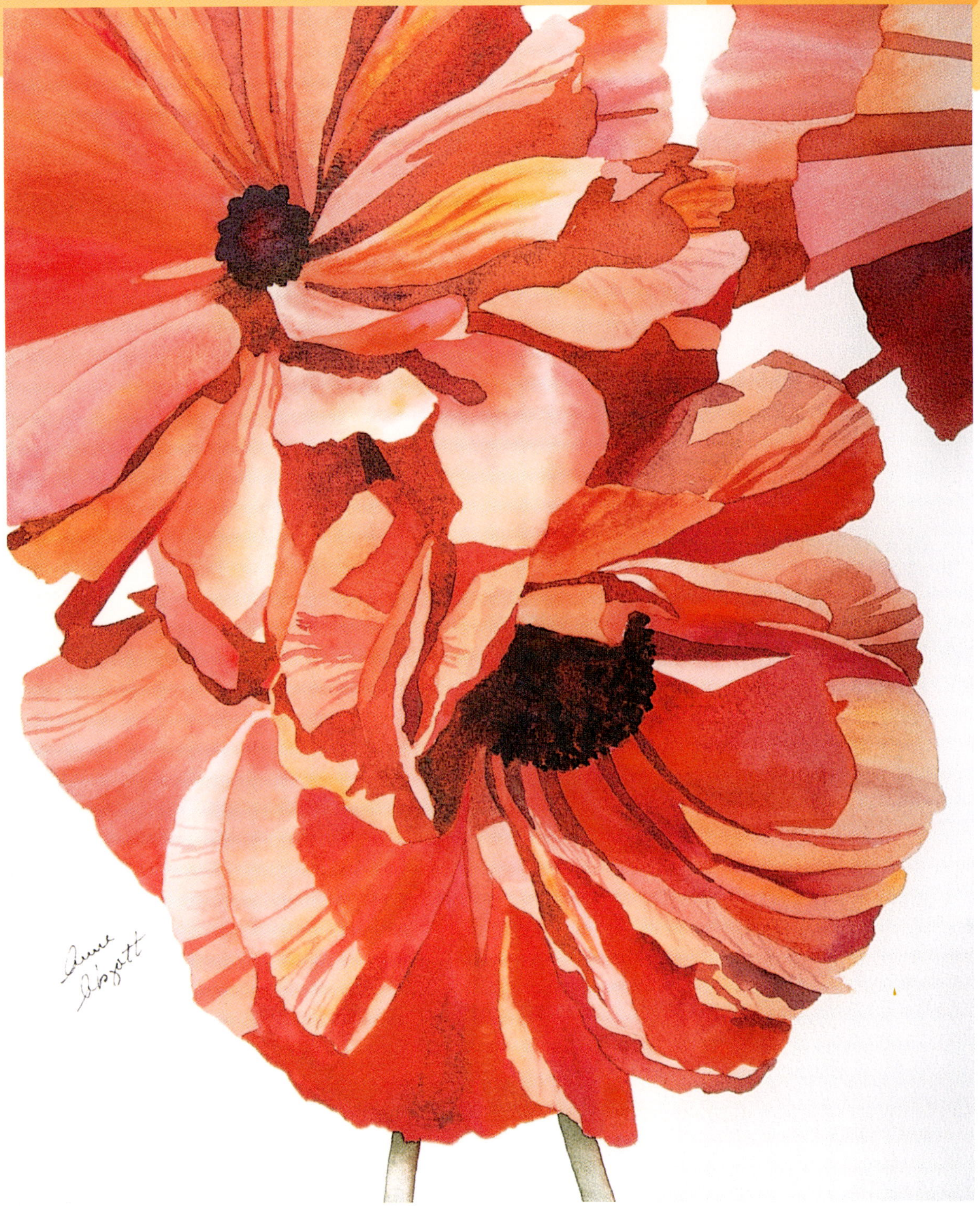

4 ADD STEMS AND COMPLETE THE PAINTING

Use a no. 12 round to mingle Permanent Sap Green, Olive Green and a little Mineral Violet for the stem's shadow side.

Finish the painting by adjusting the values and lifting some lights with the no. 8 scrubber. If necessary, turn your dry painting and black-and-white photocopy upside down so you can focus on the shapes of the value pattern. Lift lights from the dry painting by using a spray bottle to soak the area first. Lift with a wet scrubber, then blot the areas with a paper towel. I decided against a background—the color speaks for itself.

LINVILLE POPPY
20" × 16" (51cm × 41cm)
Transparent watercolor on cold-pressed paper
Collection of the artist

Reflected Colors in Shadows

MATERIALS

BRUSHES
Nos. 6, 12, 16 and 36 round • ¾-inch (19mm) flat • 1-inch (25mm) angular flat • no. 6 scrubber

COLORS
Aureolin Yellow • Brown Madder • Burnt Sienna • Cobalt Blue • Cobalt Teal Blue • Cobalt Violet • Mineral Violet • New Gamboge • Olive Green • Permanent Rose • Permanent Sap Green • Transparent Turquoise • Ultramarine Blue • Undersea Green • Verditer Blue

SURFACE
300-lb. (640gsm) Arches cold-pressed paper

OTHER
Absorbing pad • commercial masking removal pad • gesso • masking fluid • razor blade • old no. 6 round for applying masking fluid • soapy water

This painting demonstrates the way shadows reflect the colors of the surrounding objects—an important concept to keep in mind when painting any shadow shapes. These shadows were created on the yellow wall of a building by some nearby palm trees. The leaves reflect more green in the area of the shadows they are closest to. The shutters will also reflect back into the shadows.

The shapes of the shadows and the negative shapes in this painting are really exciting. Try changing the color of the building and the color of the shutters. I worked in a series and also did a vertical version.

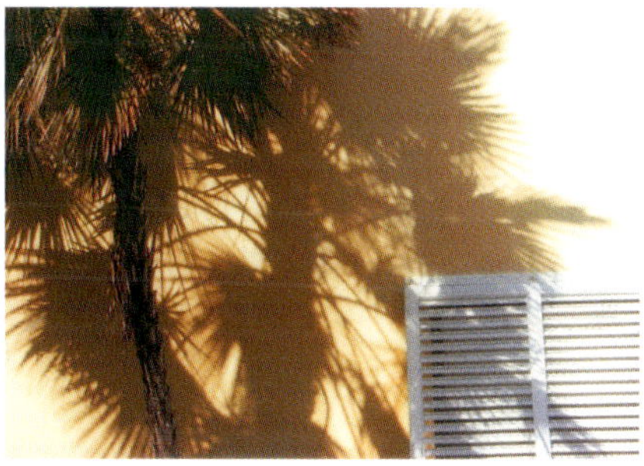

Reference Photo

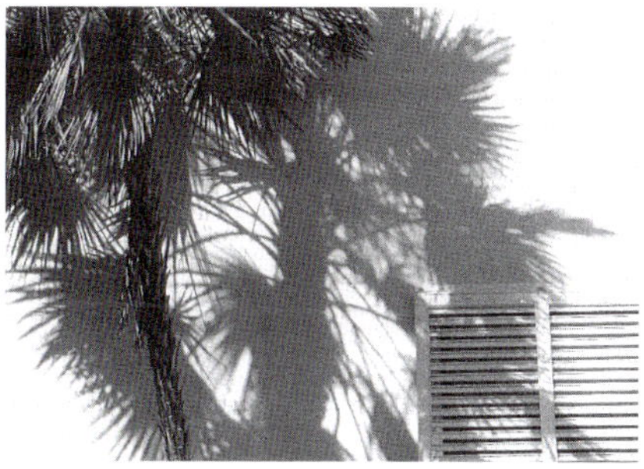

Black-and-White Photocopy

1 MASK THE NEGATIVE SPACES AND BEGIN THE SHUTTER
Make your line drawing, then use an old no. 6 round to carefully cover the negative spaces of the wall with masking fluid. Remember to dip your brush in soapy water to protect it from the masking fluid.

With a no. 16 round, mingle Transparent Turquoise and Cobalt Teal Blue on the shutter. While this is wet, gently drop in Aureolin Yellow to create the illusion of sunlight in the shutter areas that have no shadows. Let these colors dry thoroughly.

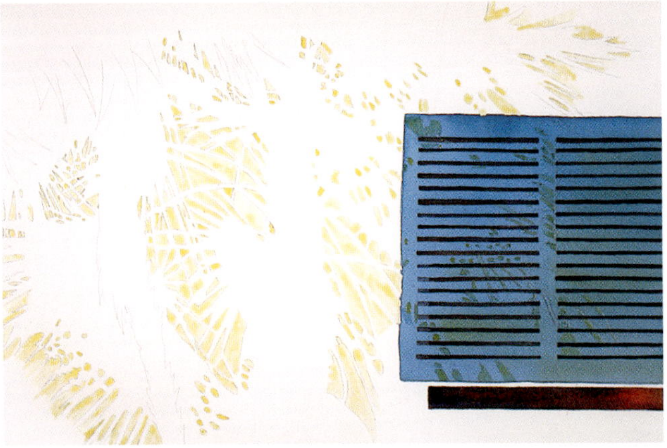

2 MASK THE NEGATIVE SPACES ON THE SHUTTER AND ADD DARK SLATS

Once the paint on the shutter is dry, use an old no. 6 round to carefully apply masking fluid to areas that will be holes in the shadows on the shutter. Let the masking fluid dry.

Use a no. 6 round to paint the dark slats on the shutter and a shadow under the shutter by mingling Brown Madder and Ultramarine Blue. Let the Brown Madder show through in some areas to suggest lighter areas.

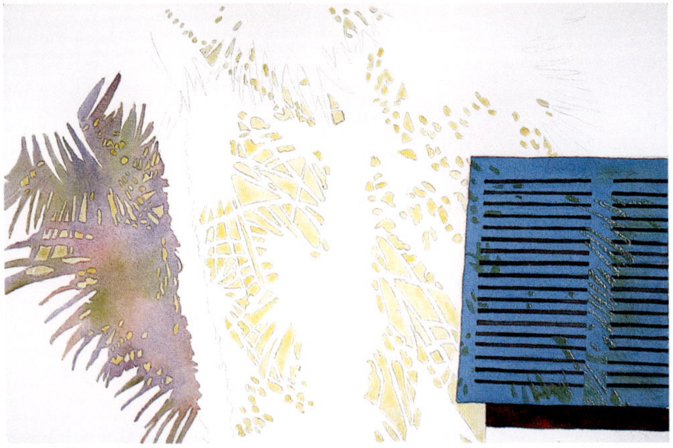

3 BEGIN MINGLING THE SHADOW ON THE WALL

Make large, separate puddles of Verditer Blue, Permanent Rose, Brown Madder, Mineral Violet, Cobalt Violet and Cobalt Blue on your palette. With a no. 36 round, lay the colors side by side on dry paper and over the masking fluid on the left of the tree trunk. Change your colors every three or four strokes, cleaning your brush between each application of a different color.

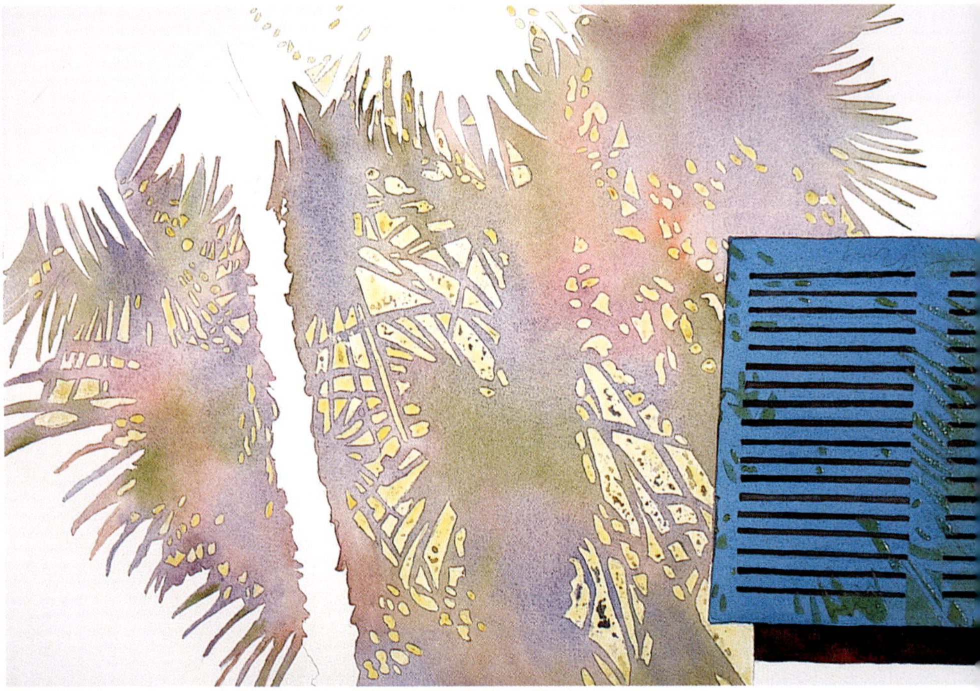

4 COMPLETE THE WALL SHADOW

Make more large puddles of Verditer Blue, Permanent Rose, Brown Madder, Mineral Violet and Cobalt Violet. With a no. 36 round, work from the top-right edge down, mingling the colors until the entire shadow shape is completed. Again, apply the colors side by side and over the masking fluid. While the shadow is still wet, use a 1-inch (25mm) angular flat to pick up some paint directly from the well. Control the amount of water on the brush with your absorbing pad and charge the extra pigment into some areas of the wet shadow to intensify and darken the value. Mingle only the shadow pattern on the wall, not the shutter.

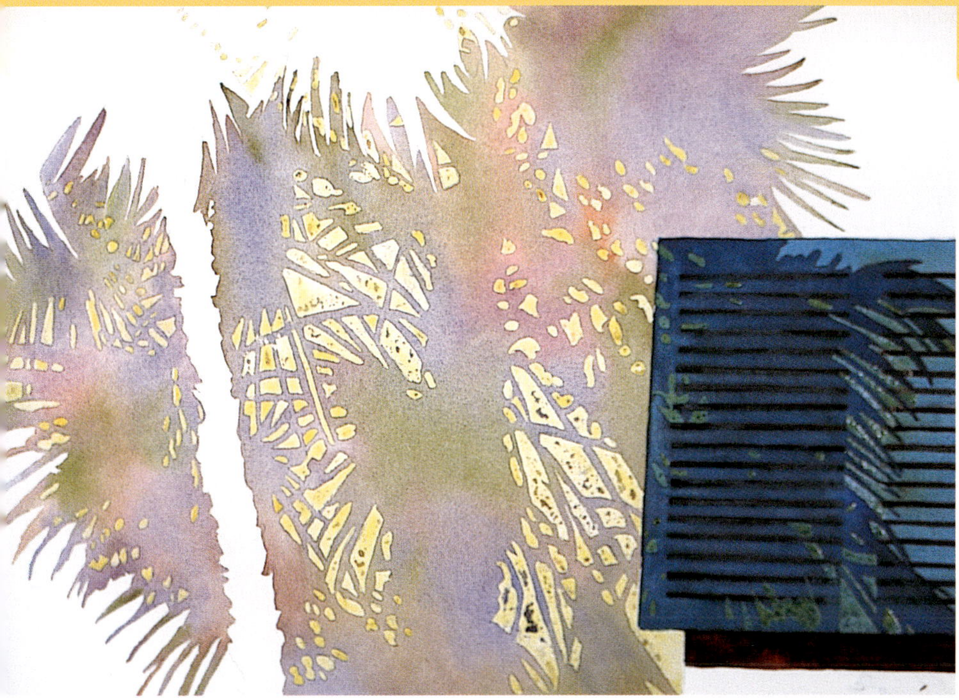

5 MINGLE SHADOWS ON THE SHUTTER

When the shadow on the wall is dry, take a no. 12 round and mingle Transparent Turquoise and Cobalt Blue over the shadow shape on the shutter, including the masked areas.

If an area is not as dark as you would like it, or if you're not satisfied with the mix of colors, you can rework the area with a glaze.

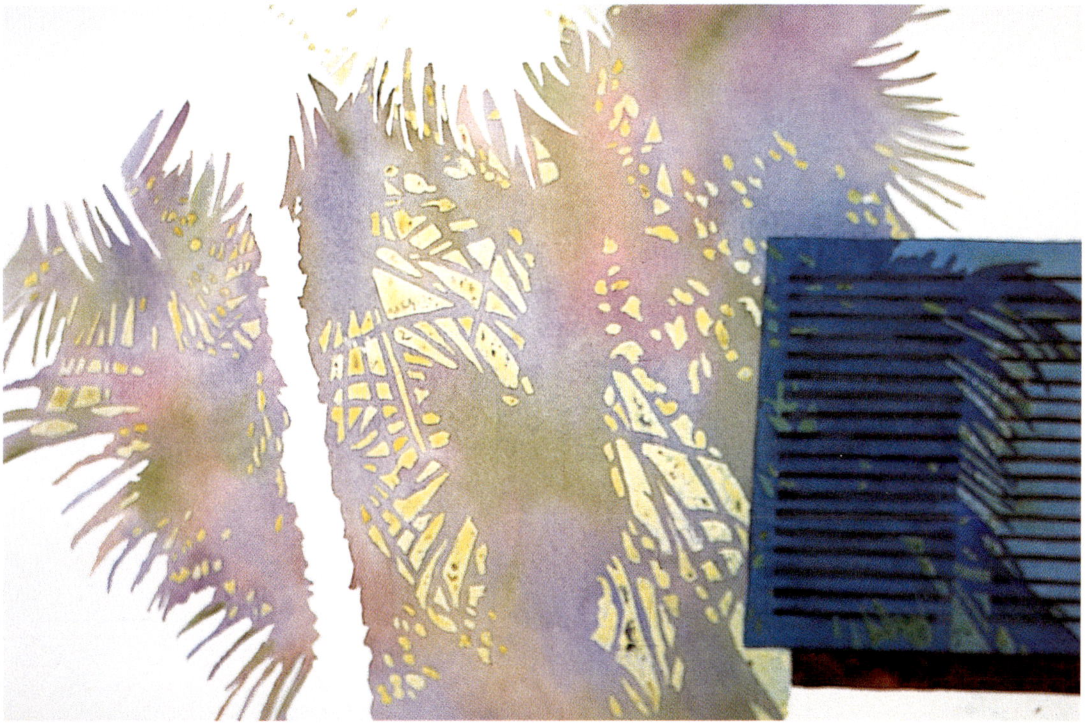

6 ADD A GLAZE TO DARKEN THE VALUES

When the paint is dry, add another layer of mingled colors to the dry shadow areas, darkening the values. (I added more reflected color into the shadows of the top left and bottom left sides of the shutters.) Load a no. 16 round with Transparent Turquoise and put your brush into the dry area of the shutter, then pull the paint out and over the shadow shape on the wall. As you move farther into the dry shadow shape, use clear water to blend. This will soften the hard edge of the shutter and connect the color of the shutter to the shadow.

7 REMOVE THE MASKING FLUID AND PAINT THE TREE TRUNK

When the painting is dry, remove the masking fluid on the wall and the shutter using a commercial removal pad. Make sure that you get all of the mask off. Run your fingertips over the whole area to check that you get it all.

Load a no. 12 round with New Gamboge and paint all of the tree trunk. With the same brush, mingle Brown Madder and Burnt Sienna into some areas of the New Gamboge. Darken the right side of the tree by switching to a ¾-inch (19mm) flat and adding Mineral Violet and Ultramarine Blue. Let the paint dry slightly, then take a razor blade and scratch and scrape the texture of the tree trunk.

I also added the shadow under the shutter by mingling Verditer Blue and Brown Madder with a no. 12 round. Begin to develop a few of the leaves using a no. 12 round and Olive Green and Ultramarine Blue.

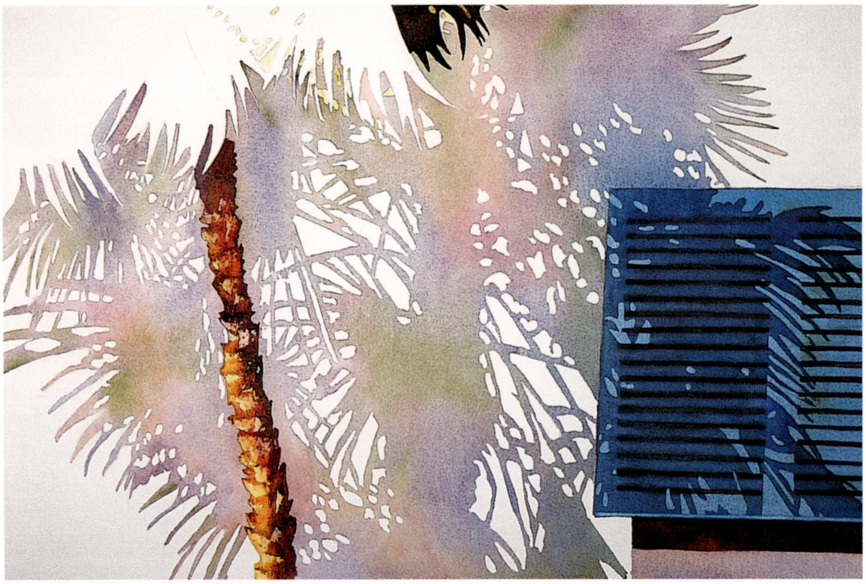

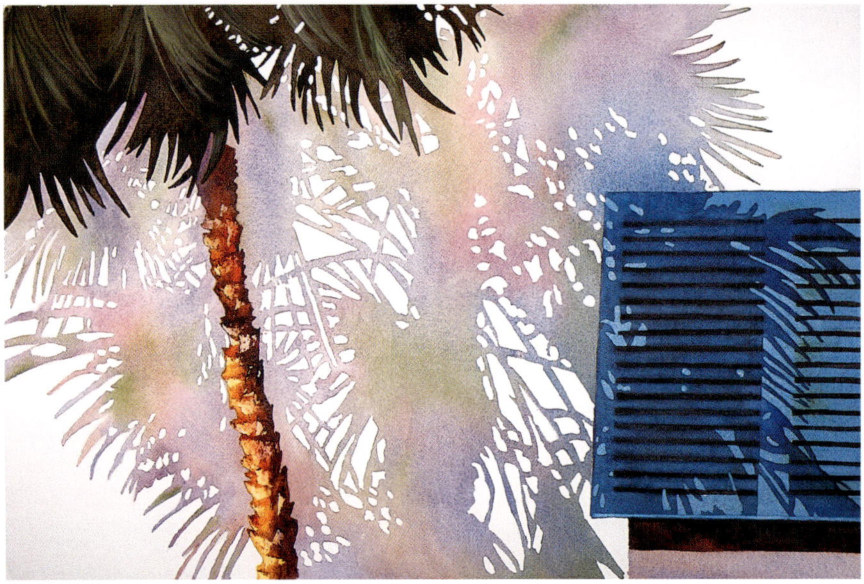

8 PAINT THE LEAVES

Paint the leaves alternating shades of green, using Permanent Sap Green, Olive Green and Undersea Green and a no. 16 brush. While the greens are still damp, mix some gesso with a little Permanent Sap Green or Aureolin Yellow and paint some of the leaf foliage that appears to be in front of the other leaves. Alternate the Permanent Sap Green and gesso and then Aureolin Yellow and gesso. Clean your brush and palette immediately after using the gesso.

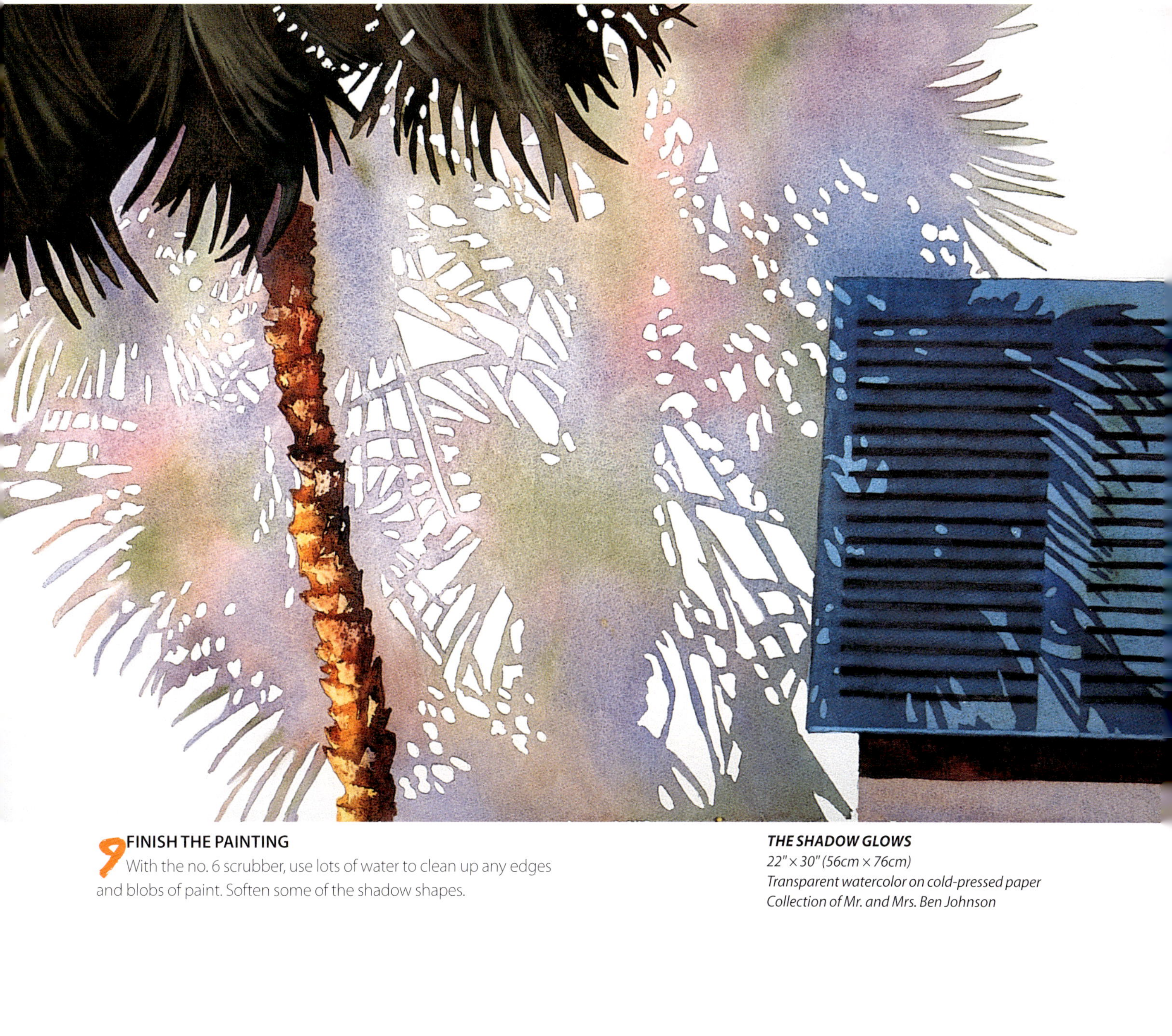

9 FINISH THE PAINTING

With the no. 6 scrubber, use lots of water to clean up any edges and blobs of paint. Soften some of the shadow shapes.

THE SHADOW GLOWS
22" × 30" (56cm × 76cm)
Transparent watercolor on cold-pressed paper
Collection of Mr. and Mrs. Ben Johnson

Glowing Shadows on Surface and Subject

MATERIALS

BRUSHES

Nos. 4, 6, 12, 16 and 26 round • ¾-inch (19mm) and 2-inch (51mm) flats • no. 6 scrubber

COLORS

Aureolin Yellow • Brown Madder • Burnt Sienna • Cobalt Blue • Greenish Yellow • Indigo • Mineral Violet • Naples Yellow • New Gamboge • Permanent Rose • Permanent Sap Green • Permanent Violet • Quinacridone Red Orange • Scarlet Lake • Ultramarine Blue • Undersea Green • Verditer Blue

SURFACE

300-lb. (640gsm) Arches cold-pressed paper

OTHER

Absorbing pad • commercial masking remover • masking fluid • paper towels

Here is an old silver colander that I got from a friend. The star design cut into the metal made for some interesting shadow shapes on the counter's surface.

In this demonstration, you'll build on the previously learned techniques of mingling grays and reflecting an object's colors into its shadows.

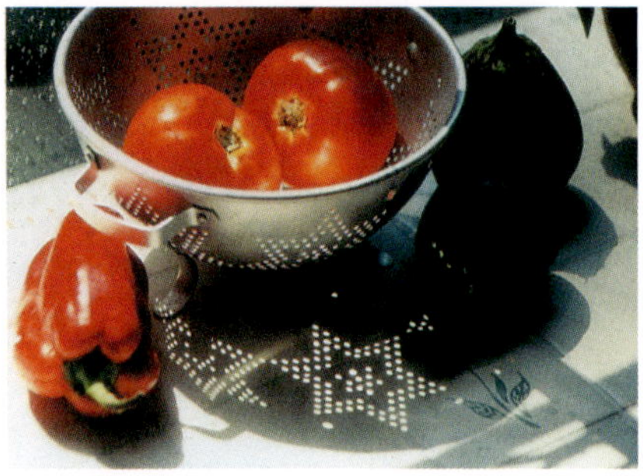

Reference Photo

I moved the eggplant out of the shadow and placed it more to the left. This put the handle's shadow on the colander, creating an interesting shape on the right side.

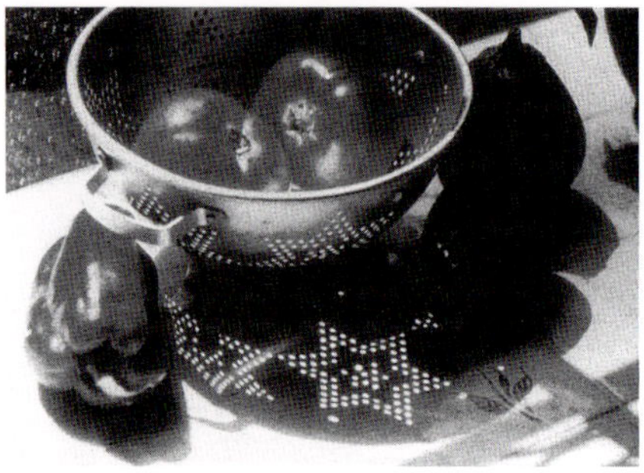

Black-and-White Photocopy

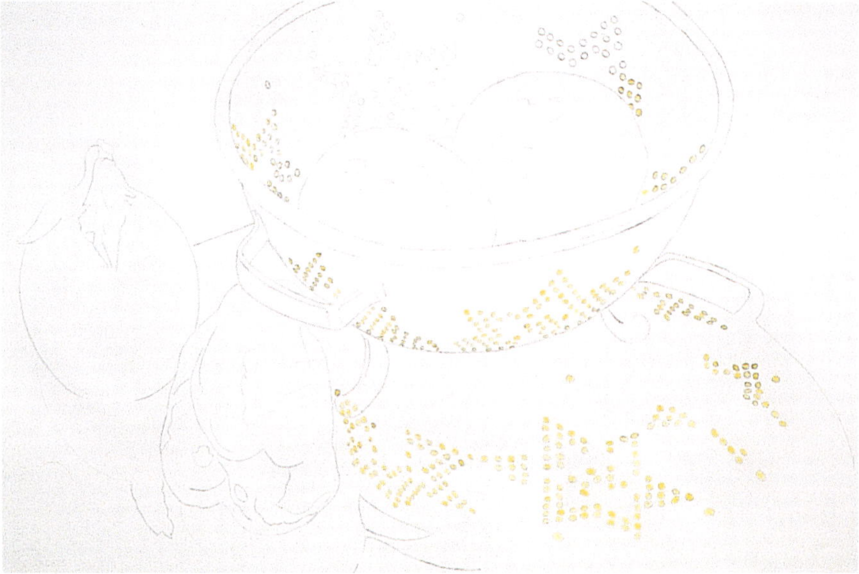

1 MASK THE HIGHLIGHTS

Draw or trace the composition. Using the black-and-white photocopy as a guide, carefully mask the star design on the surface of the counter and along the bowl's sides with an old no. 4 round. Mask any other areas where you would like to preserve the white of the paper. Let the masking fluid dry.

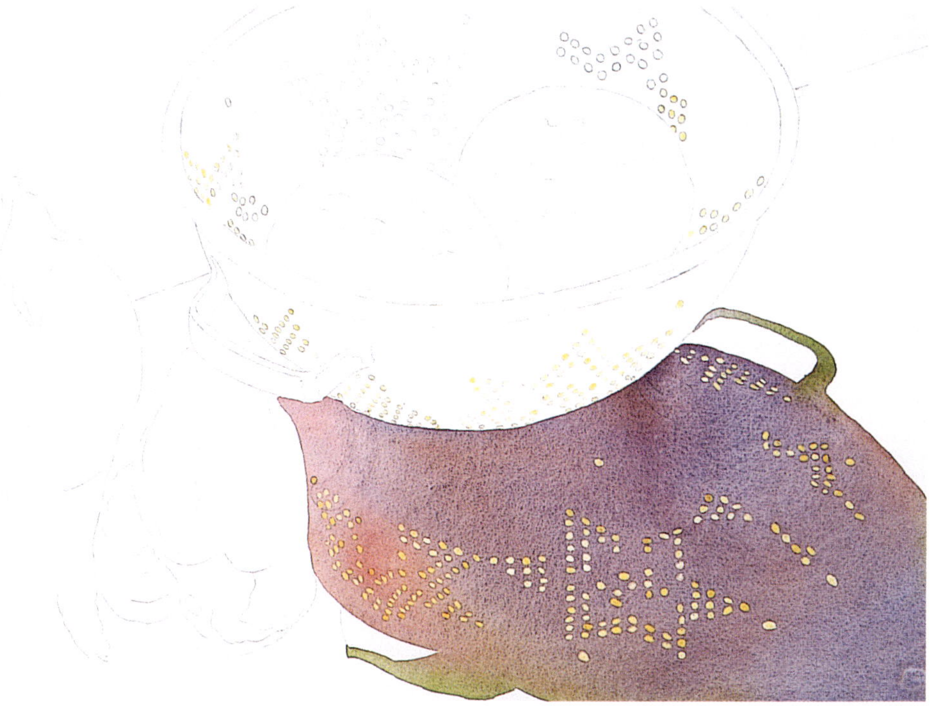

2 CREATE THE COLANDER'S SHADOW
With your paper flat on the surface, use a no. 16 round to mingle Permanent Rose, Verditer Blue, Mineral Violet and Cobalt Blue over the dry masking fluid. Use the absorbing pad to control the amount of water on your brush. Drop some Quinacridone Red Orange into the left side of the shadow to reflect the warm color of the red pepper, then drop a little Permanent Sap Green into the handle on the right side of the shadow shape.

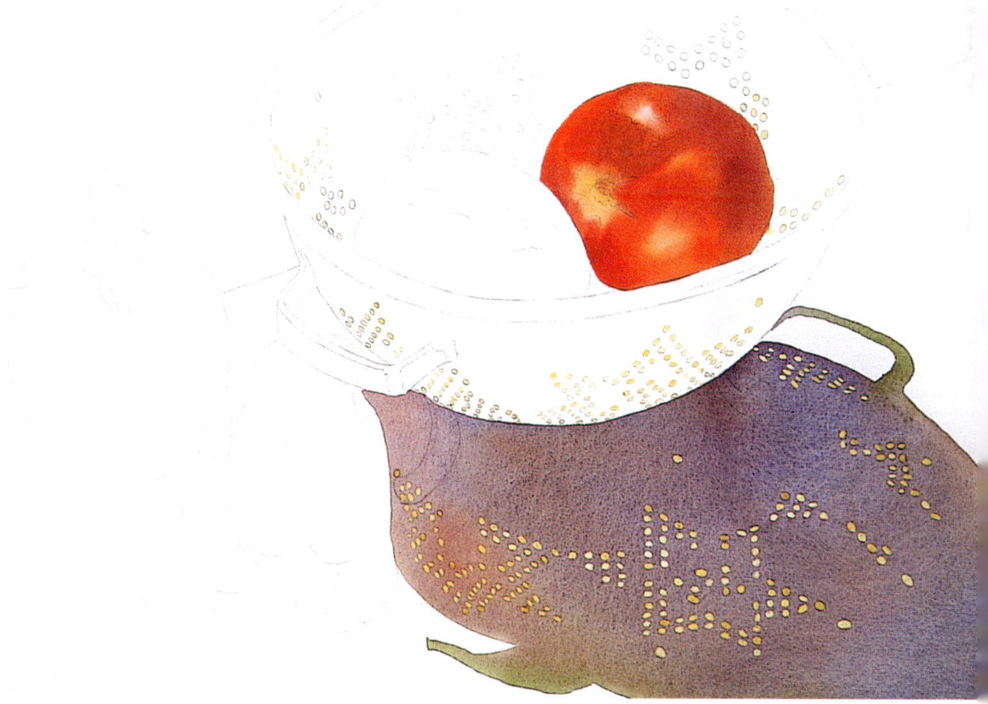

3 PAINT THE TOMATO
Take a no. 12 round and wet the highlight areas on the red tomato in the colander. Underpaint some of the areas of the tomato with New Gamboge using the no. 12 round. With a no. 16 round, cover the still-wet New Gamboge with Scarlet Lake, Permanent Rose and Quinacridone Red Orange, mingling and alternating the colors. While the tomato is wet, use a ¾-inch (19mm) flat to darken the values and shape the tomato with Brown Madder and a little Mineral Violet.

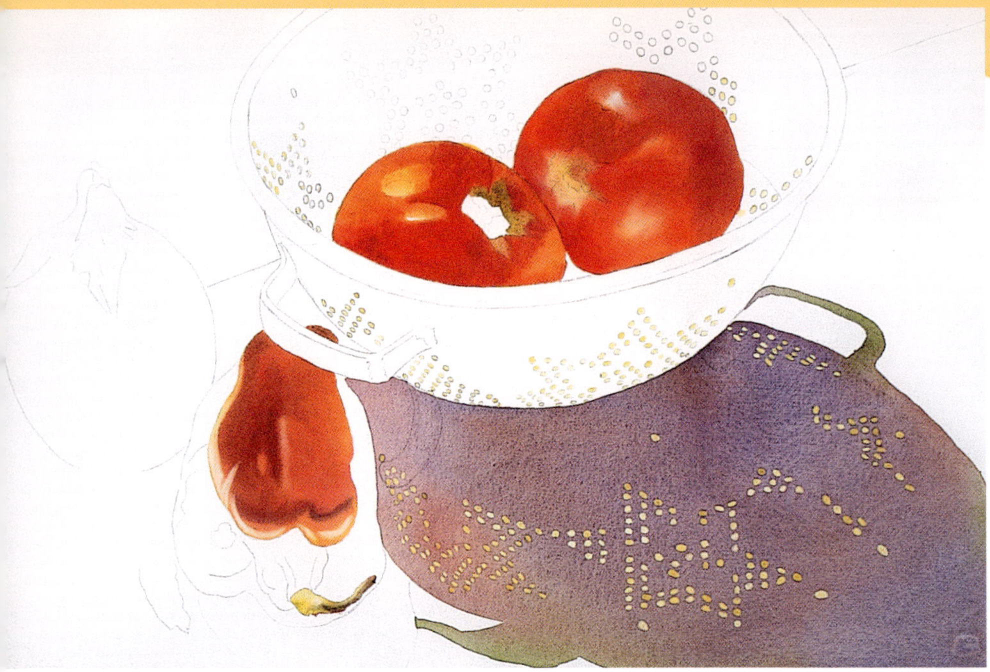

4 PAINT THE SECOND TOMATO AND THE TOP OF THE PEPPER

Finish the second tomato in the colander by using the same technique and colors in the previous step.

Underpaint the pepper's top with New Gamboge using the no. 12 round. Cover this with Scarlet Lake and Quinacridone Red Orange. Carve out the shape of the pepper with Brown Madder and more Mineral Violet in the darker areas, using the black-and-white photocopy as your guide. Use a ¾-inch (19mm) flat to get more pigment into the darker areas. While this is damp, use the same brush to lift some lights out of the top of the pepper. Use a paper towel to keep your brush clean of any excess liquids.

With a no. 4 round, begin to paint the stem on the pepper. Use Greenish Yellow, mingled with Undersea Green and a little Brown Madder.

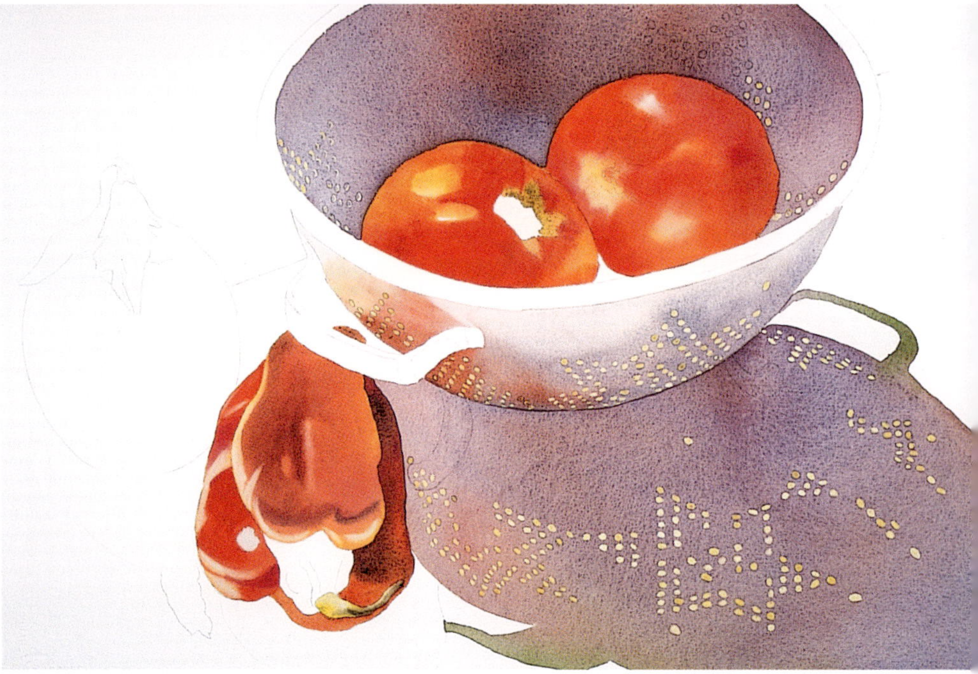

5 FINISH THE PEPPER AND PAINT THE COLANDER

Finish the underside of the pepper by mingling reds with Brown Madder and lots of Mineral Violet with a no. 12 round. Be sure to paint around the highlight.

To paint the silver colander, make three large, separate puddles of Verditer Blue, Brown Madder and Burnt Sienna on your palette. With a no. 16 round, mingle the colors across the surface of the colander and over the dry masking fluid. While the paint is wet, drop some Quinacridone Red Orange into the left side of the colander near the handle to reflect the glow from the pepper. Also, drop some Cobalt Blue into the underside where the colander meets the table to darken the edge. Mingle Verditer Blue, Brown Madder, Mineral Violet and Quinacridone Red Orange into the inside of the colander around the tomatoes. Use more red to create the glow from the tomatoes.

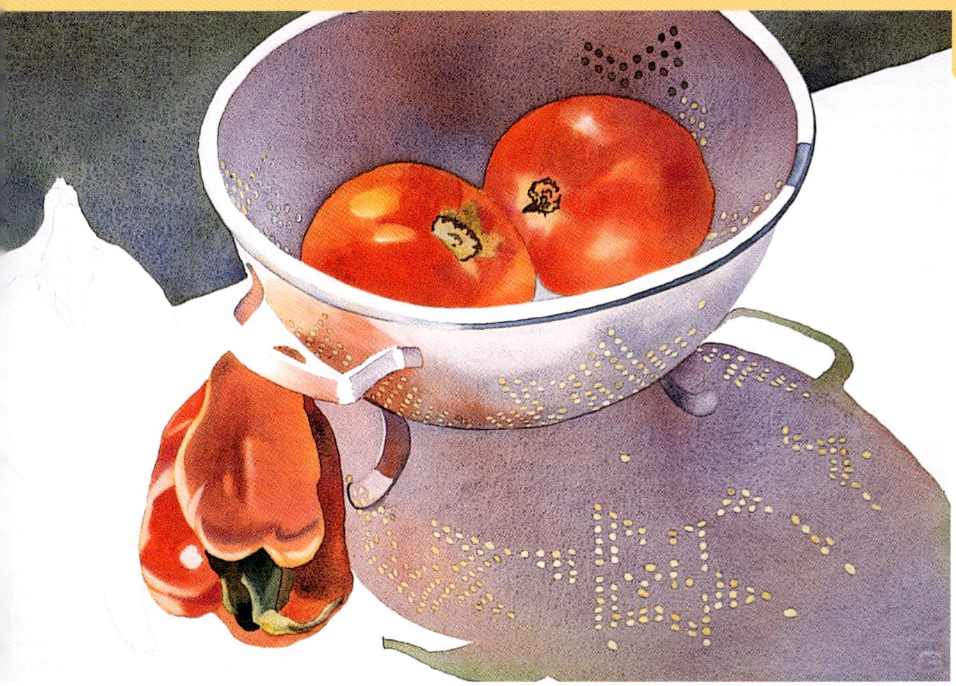

6 PAINT THE BACKGROUND AND VEGETABLE STEMS

With a no. 26 round, mingle Permanent Sap Green and Cobalt Blue for the background. With a no. 6 round, paint the darks of the tomatoes' stems. Use some Naples Yellow, mingling in some Brown Madder and Ultramarine Blue to darken. Paint the stem on the pepper with Permanent Sap Green, Undersea Green, Aureolin Yellow and Greenish Yellow. Pay attention to the lights and darks.

Make separate puddles of Brown Madder and Ultramarine Blue on your palette. Mingle them with a no. 4 round for the dark holes in the colander. Use more pigment in some places to create intense darks.

With a no. 6 round, mingle Brown Madder and Ultramarine Blue on the feet of the colander. Carefully paint around the highlights on the feet. Reflect more red into the foot closest to the pepper on the table.

Use a small no. 4 round and Indigo to add some darker shadow areas along the upper edge of the colander and a shadow shape on the lip.

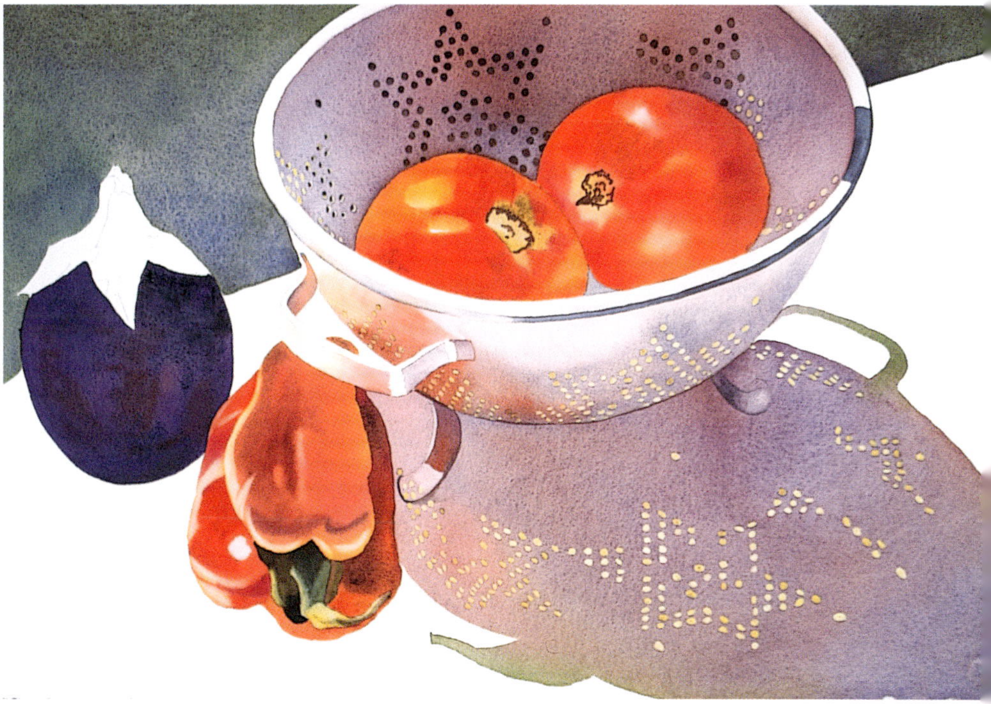

7 PAINT THE EGGPLANT

With a no. 16 round, mingle Permanent Violet, Brown Madder and Mineral Violet across the shape of the eggplant. Finish the darks in the colander's star shapes using a no. 4 round with Brown Madder and Ultramarine Blue. Add a little Indigo if you feel it needs it. Indigo is an intense dark blue and will really darken the previous colors.

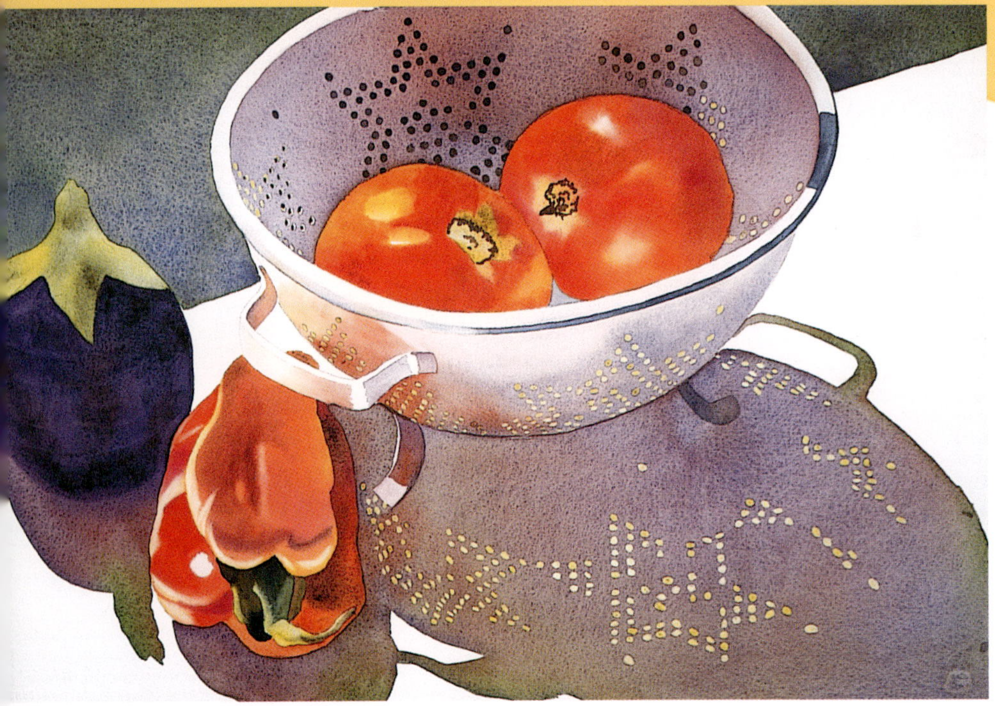

8 ADDS SHADOWS UNDER THE EGGPLANT AND PEPPER

Beginning under the eggplant, use a no. 12 round to mingle Brown Madder, Mineral Violet and some Cobalt Blue. Pull the paint up around the red pepper and drop a little Permanent Sap Green into the shadow area of the stem.

Under the pepper, begin with Brown Madder then mingle some Verditer Blue and Mineral Violet, joining that shadow to the colander's shadow.

Paint the stem on the eggplant by mingling Aureolin Yellow, Permanent Sap Green and Undersea Green with a no. 6 round.

9 PICK OUT THE HIGHLIGHTS, FINISH THE PAINTING

To tone down the bright, white surface, use a 2-inch (51mm) flat to add some Verditer Blue to the tabletop area. Following the value pattern in the black-and-white photocopy, dampen the light areas with water using a 2-inch (51mm) flat, then use the no. 6 scrubber to lift out the highlights. Lift, blot and wet again until the process is complete. Clean up the edges with the scrubber, if necessary. Use the scrubber to lift out the highlights on the eggplant's stem. Finally, use a commercial mask remover to remove all of the masking fluid from the paper.

STAR STRUCK
15" × 22" (38cm × 51cm)
Transparent watercolor on cold-pressed paper
Collection of the artist

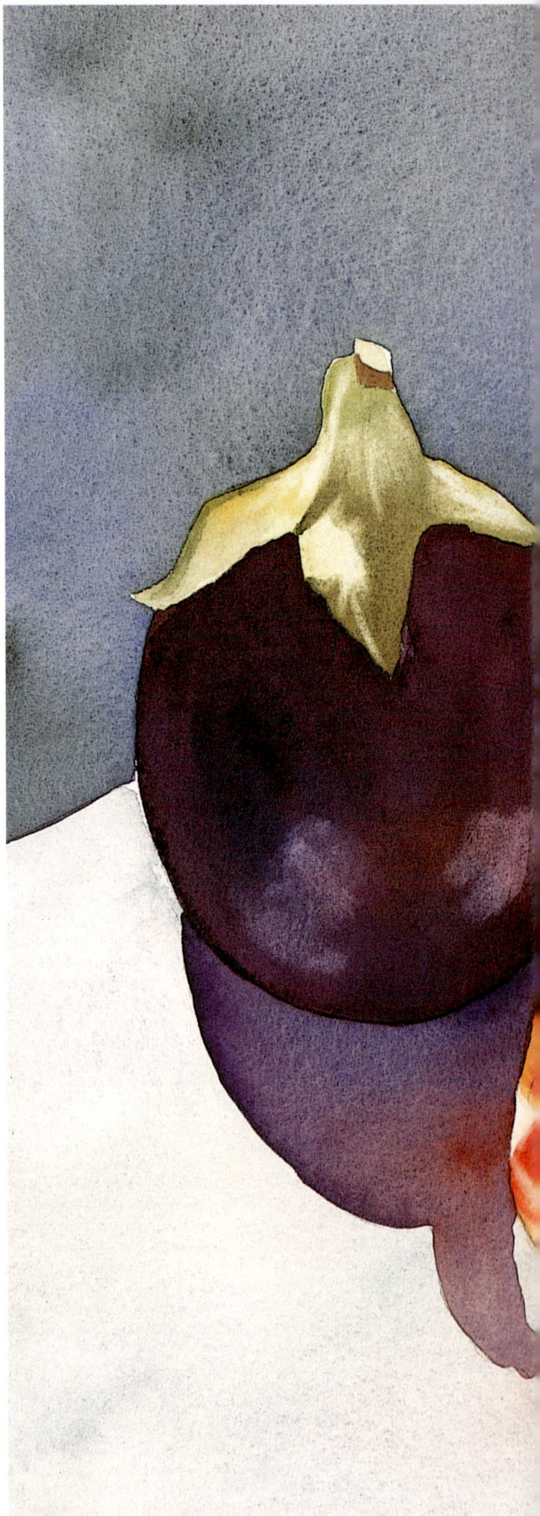

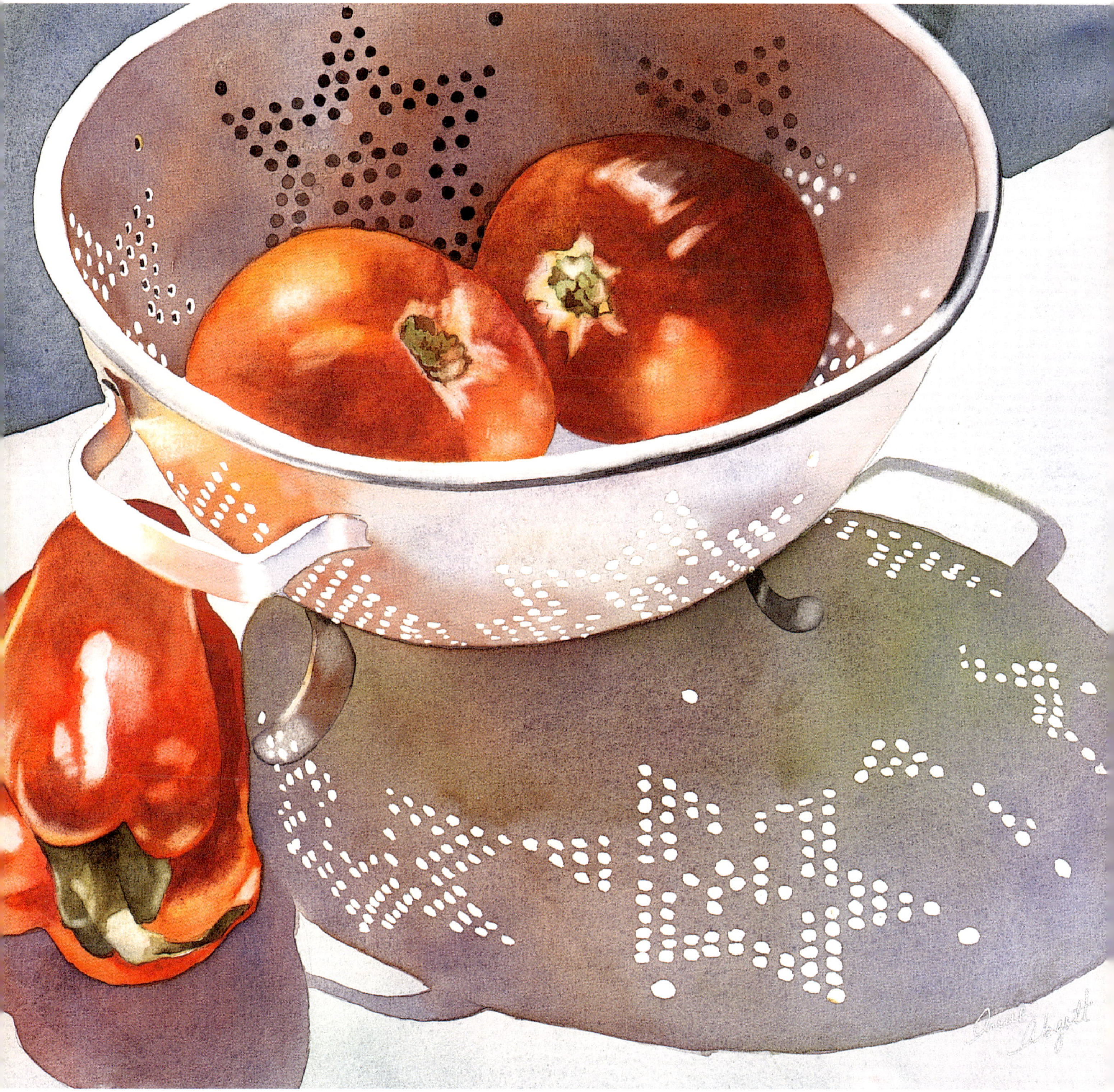

Index

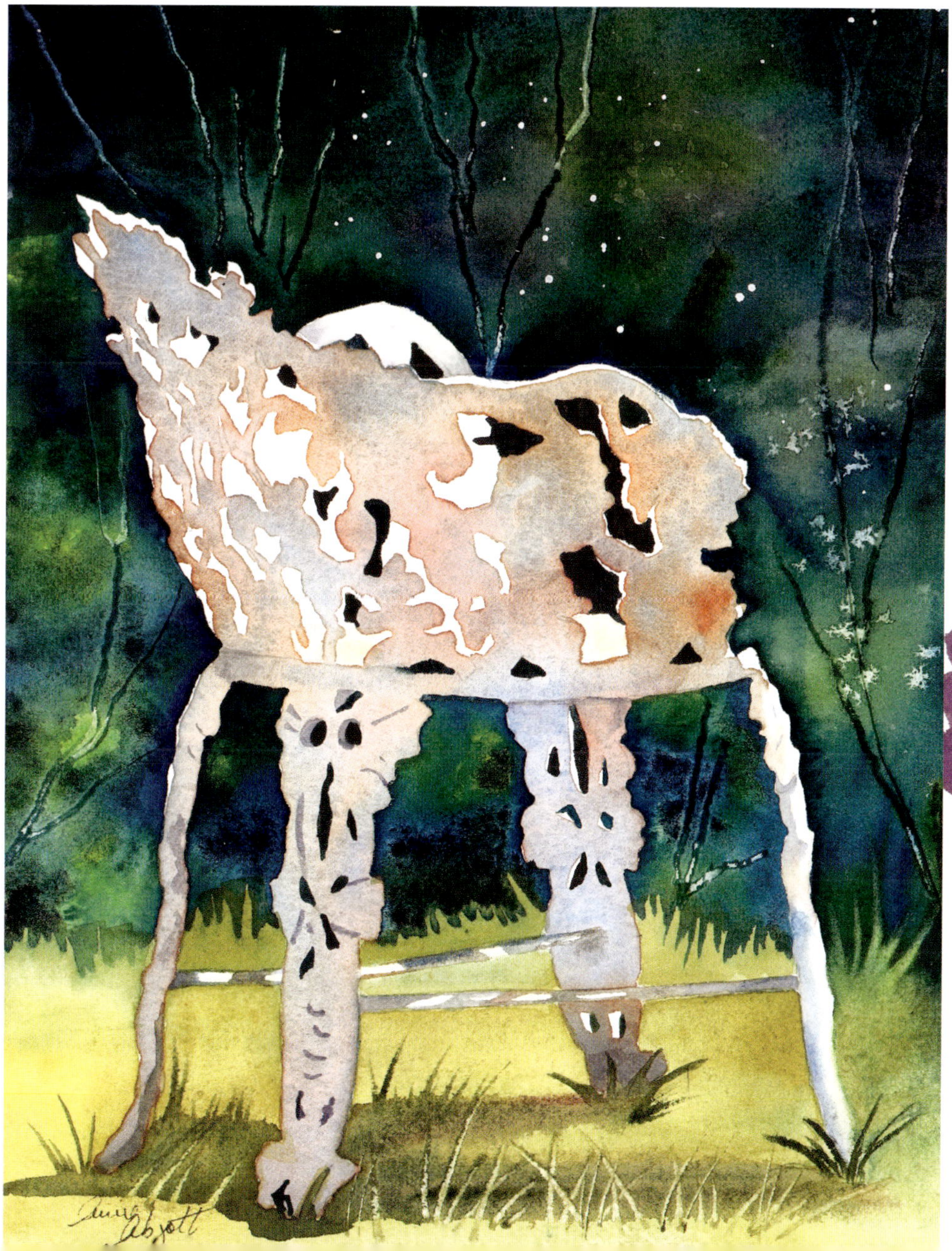

SOLITUDE ON THE GRASS
14" × 11" (36cm × 28cm)
Transparent watercolor on cold-pressed paper
Collection of Mrs. Louise Adler

Paint like the pros with North Light!

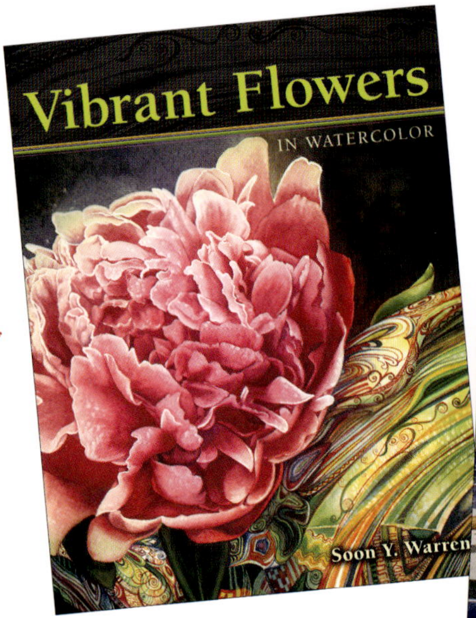

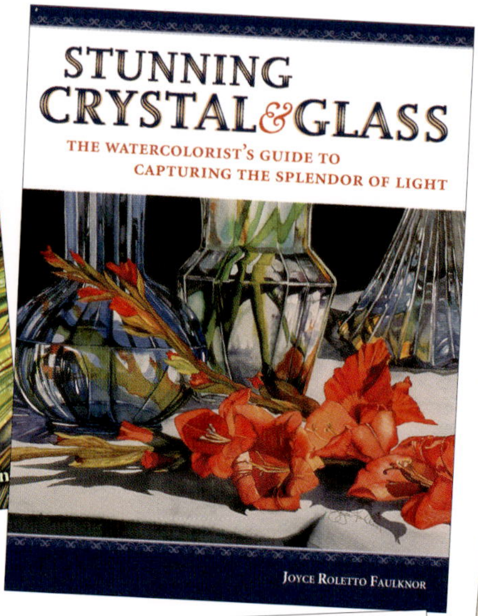

In *Stunning Crystal and Glass*, dramatic light-filled paintings become possible no matter what your skill level. Where most watercolorists paint from light to dark, expert Joyce Faulknor teaches you how to go from dark to light—a technique that is easy to learn and adds more depth and texture to any work.

ISBN 10: 1-58180-753-8,
ISBN 13: 978-1-58180-753-0,
HARDCOVER, 128 PAGES, #33420

In 14 eye-popping step-by-step demonstrations, author Soon Y. Warren reveals her techniques for painting bold, intense florals. Learn how to take the glowing, light-drenched scenes watercolor is known for and elevate them to another level.

ISBN 10: 1-58180-707-4,
ISBN 13: 978-1-58180-707-3,
HARDCOVER, 144 PAGES, #33373

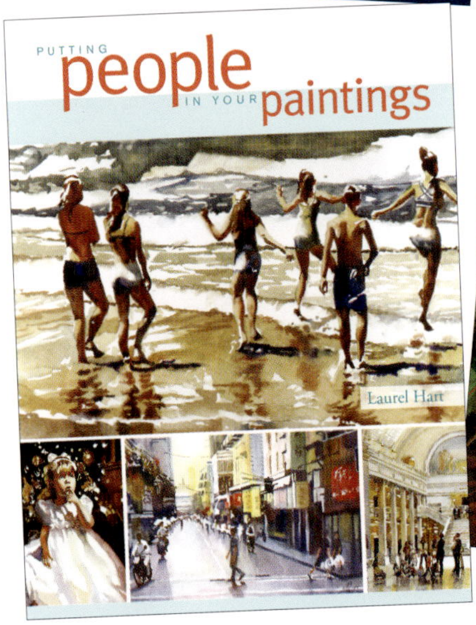

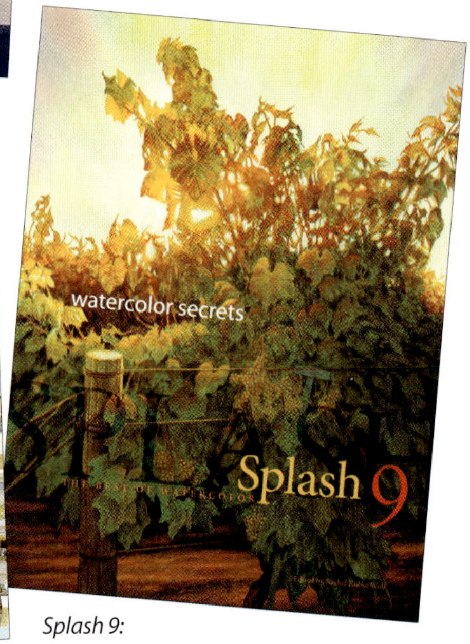

These books and other fine North Light titles are available at your local fine art retailer or bookstore or from online suppliers.

Watercolor artist Laurel Hart is a master at putting people into realistic scenes. No other book provides such clear instruction for painting people as important elements within such settings as landscapes, cityscapes, interiors and more. *Putting People in Your Paintings* covers all the basics including shape, value, composition, color and watercolor technique to help your watercolor paintings be filled with life. There is more to people than portraits!

ISBN-10: 1-58180-780-5,
ISBN-13: 978-1-58180-780-6,
PAPERBACK, 128 PAGES, #33450

Splash 9: Watercolor Secrets provides an inside look at the style of successful artists. You are given tips on techniques including light, color, composition and brush application, as well as insights into the methods and ideas behind great watercolor painting. With more than 100 paintings on subjects including street scenes, landscapes, animals and people, this is one book that will make a splash in your studio!

ISBN 10: 1-58180-694-9,
ISBN 13: 978-1-58180-694-6,
HARDCOVER, 144 PAGES, #33353